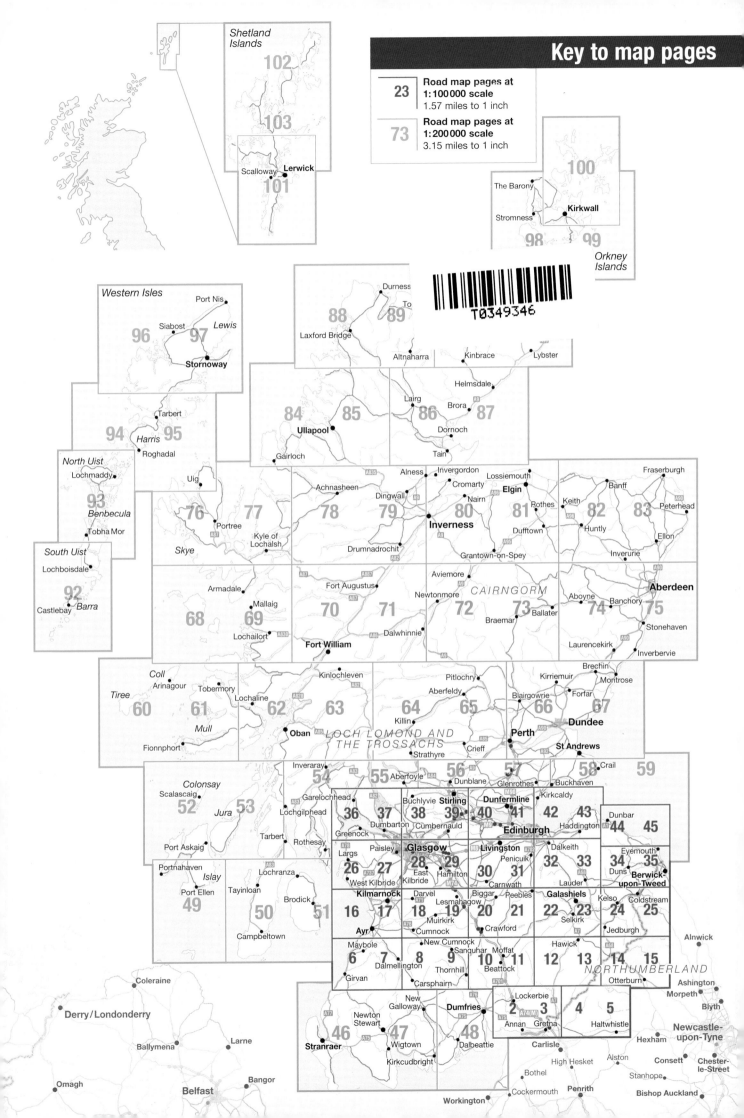

Best places to visit

Outdoors

Nature reserves, national parks and conservation areas

Aberdeen and Moray

Cairngorm National Park *Braemar, Aberdeenshire.* The Cairngorm National Park covers 2375 square miles of the Highlands, Moray and Aberdeenshire. It holds more than a quarter of Scotland's remaining native woodland and is home to over a quarter of Scotland's threatened species. ⌨ www.cairngorms.co.uk **73 C6**

Forvie National Nature Reserve *Collieston, Aberdeenshire.* The Ythan estuary, riverside, sand dunes, coastal heath and seacliffs make this a rich area for a variety of plants and wildlife, including seals which can be seen at the mouth of the Ythan. It is renowned for its birdlife with breeding eider duck, four species of breeding terns and large groups of geese and waders in winter. There is a visitor centre at Collieston with level access for wheelchair users. ⌨ ww.nature.scot/enjoying-outdoors/scotlands-national-nature-reserves/forvie-national-nature-reserve **83 F7**

Fowlsheugh *Crawton, Aberdeenshire.* In spring and summer the cliffs are crammed with breeding fulmars, guillemots, herring gulls, kittiwakes, puffins, razorbills and shags. ⌨ www.rspb.org.uk/reserves-and-events/reserves-a-z/fowlsheugh **75 D5**

Loch of Strathbeg *Crimond, Aberdeenshire.* Pink-footed geese and whooper swans winter here regularly, while summer breeders include lapwings, redshanks, common and Sandwich terns. There are nature trails, hides and visitor centre with a viewing area. ⌨ www.rspb.org.uk/reserves-and-events/reserves-a-z/loch-of-strathbeg **83 C7**

St Cyrus National Nature Reserve *St Cyrus, Aberdeenshire.* The cliffs and dunes of St Cyrus support a range of plants, including some you would not expect to find this far north. These provide suitable habitat for a rich variety of insects, particularly moths and butterflies. Breeding birds include terns, stonechats and whinchats, as well as fulmars on the cliffs. No access to tern breeding area April to August. ⌨ www.nature.scot/enjoying-outdoors/scotlands-national-nature-reserves/st-cyrus-national-nature-reserve **67 A7**

Argyll, Bute, Stirling, Trossachs

Flanders Moss National Nature Reserve *Thornhill, Stirling.* This reserve is a remnant of one of the largest lowland bog areas in Britain. Its colourful sphagnum mosses support a variety of insects in summer and birdlife, including birds of prey in the autumn. The viewing tower provides the best overview. Visitors should keep to the circular path. ⌨ www.nature.scot/enjoying-outdoors/scotlands-national-nature-reserves/flanders-moss-national-nature-reserve **56 C1**

Loch Gruinart *Aoradh, Islay, Argyll and Bute.* Hundreds of lapwings, redshanks and snipe breed by the loch in spring, while hen harriers nest up on the moorland in early summer. Corncrake can be heard at night during the summer. Large numbers of barnacle and white-fronted geese winter here, while golden eagles and peregrine falcons can be seen hunting all year. ⌨ www.rspb.org.uk/reserves-and-events/reserves-a-z/loch-gruinart/ **52 F2**

Loch Lomond and the Trossachs National Park *Aberfoyle, Stirling.* Scotland's first national park opened in July 2002. It contains a wide variety of special habitats and large amounts of protection for wildlife. It is divided into four areas: Lomond, which centres on the Loch and Ben Lomond and is good for watersports among other activities; the Trossachs, which includes Queen Elizabeth Forest Park and Loch Katrine and is an excellent place for scenery and walking; Breadalbane, which has spectacular scenery and some good hillwalking; and Argyll, which has extensive forests and sea lochs. ⌨ www.lochlomond-trossachs.org **55 B8**

Moine Mhor National Nature Reserve *Bellanoch, Argyll and Bute.* This water-logged system of pools and bogs is home to otters, ospreys, curlews and hen harriers, as well as a wide range of dragonflies in summer. The best views over the reserve are from the Crinan Canal, near Bellanoch, or the ancient hill fort of Dunadd. Stay on the paths. ⌨ www.nature.scot/enjoying-outdoors/scotlands-national-nature-reserves/moine-mhor-national-nature-reserve **53 C8**

Staffa National Nature Reserve *Staffa, Argyll and Bute.* The distinctive hexagonal rock columns of this uninhabited island are formed from basalt, just like those of the Giant's Causeway on the opposite side of the Irish Sea. In spring and early summer, the cliffs and grassy clifftops provide nesting sites for guillemots, puffins and razorbills, as well as other seabirds. Tour boats operate from Iona, Mull and Oban See also Fingal's Cave. ⌨ www.nts.org.uk/visit/places/staffa **61 D6**

Taynish National Nature Reserve *Tayvallich, Argyll and Bute.* This ancient deciduous woodland lies on a scenic peninsula overlooking Loch Sween. Its dripping ferns and mosses, mixed with marshland and grassland, support otters, red squirrels, more than 300 plant species and 20 kinds of butterfly in summer. ⌨ www.nature.scot/enjoying-outdoors/scotlands-national-nature-reserves/taynish-national-nature-reserve **53 D7**

Loch Barnluasgan and Knapdale Nature Reserve *Near Bellanoch, Argyll and Bute* The ancient Atlantic oak woodlands and lochs at Knapdale are home to Scotland's reintroduced beaver population, which are most likely to be spotted around dawn or dusk. Evidence of their activities in the form of stripped branches, felled trees and beaver canals may be seen when exploring the nature trails. Other wildlife includes eagles, ospreys, otters and red squirrels. There is a visitor centre at Barnluasgan with an accessible trail and wildlife hide. ⌨ https://scottishwildlifetrust.org.uk/reserve/knapdale-habitats-partnership-area ⌨ https://www.scottishbeavers.org.uk/visit-knapdale ⌨ https://forestryandland.gov.scot/visit/barnluasgan **53 C7**

The Oa (Upper Killeyan) *Port Ellen, Islay, Argyll and Bute.* Choughs and, sometimes, golden eagles can be seen from the coast, while Greenland white-fronted geese use the bog in winter. ⌨ www.rspb.org.uk/reserves-and-events/reserves-a-z/the-oa/ **49 B2**

Glasgow and the Clyde

Baron's Haugh *Motherwell, North Lanarkshire.* More than 170 species of birds have been recorded in this small urban nature reserve. Kingfishers can be seen by the river and whooper swans winter on the meadows. ⌨ www.rspb.org.uk/reserves-and-events/reserves-a-z/barons-haugh/ **29 C5**

Clyde Valley Woodlands National Nature Reserve *Lanark, South Lanarkshire.* This reserve features steep gorges with woodland typical of the Clyde Valley, including ash, oak and wych elm. Birdlife includes flycatchers, redstarts and warblers during the breeding season. The steepness of the terrain means that the paths can be dangerous when wet. ⌨ www.nature.scot/enjoying-outdoors/scotlands-national-nature-reserves/clyde-valley-woodlands-national-nature-reserve **29 E8**

Lochwinnoch *Renfrewshire.* In winter the large variety of wildfowl on the loch includes goosanders, while in spring lapwings display and sedge warblers can be heard singing. ⌨ www.rspb.org.uk/reserves-and-events/reserves-a-z/lochwinnoch/ **27 C6**

Perth, Angus, Dundee and Fife

Ben Lawers National Nature Reserve *Milton Morenish, Perth and Kinross.* This reserve, on the north side of Loch Tay, has a unique range of mountain plants because the soils are unusually rich at high altitude, supporting a superb collection of arctic-alpine plants that flower in early to mid- summer. Work is being undertaken to restore the natural montane willow scrub. There is a nature trail and ranger-led walks are available. Birds that can be seen in season include curlew, dipper, ptarmigan, raven and red grouse. ⌨ www.nts.org.uk/visit/places/ben-lawers **64 D4**

Isle of May National Nature Reserve *Isle of May, Fife.* As well as containing one of the largest puffin colonies in Scotland, together with guillemots and razorbills, this tiny island in the Firth of Forth has a lighthouse, a 12th-century chapel and a bird observatory. Boat trips to the island depart from Anstruther or North Berwick from April to September. ⌨ www.nature.scot/enjoying-outdoors/scotlands-national-nature-reserves/isle-may-national-nature-reserve **58 C4**

Loch Leven National Nature Reserve *Kinross, Perth and Kinross.* Loch Leven is Scotland's largest lowland freshwater loch. Among the wildfowl that depend on it are up to 20,000 pink-footed geese in winter. See also Loch Leven Nature Reserve. ⌨ www.nature.scot/enjoying-outdoors/scotlands-national-nature-reserves/loch-leven-national-nature-reserve **57 B6**

Loch Leven Nature Reserve *Loch Leven NNR, Kinross, Perth and Kinross.* Thousands of ducks overwinter here, along with greylag and pink-footed geese and whooper swans. The wet grassland provides a haven for nesting ducks, lapwings, redshanks and snipe. Birds that breed in the woodland on Vane Hill include great spotted woodpeckers, tree pipits and willow warblers. Nature trails. See also Loch Leven National Nature Reserve. ⌨ www.rspb.org.uk/reserves-and-events/reserves-a-z/loch-leven/ **57 B6**

Loch of Kinnordy *Kinnordy, Angus.* The lochs, mires and fens of the reserve are surrounded by farmland. On the reserve, wildfowl, wading birds and ospreys visit regularly in the spring and summer, when black-necked grebes may also occur. In winter, the reserve is full of wildfowl. ⌨ www.rspb.org.uk/reserves-and-events/reserves-a-z/loch-of-kinnordy **66 B3**

Montrose Basin Nature Reserve *Montrose, Angus* This 750-hectare enclosed tidal basin at the mouth of the South Esk contains a variety of estuary habitats including reedbeds and tidal mudflats. It attracts such species as pink-footed geese, eider, Arctic terns, knots and sedge warblers. The visitor centre is on the A92 just outside Montrose. Bird hides, guided walks and audio guides are available. See also House of Dun. ⌨ https://scottishwildlifetrust.org.uk/reserve/montrose-basin/ **67 B6**

Tentsmuir National Nature Reserve *Tayport, Fife.* The dunes and beach on the south side of the mouth of the Tay Estuary form an important habitat for huge numbers of waders and wildfowl, especially in the winter for the latter, as well as a place for more common and grey seals to rest. In summer, the grasslands behind the dunes are a haven for butterflies. ⌨ www.nature.scot/enjoying-outdoors/scotlands-national-nature-reserves/tentsmuir-national-nature-reserve ⌨ https://forestryandland.gov.scot/visit/tentsmuir **67 E4**

1 South of Scotland
2 Glasgow and the Clyde
3 Edinburgh and East Central Scotland
4 Perth, Angus, Dundee and Fife
5 Argyll, Bute, Stirling, Trossachs
6 Aberdeen and Moray
7 The Highlands
8 Western Isles, Orkney and Shetland

Shetland Islands

Orkney Islands

Ben Lawers and Loch Tay
DGP_Scotland / Alamy

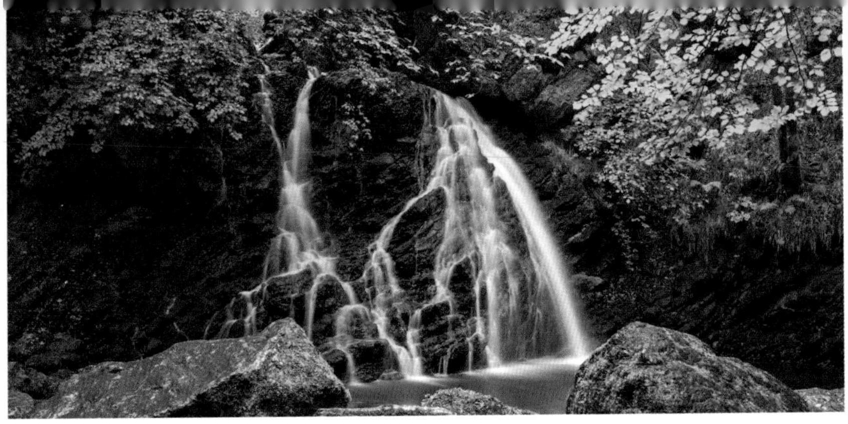

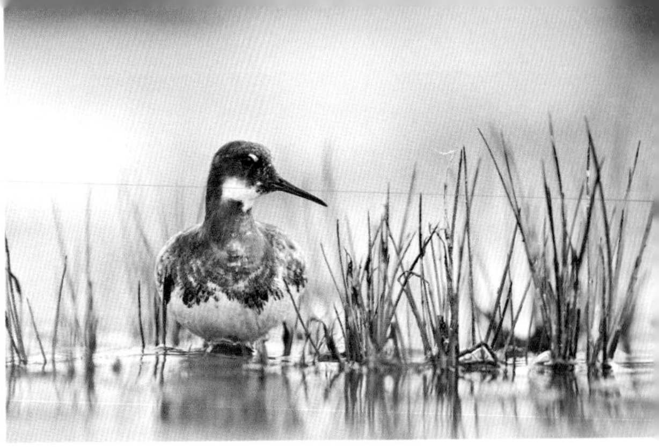

South of Scotland

Caerlaverock National Nature Reserve *Bankend, Dumfries and Galloway.* Thousands of wildfowl, including barnacle geese from the Arctic, winter on the estuary and feed on the tidal saltmarsh. 💻www.wwt.org.uk/wetland-centres/caerlaverock 💻www.nature.scot/enjoying-outdoors/scotlands-national-nature-reserves/caerlaverock-national-nature-reserve **2 F2**

Grey Mare's Tail Nature Reserve *Moffat, Dumfries and Galloway.* The spectacular 200ft waterfall is formed by the Tail Burn dropping from Loch Skene. The surrounding reserve is rich in wild flowers. Feral goats, ospreys, ring ouzels and peregrine falcons can sometimes be seen in the area. 💻www.nts.org.uk/visit/places/grey-mares-tail **11 B7**

Ken-Dee Marshes *Glenlochar, Dumfries and Galloway.* In winter, many wildfowl, including white-fronted geese, can be seen on the wetlands, while in spring, pied flycatchers and redstarts arrive to breed in the woodlands. Red kites hunt in the area and mammals present include red squirrels and otters. 💻www.rspb.org.uk/reserves-and-events/reserves-a-z/ken-dee-marshes **48 C1**

Mull of Galloway *Drummore, Dumfries and Galloway.* Guillemots, black guillemots, kittiwakes, razorbills, shags and a small number of puffins nest on the cliffs in spring and early summer. Offshore, the Scar Rocks are home to a colony of around 4000 gannets. Onshore, the coastal habitat is managed to encourage breeding stonechats, wheatears and twites. 💻www.rspb.org.uk/reserves-and-events/reserves-a-z/mull-of-galloway/recent-sightings **46 F3**

St Abb's Head National Nature Reserve *St Abbs, Scottish Borders.* The stunning cliffs supports large breeding colonies of fulmars, guillemots, kittiwakes, puffins, razorbills and shags in May–July. In spring and high summer the grasslands are full of flowers, which in summer attract large numbers of butterflies. In autumn and spring large numbers of migrant birds pass close to the cliffs. 💻www.nts.org.uk/visit/places/st-abbs-head **35 A7**

Whitlaw Mosses National Nature Reserve *Selkirk, Scottish Borders.* These four low-lying areas contain a variety of wetland habitats including moss carpets, swamps of sedges, willow scrub, meadows and grasslands. The fragile surfaces are easily damaged and look deceptively solid. Keep to the firm ground. 💻https://scottishwildlifetrust.org.uk/reserve/whitlaw-wood/ **23 D6**

Wood of Cree *Minnigaff, Dumfries and Galloway.* The Wood of Cree is the largest ancient wood in southern Scotland. In spring, migrant pied flycatchers, redstarts, tree pipits and wood warblers arrive from Africa. There is a resident population of willow tits. Otters can sometimes be seen. 💻www.rspb.org.uk/reserves-and-events/reserves-a-z/wood-of-cree/ **47 B5**

The Highlands

Abernethy National Nature Reserve *Nethy Bridge, Highland.* The largest remnant native Scots pinewood in Britain, Abernethy Forest offers a unique mix of woodland and northern bog (keep to the tracks). Birds include capercaillie, crossbill, crested tit, goldeneye and osprey, which breed in the wide variety of habitats. See also Loch Garten. 💻www.nature.scot/enjoying-outdoors/scotlands-national-nature-reserves/abernethy-national-nature-reserve **72 A5**

Beinn Eighe National Nature Reserve *Kinlochewe, Highland.* Among Beinn Eighe's wonderful mountain scenery, overlooking Loch Maree, are some of the few remaining fragments of ancient pinewood in Scotland. The wildlife includes golden eagles, pine martens and red deer, as well as a wide variety of dragonflies over the bogland. The visitor centre provides information on the various woodland and mountain trails. 💻www.nature.scot/enjoying-outdoors/scotlands-national-nature-reserves/beinn-eighe-and-loch-maree-islands-national-nature-reserve **78 B1**

Ben Wyvis National Nature Reserve *Garve, Highland.* Animals that are found in the area include red and roe deer, pine martens and golden eagles. The habitats vary from the moss-covered upper slopes to the dwarf shrub heath and boglands lower down that support plants like dwarf birch, cloudberry and dwarf cornel. Some areas may be closed for deer stalking between August and October. 💻www.nnr-scotland.org.uk **79 B6**

Corrieshalloch Gorge National Nature Reserve *Braemore, Highland.* This spectacular, mile-long gorge, a box canyon, is 200ft deep. The river that carved this channel, the Abhainn Droma, plunges over the Falls of Measach. These can be seen from the suspension bridge, built by Sir John Fowler – a co-designer of the Forth Bridge. The gorge is home to a rich variety of liverworts and mosses. 💻www.nts.org.uk/visit/places/corrieshalloch-gorge **85 F6**

Corrimony *Highland.* Set in a superb landscape, this reserve has conifer plantations, native woodland and open moorland. In summer, Loch Comhnard has breeding common sandpipers, curlews and greenshanks, with ospreys and red-throated divers sometimes seen. Goldeneyes and whooper swans are among the winter visitors. Black grouse can be seen in the birchwoods, while the pinewoods have breeding bullfinches, Scottish crossbills, spotted flycatchers and wood warblers. 💻www.rspb.org.uk/reserves-and-events/reserves-a-z/corrimony/ **79 E5**

Craigellachie National Nature Reserve *Aviemore, Highland.* Scenic trails through the mature birchwood that cloaks the lower slopes of the hill of Craigellachie provide fine views across Aviemore and Strathspey to the Cairngorms. Peregrines nest on the cliff between April and July, while spring is the best time to see the woodland flowers. 💻www.nature.scot/enjoying-outdoors/scotlands-national-nature-reserves/craigellachie-national-nature-reserve **72 A3**

Culbin Sands *Nairn, Highland.* Culbin Sands is one of the largest shingle and sand dune bars in Britain. Bar-tailed godwits, knot and oystercatchers can be seen at high tide. In winter, large numbers of sea ducks are visible offshore. 💻www.rspb.org.uk/reserves-and-events/reserves-a-z/culbin-sands/ **80 C3**

Fairy Glen *Rosemarkie, Highland.* A small area of broadleaved woodland in a pretty, steep-sided glen with a fast-flowing stream. Dippers can be seen in the stream. 💻www.rspb.org.uk/reserves-and-events/reserves-a-z/fairy-glen/ **80 C2**

Forsinard Flows *Highland.* The blanket-bog peatlands of Forsinard are at the heart of the Flow Country. Breeding birds include dunlin, golden plovers and merlins. Visitor centre, bog pool trail and guided walks. 💻www.rspb.org.uk/reserves-and-events/reserves-a-z/forsinard-flows/ **90 D2**

Glen Affric National Nature Reserve *Cannich, Highland.* Glen Affric is among the most beautiful glens and has one of the largest remaining ancient pinewoods in Scotland. Wildlife present includes some of Scotland's most elusive species – black

▲ Fairy Glen waterfalls, Rosemarkie
Jonathan W Cohen / iStockphoto

grouse, capercaillies, crested tits, crossbills, golden eagles, otters, red-throated divers and pine martens. Activities include hillwalking, mountain biking on forest tracks and open water canoeing. 💻https://forestryandland.gov.scot/visit/glen-affric **78 F3**

Glen Roy National Nature Reserve *Roybridge, Highland.* The famous 'Parallel Roads' of Glen Roy were created during the last ice age when glaciers dammed the end of the glen and created a succession of lakes in it. The shorelines of these form the 'Roads' on the hillsides that can be seen from the viewpoint. 💻www.nature.scot/enjoying-outdoors/scotlands-national-nature-reserves/glen-roy-national-nature-reserve **71 D5**

Glenborrodale *Highland.* An ancient oakwood on the north shore of Loch Sunart. In spring, wood warblers, redstarts and spotted flycatchers nest. Otters and seals can be seen in the loch. 💻www.rspb.org.uk/reserves-and-events/reserves-a-z/glenborrodale/ **62 A1**

Handa Island *Scourie, Highland.* This internationally important nature reserve, is a mass of red Torridon sandstone. In summer it has breeding populations of razorbills, guillemots and puffins. There are also remnants of the cottages of the crofters who lived on the island until the 19th century. A walk around the island offers views across the Minch and of the Great Stack rock formation. Access is by passenger ferry from Tarbet. 💻https://scottishwildlifetrust.org.uk/reserve/handa-island/ **88 D3**

Insh Marshes National Nature Reserve *Kingussie, Highland.* This is one of Europe's most important wetlands, primarily because about half of all British goldeneyes breed here, as do substantial numbers of wigeon. Waders that visit the site include curlews,

▼ A juvenile pine marten in Beinn Eighe National Nature Reserve
Nature Picture Library / Alamy

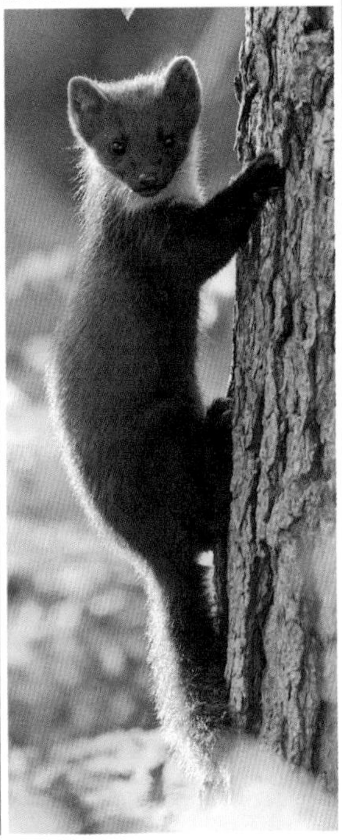

▲ A female red-necked phalarope on Loch Funzie, Fetlar David Tipling / Alamy

lapwings, oystercatchers, redshanks and snipe. In winter, the flooded marshes are home to large groups of whooper swans and greylag geese. 💻www.rspb.org.uk/reserves-and-events/reserves-a-z/insh-marshes/ **72 B2**

Loch Fleet National Nature Reserve *Golspie, Highland.* This tidal basin is home to common seals, and waders and wildfowl are easy to spot on the mudflats. The sand dunes, coastal heath and pinewood plantations are rich in wild flowers. Among the annual highlights are the ospreys that can be seen fishing in early to mid-summer. 💻https://scottishwildlifetrust.org.uk/reserve/loch-fleet 💻www.nature.scot/enjoying-outdoors/scotlands-national-nature-reserves/loch-fleet-national-nature-reserve **86 D5**

Loch Garten *Boat of Garten, Highland.* In summer, ospreys can be seen from the osprey centre, which also has a video feed of the nest. In April and early May, male capercaillies display (lek) around dawn. Other rarities include crested tits, Scottish crossbills and red squirrels. Visitor centre. See also Abernethy Forest National Nature Reserve. 💻www.rspb.org.uk/reserves-and-events/reserves-a-z/loch-garten/ **72 A4**

Loch Ruthven *East Croachy, Highland.* This lovely loch is the most important site in the UK for Slavonian grebes. Ospreys can be seen in summer and hen harriers and peregrines can also sometimes be spotted. 💻www.rspb.org.uk/reserves-and-events/reserves-a-z/loch-ruthven/ **80 F1**

Rùm National Nature Reserve *Kinloch, Rùm, Highland.* The spectacular Isle of Rùm is home to otters, red deer, sea eagles and a mountaintop colony of Manx shearwaters. Access is via ferry from Mallaig. 💻www.nature.scot/enjoying-outdoors/scotlands-national-nature-reserves/rum-nnr/rum-nnr-visiting-reserve **68 C3**

The Outer Islands

Birsay Moors *Finstown, Mainland, Orkney.* In the summer, hen harriers, short-eared owls and Arctic skuas nest on the moorland. The Orkney vole is also common on the reserve. 💻www.rspb.org.uk/reserves-and-events/reserves-a-z/birsay-moors/ **98 A4**

Brodgar *Hestwall, Mainland, Orkney.* Snipe can be heard drumming in the summer, and other breeding waders include curlews, dunlin, lapwings, oystercatchers and redshanks. Wildfowl present on the reserve in summer includes, gadwalls, wigeon, shovelers and teal. See also Ring of Brodgar. 💻www.rspb.org.uk/reserves-and-events/reserves-a-z/brodgar/ **98 B3**

Cottascarth and Rendall Moss *Finstown, Mainland, Orkney.* Hen harriers, merlins and short-eared owls can be seen, while nearby Rendall Moss is great for breeding curlews. 💻www.rspb.org.uk/reserves-and-events/reserves-a-z/cottascarth-and-rendall-moss/ **98 B4**

Fair Isle *Stoneybreck, Shetland.* This isolated island is home to around 70 people. It has a bird observatory, which is open to the public in summer, and the Shetlands council and National Trust for Scotland encourage traditional crofting practices and conservation. Chiefly famous for its traditional knitted garments, additional crafts now include traditional wooden boat building, fiddle making and the manufacture of stained glass windows. Accessible in summer by boat from Grutness, on Shetland or flights from Tingwall (Lerwick) airport and Kirkwall, Orkney. 💻www.nts.org.uk/visit/places/fair-isle 💻www.fairisle.org.uk **101 E4**

Fetlar *Houbie, Shetland.* In summer, the breeding birds include nine-tenths of all British red-necked phalaropes, as well as arctic and great skuas, red-throated divers and whimbrels. 💻www.rspb.org.uk/reserves-and-events/reserves-a-z/fetlar/ **102 D6**

Hermaness National Nature Reserve *Burrafirth, Unst, Shetland.* National Nature Reserve overlooking Muckle Flugga, the cliffs and stacks of Herma Ness are a haven for more than 100,000 seabirds, including over 50,000 nesting puffins and 30,000 gannets, while the inland moors hold the third largest colony of great skuas in the world. The walk to the cliffs takes 3–4 hours. 💻www.nature.scot/enjoying-outdoors/scotlands-national-nature-reserves/hermaness-national-nature-reserve **102 B6**

Hobbister *Kirkwall, Mainland, Orkney.* Hen harriers, red-throated divers and short-eared owls breed on the moorland in early summer, while black guillemots and red-breasted mergansers can be seen from the coast. 💻www.rspb.org.uk/reserves-and-events/reserves-a-z/hobbister/ **98 C4**

Hoy *Rackwick, Orkney.* The reserve is a mixture of moorland and cliffs and includes the Old Man of Hoy rock stack. Dunlin, golden plovers, great skuas and red grouse breed on the moor and guillemots, kittiwakes and razorbills on the cliffs. See also Old Man of Hoy. 💻www.rspb.org.uk/reserves-and-events/reserves-a-z/hoy **100 B2**

Marwick Head *Marwick, Mainland, Orkney.* Thousands of pairs of seabirds crowd onto the cliffs during the breeding season. Among the coastal specialities in the grasslands on the cliff top are sea campion, spring squill and thrift. 💻www.rspb.org.uk/reserves-and-events/reserves-a-z/marwick-head/ **98 A3**

Monach Isles National Nature Reserve *Monach Isles, Western Isles.* Breeding birds in the summer include terns and black guillemots and there is a rich variety of plants on the machair, but these islands are primarily known for the internationally important colonies of Atlantic grey seals that breed here in the autumn. The islands are part of a Marine Protected Area. Permission is required from Scottish Natural Heritage to land. 💻www.scotland.com/attractions/nature-reserves/monach-islands/ **93 B1**

Mousa *Shetland.* Many of the island's 12,000 storm petrels nest near Mousa broch, and arctic skuas, arctic terns, black guillemots, great skuas, oystercatchers and ringed plovers also breed. Common seals breed on the shoreline. Harbour porpoises, minke whales and orcas can sometimes be seen en route to the island. 💻www.rspb.org.uk/reserves-and-events/reserves-a-z/mousa/ **101 D3**

North Hill *Papa Westray, Orkney.* The cliffs house breeding guillemots, kittiwakes and razorbills, with arctic skuas and arctic terns nests, eiders, oystercatchers and ringed plovers. 💻www.rspb.org.uk/reserves-and-events/reserves-a-z/north-hill/ **100 A2**

Noss National Nature Reserve *Noss, Shetland.* Some 45,000 guillemots, 7000 pairs of gannets and thousands of fulmars, kittiwakes and puffins breed on the ledges of this island's cliffs. Seals are often seen in the surrounding seas and great skuas over the moorland. 💻www.nature.scot/enjoying-outdoors/scotlands-national-nature-reserves/noss-national-nature-reserve **101 E2**

Noup Cliffs *Westray, Orkney.*
More than 44,500 guillemots and 12,700 pairs of kittiwakes breed on these lonely cliffs, as well as good numbers of fulmars and razorbills.
www.rspb.org.uk/reserves-and-events/reserves-a-z/noup-cliffs/ **100 B1**

Sumburgh Head *Sumburgh, Mainland, Shetland.* The cliffs attract thousands of breeding birds, including fulmars, guillemots and puffins. Gannets can be seen offshore, and occasionally whales and dolphins. www.rspb.org.uk/reserves-and-events/reserves-a-z/sumburgh-head/ www.sumburghhead.com **101 F3**

Trumland *Brinian, Rousay, Orkney.* The heather moorland of this reserve provides ideal nesting grounds for hen harriers, merlins and red-throated divers. www.rspb.org.uk/reserves-and-events/reserves-a-z/trumland/ **100 D2**

Country and forest parks

Aberdeen and Moray
Aden Country Park *Mintlaw, Aberdeenshire.* Some 230 acres of woodlands, a large lake and a variety of wildlife. www.visitabdn.com/listing/aden-country-park **83 D6**

Argyll, Bute, Stirling, Trossachs
Argyll Forest Park *Lochgoilhead, Argyll and Bute.* The Argyll Forest Park occupies 60,000 acres of southern Argyll. Activities available include rock climbing, hill walking, boating and hiking. Among the wildlife that may be seen in the sea lochs are sea otters, sharks and grey seals. https://forestryandland.gov.scot/visit/forest-parks/argyll-forest-park **54 C4**

Queen Elizabeth Forest Park *David Marshall Lodge, near Aberfoyle, Stirling.* Nestling between the eastern shore of Loch Lomond and the Trossachs, 45,000 acres of woodland, moorland and mountainside have been reserved for walkers and hikers; also Go Ape high wire forest adventure. https://forestryandland.gov.scot/visit/forest-parks/queen-elizabeth-forest-park **55 B8**

Glasgow and the Clyde
Calderglen Country Park *Strathaven Road, East Kilbride, South Lanarkshire.* As well as miles of nature trails, this country park has a children's zoo with exotic animals, adventure play areas and a visitor centre. www.slleisureandculture.co.uk/info/113/calderglen_country_park **28 D4**

Gleniffer Braes Country Park *Glenfield Road, Paisley, Renfrewshire.* A large area of woodland and moorland with an adventure playground. www.renfrewshire.gov.uk/article/3690/Gleniffer-Braes-Country-Park **27 B8**

Strathclyde Country Park *336 Hamilton Road, Motherwell, North Lanarkshire.* Centred on Strathclyde Loch, this park consists of 1100 acres of mature woodland, wetland, wildlife areas and open parkland. See also activities. www.northlanarkshire.gov.uk/index.aspx?articleid=6760 **29 C5**

Perth, Angus, Dundee and Fife
Crombie Country Park *Monikie, Broughty Ferry, Dundee City.* Woodland country park with guided nature trails, interpretation of forestry in the area as far back as 2000 BCE, an orienteering course, a children's play area. www.visitscotland.com/info/see-do/crombie-country-park-p252661 **67 D4**

Gartmorn Dam Country Park *Sauchie, Clackmannanshire.* This local nature reserve and Site of Special Scientific Interest includes the oldest man-made reservoir still working in Scotland, built by the 6th Earl of Mar in 1713 to provide water to drive the pumps in his nearby coal mines. There are extensive footpaths, links to national cycleways and horse riding routes. www.clacks.gov.uk/culture/gartmorndam/ **40 B2**

South of Scotland
Galloway Forest Park *New Galloway, Dumfries and Galloway.* Britain's largest forest park covers more than 300 square miles with habitat ranging from forest, moorland and loch to mountains and beaches. Excellent stargazing conditions have led to it being designated a Dark Sky Park by the International Dark Sky Association, the first in the UK. There are extensive walking and cycle trails, horse riding, fishing, a wide variety of wildlife, forest drives, and stunning views. https://forestryandland.gov.scot/visit/forest-parks/galloway-forest-park https://forestryandland.gov.scot/visit/forest-parks/galloway-forest-park/dark-skies **47 B8**

Other natural features

Argyll, Bute, Stirling, Trossachs
Fingal's Cave *Staffa, Argyll and Bute.* The uninhabited isle of Staffa inspired Mendelssohn to compose his 'Hebridean Overture', of which the most famous movement is named after this cave. The hexagonal shape of the rocks that make up its walls, floor and roof occurred when Tertiary basalt lava flows shrank and cracked as they cooled after a volcanic eruption. Tour boats operate from Iona, Mull and Oban. See also Staffa National Nature Reserve. www.nts.org.uk/visit/places/staffa **61 D6**

Mackinnon's Cave *Balnahard, Mull, Argyll and Bute.* Accessible only at low tide, this is the largest sea-cave in the Hebrides. The grisly legend asserts that evil spirits once devoured a group of people here. www.isle-of-mull.net/attractions/geology/mackinnons-cave **61 D7**

Edinburgh and East Central
Arthur's Seat *Holyrood Park, Edinburgh, City of Edinburgh.* At 823 ft high, this extinct volcanic plug looms over the city. The hike to the top affords spectacular views. www.visitscotland.com/info/see-do/holyrood-park-and-arthurs-seat-p914341 **42 F1**

The Highlands
Falls of Shin *Lairg, Highland.* Between June and September, these falls are one of the best places to watch salmon going upriver to spawn. https://forestryandland.gov.scot/visit/falls-of-shin **86 D2**

Smoo Cave *Durness, Highland.* A 200ft long complex of three caves etched into the limestone cliffs by the stream and the sea. The central cave is crossed by rubber dinghy. www.visitscotland.com/info/towns-villages/smoo-cave-p245631 **89 B6**

Parks and gardens

Aberdeen and Moray
Cruickshank Botanic Garden *St Machar Drive, Aberdeen, Aberdeen City.* Pretty displays of shrubs, alpine and herbaceous plants, with water and rock gardens. There is also a small zoological museum. http://abdn.ac.uk/botanic-garden/ **75 B6**

Pitmedden Garden *Ellon, Aberdeenshire.* The centrepiece of this garden, known as the Great Garden, was originally laid out in 1675. The parterres were relaid in the 1950s with designs that may have been used in the gardens of Holyrood House and the original owner's coat of arms. The gardens include a visitor centre, woodland walks, a herb garden and a small museum devoted to farming life. www.nts.org.uk/visit/places/pitmedden-garden **83 E6**

Argyll, Bute, Stirling, Trossachs
Achamore House Gardens *Ardminish, Gigha, Argyll and Bute.* Sir James Horlick, one of the world's greatest gardeners, created this landscape filled with azaleas, rhododendrons, camellias, hydrangeas and roses. http://www.gigha.org.uk/viewItem.php?id=8845 **50 B2**

Ardencraig Gardens *Rothesay, Bute, Argyll and Bute.* In summer the gardens and hothouses are overflowing with flowering plants. Also has aviaries with exotic birds. www.visitbute.com/ardencraig-gardens-a-secret-garden/ www.gardens-of-argyll.co.uk/view-details.php?id=471 **54 F3**

Ardkinglas Woodland Garden *Cairndow, Argyll and Bute.* One of Scotland's best collections of conifers, with spectacular views over Loch Fyne and rhododendrons in flower in June. www.ardkinglas.com/ardkinglas-woodland-gardens.html **54 A4**

Arduaine Garden *Arduaine, Argyll and Bute.* This outstanding garden, with an important collection of rare trees and shrubs, lies on a promontory bounded by Loch Melfort and the Sound of Jura, and benefits from the warmth brought by the Gulf Stream. Among the seasonal highlights are rhododendrons, azaleas and magnolias. www.nts.org.uk/visit/places/arduaine-garden **53 A7**

Ascog Fernery and Gardens
Ascog Hall, Ascog, Argyll and Bute. Restored Victorian conservatories, containing a wide range of ferns, including one that is alleged to be more than 1000 years old. www.ascogfernery.com **54 F4**

Benmore Botanic Gardens *Benmore, Argyll and Bute.* An offshoot of Edinburgh's Royal Botanic Gardens, with masses of rhododendrons and azaleas flowering in late spring. Among the trees from all over the world is an avenue of giant redwoods. www.rbge.org.uk/visit/benmore-botanic-garden **36 C1**

Crarae Gardens *Crarae, Argyll and Bute.* Beautiful gardens overlooking Loch Fyne, with panoramic vistas, spectacular waterfalls, rhododendrons in late spring and various walking trails. www.nts.org.uk/visit/places/crarae-garden **54 C2**

Edinburgh and East Central
Holyrood Park *Queen's Drive, Edinburgh, City of Edinburgh.* The former royal hunting ground occupies 650 acres, and includes moorland, a loch and the towering 'Arthur's Seat'. www.historicenvironment.scot/visit-a-place/places/holyrood-park **42 F1**

Royal Botanic Gardens *Inverleith Row, Edinburgh, City of Edinburgh.* One of the most beautiful botanic gardens in Britain, spread across 70 acres and dating from the late 17th century. Highlights include the Glasshouse Experience, the Palm House and the Chinese Garden. www.rbge.org.uk **41 E8**

Glasgow and the Clyde
Glasgow Botanic Gardens *Great Western Road, Glasgow, City of Glasgow.* An extensive collection of herb gardens and tropical plants, founded in 1871. www.glasgowbotanicgardens.com **28 A2**

Perth, Angus, Dundee and Fife
Branklyn Garden *116 Dundee Road, Perth, Perth and Kinross.* A small garden holds a magnificent collection of alpines and rhododendrons as well as peat-garden and herbaceous plants from all over the world. It was founded in 1922 and now belongs to the National Trust for Scotland. www.nts.org.uk/visit/places/branklyn-garden **66 E1**

South of Scotland
Dawyck Botanic Garden *Drumelzier, Scottish Borders.* The collection – an offshoot of the Royal Botanic Garden in Edinburgh – includes conifers, and flowering shrubs. www.rbge.org.uk/visit/dawyck-botanic-garden **21 B7**

Harestanes Countryside Visitor Centre *Bonjedward, Scottish Borders.* Trails and guided walks. Discovery room with wildlife displays. www.liveborders.org.uk/play/harestanes **24 E1**

Kailzie Gardens *Kirkburn, Scottish Borders.* Series of formal walled Victorian gardens, with woodland and waterside walks, as well as waterfowl and owl collections. www.kailziegardens.com **22 B1**

Logan Botanic Garden *Port Logan, Dumfries and Galloway.* The mild climate of south western Scotland allows this beautiful annexe of the Royal Botanic Garden in Edinburgh to grow a larger range of plants from temperate regions, such as palms and tree ferns. www.rbge.org.uk/visit/logan-botanic-garden **46 E2**

The Highlands
Inverewe Gardens *Poolewe, Highland.* This extensive garden was created on an area of bare rocks on this treeless, barren peninsula in the 1860s. It now holds more

▲ **Arduaine Garden** Allan wright / Alamy
◄ **Arthur's Seat** Davide Belpanno / Alamy

◄ **Glasgow Botanic Gardens**
Bill Miller / Alamy

than 100 acres of one of the greatest exotic plant collections in the world. Sheltered from the winds by extensive belts of trees, it benefits from the warmth of the Gulf Stream. www.nts.org.uk/visit/places/inverewe **84 E2**

Boat trips

Argyll, Bute, Stirling, Trossachs

Staffa Boat Trips *Fionnphort, Mull, Argyll and Bute.* Boat trips to Fingal's Cave on Staffa. Weather permitting, the boat sails right into the cave, allowing passengers to land. www.staffatrips.co.uk **61 E6**

Seafari (Oban) *Easdale near Oban, Argyll and Bute.* Boat trips to Iona and Staffa, also marine wildlife-watching trips in the Firth of Lorn and visits to the Corryvreckan Whirlpool. www.seafari.co.uk/oban **62 F2**

Sea Life Surveys and Eco-cruz *Ledaig, Mull, Argyll and Bute.* Research vessels that take passengers while conducting surveys of the area's dolphins and whales. www.sealifesurveys.com **62 D4**

SS Sir Walter Scott *Trossachs Pier, Loch Katrine, Aberfoyle, Stirling.* A small steamship that makes trips across Loch Katrine, made famous by Scott's evocative poem, 'The Lady of the Lake'. www.lochkatrine.com/cruises/loch-cruises **55 B7**

Turus Mara *Penmore Mill, Dervaig, Isle of Mull, Argyll, PA75 6QS.* Boat trips to Fingal's Cave on Staffa, to the Trennish Isles or whale- and dolphin-watching. www.turusmara.com **61 B7**

Edinburgh and East Central

Maid of the Forth *Hawes Pier, South Queensferry, City of Edinburgh.* Trips to see the birds and sealife of the islands in the Firth of Forth. www.maidoftheforth.co.uk **41 E6**

Seafari (Edinburgh) *North Berwick, East Lothian* Wildlife watching and photographic boat trips depart from North Berwick to Bass Rock and the Isle of May. Also from South Queensferry to view the three Forth bridges. www.seafari-edinburgh.co.uk **43 C7**

Sula *North Berwick, East Lothian.* The boat 'Sula' provides trips around Bass Rock from North Berwick harbour. Breeding birds that may be seen include fulmars, guillemots, puffins, razorbills and terns, as well as Scotland's second biggest gannet colony. www.sulaboattrips.co.uk **43 C7**

Perth, Angus, Dundee and Fife

May Princess *Anstruther Easter, Fife.* This ferry runs daily boat trips to the nature reserve on the Isle of May from the lifeboat station. Also fast boat trips in the RIB 'Osprey'. www.isleofmayferry.com **58 B3**

The Highlands

Aquaxplore *Elgol, Skye, Highland.* Trips to otherwise inaccessible locations around Skye and the neighbouring islands by rigid inflatable boat. www.aquaxplore.co.uk **68 A5**

Bella Jane Boat Trips *Elgol, Skye, Highland.* Trips from Elgol to Loch Coruisk and the seal colony. www.bellajane.co.uk **68 A5**

Crannog Cruises *The Town Pier, Fort William, Highland.* Short wildlife cruises on Loch Linnie. www.crannog.net/cruises **70 E3**

Ecoventures *Harbour Workshop, Victoria Place, Cromarty, Highland.* Full-day trips to see the dolphins and seals in the outer regions of the Moray Firth. www.ecoventures.co.uk **80 B2**

Handa Island Ferry *Tarbet, Scourie, Highland.* Trips run from the tiny hamlet of Tarbet to the internationally important wildlife reserve throughout the day during summer. www.handa-ferry.com **88 D3**

Jacobite Cruises Loch Ness *Tomnahurich Bridge, Glenurquhart Road, Inverness, Highland.* A range of cruises on Loch Ness, with options for visiting various attractions around the Loch. www.jacobite.co.uk **79 D8**

John o'Groats Wildlife Cruises *Ferry Office, John o'Groats, Highland.* Half-day trips on the local ferry in high summer. Whales and dolphins are sometimes spotted and seabirds almost guaranteed. www.jogferry.co.uk **91 A7**

MV Shearwater *The Harbour, Arisaig, Highland.* Boat trips run by Arisaig Marine between Arisaig and the nature reserve on Rùm, as well as Eigg, Muck and Canna. Whales and porpoises are sometimes seen en route. www.arisaig.co.uk **69 D6**

Animal attractions

Aberdeen and Moray

Doonies Farm *Coast Road, Nigg, Aberdeen City.* One of the largest collections of rare-breed farm animals, including horses, goats, cattle, sheep, pigs and poultry. Children's play area. www.dooniesfarm.co.uk **75 B6**

Macduff Marine Aquarium *11 High Shore, Macduff, Aberdeenshire.* This aquarium concentrates on the sealife of the Moray Firth, with rays, native fish, crustaceans and touch tanks. www.macduff-aquarium.org.uk **82 B4**

North East Falconry Centre *Broadland, Carnie, Huntly, Aberdeenshire.* Daily demonstrations of falconry, with flying eagles and falcons. There are also owls in the collection. www.huntly-falconry-centre.com **82 E2**

Argyll, Bute, Stirling, Trossachs

Blair Drummond Safari and Adventure Park *Blair Drummond, Stirling.* The animal collection includes chimpanzees, elephants, monkeys, lemurs, zebras, bears, giraffes, ostriches, rhinoceroses, camels, bison, wallabies and penguins. Sea lion displays take place regularly and other attractions include a pets farm, boating and an adventure playground. www.blairdrummond.com **56 C2**

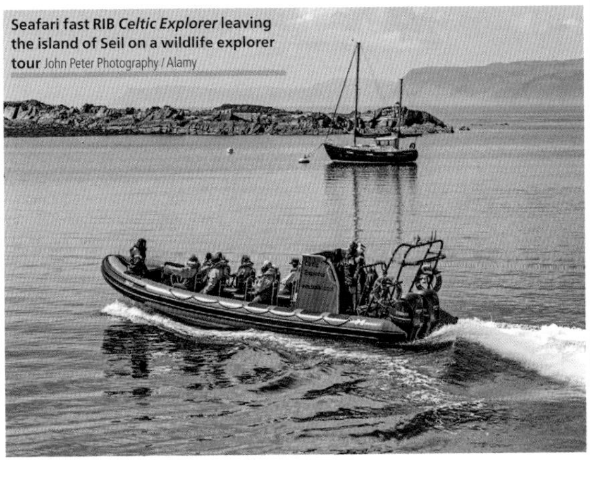

Seafari fast RIB *Celtic Explorer* leaving the island of Seil on a wildlife explorer tour John Peter Photography / Alamy

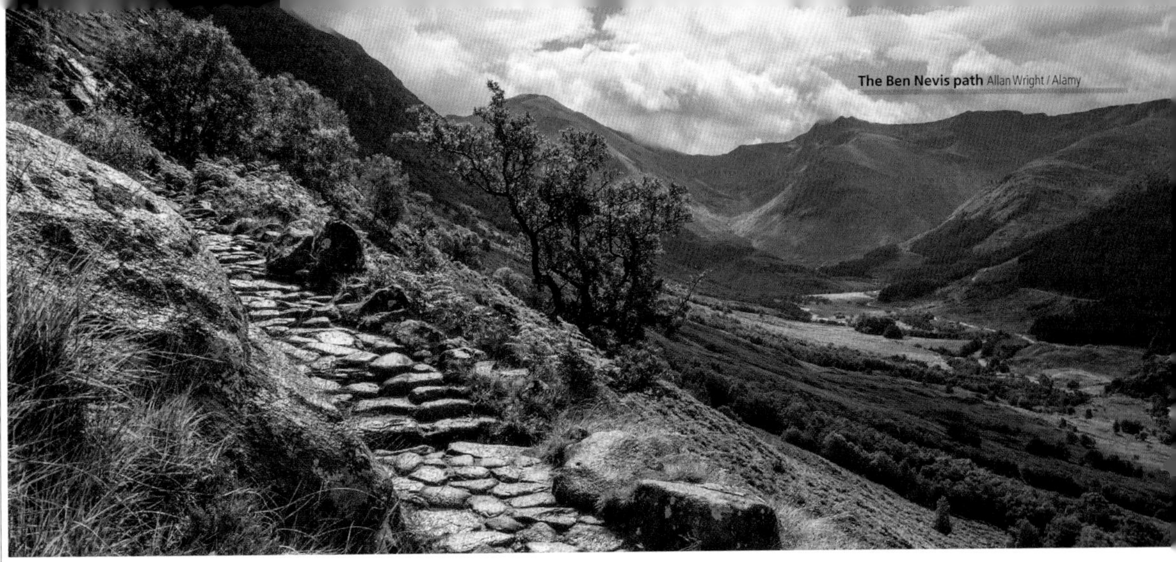

The Ben Nevis path Allan Wright / Alamy

Walking, cycling and riding trails

Aberdeen and Moray

Moray Monster Trails *Balnacoul, Fochabers, Moray* A winding woodland mountain bike trail with spectacular views over the nearby gorge, accessed from the Winding Walks car park. http://scotland.forestry.gov.uk **81 C8**

Speyside Way *Buckie, Moray* This challenging route follows the river Spey for 66 miles, south from the coast, via Craigellachie uphill to the ski resort of Aviemore. www.speysideway.org **82 B1**

Winding Walks Forest Walks *Balnacoul, Fochabers, Moray* Waymarked paths of varying degrees through mature conifer and beech woodland, near a steep gully. http://scotland.forestry.gov.uk **81 C8**

Argyll, Bute, Stirling, Trossachs

An Caisteal *Crianlarich, Stirling* The hike to the top of this 3265 ft peak from the layby 2 miles from Crianlarich takes around 5 hours there and back. **64 E1**

Ben Cruachan Walk *Lochawe, Argyll and Bute* The challenging hikes on this ben take between 6 and 9 hours from Cruachan Dam Visitor Centre. **63 E6**

Ben Lui *Tyndrum, Stirling* One of the more popular walks on this mountain goes up the south-eastern ridge from Cononish Farm and takes 7 hours up and back. **63 D8**

Campsies Fells Trail *Stirling, Stirling* A local trail that links villages in the region, such as Fintry and Gargunnock, with open country and forest paths. Stirling TIC **39 B6**

Cruach Tairbeirt *Arrochar, Argyll and Bute* A waymarked 2 mile forest walk on the flanks of Cruach Tairbeirt from Arrochar and Tarbet railway station. The climb to the viewpoints is fairly easy, but allow at least 2 hours. http://scotland.forestry.gov.uk **55 B5**

Rob Roy Way *Drymen, Stirling* An unmarked, unofficial path from Drymen to Loch Tay and then north-east along Strathtay. Its 80 miles includes woodlands, heaths and remote moorland. **37 C8**

The Trossachs Trail *Brig o'Turk, Stirling* Not a single route but a network of interlinking pathways in an area roughly bounded by Callander in the East, Doune and Aberfoyle in the south, Loch Lomond in the west and the Crianlarich Hills in the north. Among the good starting points is Brig o'Turk. **55 B8**

West Island Way *Port Bannatyne, Bute, Argyll and Bute* This relatively easy route leads for 30 miles from Kilchattan Bay round the Isle of Bute via Port Bannatyne across varied scenery including seashore, moorland, forest and farmland. **54 F3**

Glasgow and the Clyde

Clyde Walkway *New Lanark, South Lanarkshire* A 40 mile route tracing the river Clyde downstream from the spectacular Falls of Clyde at New Lanark to where it meets the river Kelvin. **19 A8**

Glasgow to Gourock *Gourock, City of Glasgow* A 14 mile cycle route that runs to the west of Glasgow via Paisley, Kilmacolm and Greenock along minor roads and a disused railway line. **36 E3**

Kelvin Allander Walkway *Glasgow, City of Glasgow* This 9-mile gentle route follows the rivers Kelvin and Allander from the Tall Ship in Glasgow Harbour through Kelvingrove Park and Maryhill to Milngavie, where the West Highland Way starts. **28 A2**

West Highland Way *Milngavie, East Dunbartonshire* This hike stretches 95 miles from Milngavie to Fort William, via Loch Lomond, Rannoch Moor and Glen Nevis. The path itself is not difficult and passes through some of Scotland's most spectacular scenery, using old drove roads, a military road built to help in moving troops during the suppression of the Highlands during the 18th century and old railway lines. **38 F2**

Perth, Angus, Dundee and Fife

Dollar Glen *Dollar, Clackmannanshire* A waymarked path through this spectacular wooded glen provides a beautiful approach to Castle Campbell. **56 C4**

Fife Coastal Path *North Queensferry, Fife* A 78 mile route running along the north shore of the Firth of Forth between North Queensferry and Newport on Tay via Crail and St Andrews. As well as coastal paths, it takes in some pretty villages and seaside towns. **41 D6**

Loch Leven *Leven, Fife* The views from the 20-mile circuit of roads around the loch are stunning. **58 B1**

South of Scotland

Berwickshire Coastal Path *St. Abbs, Scottish Borders* A 15 mile path that leads along the east coast from Berwick-upon-Tweed, just over the English Border to St Abbs. **35 A7**

Cock of Arran Coast Walk *Lochranza, Arran, North Ayrshire* This 8 mile route runs along the north-east coast between Lochranza and Sannox. The route takes about 4 to 5 hours to complete. **51 A5**

Goat Fell *Brodick, Arran, North Ayrshire* There are several routes to the summit of Arran's highest mountain (2866 ft), including from Brodick itself to the south and Corrie to the east. Most of the routes take about 8 hours. **51 C6**

Isle of Arran Coastal Way *Brodick, Arran, North Ayrshire* The coastal paths make a 60 mile circuit around the island. The north of the island has steeper climbs, but these provide magnificent views. In some stretches, demanding paths have road-based alternatives. **51 C6**

Newton Stewart to Glenluce *Newton Stewart, Dumfries and Galloway* A 50 mile route through farmland and pretty villages, along the coast of the Machars peninsula. **47 C6**

The Pilgrims Way *Newton Stewart, Dumfries and Galloway* A 25 mile route between Newton Stewart to the Isle of Whithorn near the tip of the Machars peninsula. It is associated with St Ninian, who introduced Christianity to Scotland and ends at the ruined 13th-century chapel dedicated to the saint. **47 C6**

St Cuthbert's Way *Melrose, Scottish Borders* This 60 mile route links sites associated with St Cuthbert, from Melrose to Holy Island in Northumberland. It crosses the Eildon Hills and follows the course of the Tweed and then, once over the border, traverses the Cheviot Hills to Fenwick. Part of its course follows Roman Dere Street. **23 C6**

Southern Uplands Way *Portpatrick, Dumfries and Galloway* This scenic coast-to-coast route runs for 210 miles and is demanding in places. It starts in Portpatrick on the west coast and its often remote track goes via Sanquar, Moffat and Melrose to Cockburnspath a few miles south of Dunbar. **46 D2**

Tweed Cycle Way *Biggar, Scottish Borders* This route runs from Biggar along the Tweed Valley to Berwick-upon-Tweed just over the English border. **20 B4**

The Highlands

Ben More *Crianlarich, Highland* Allow at least 6 hours for the strenuous hike to the summit and back from Benmore Farm. **64 E1**

Ben Nevis Summit *Fort William, Highland* One route to the summit starts from the Glen Nevis Visitor Centre and uses a zig-zagging pony path to reach the summit. Whether returning via the same route, or descending via the Allt a'Mhuilinn, the walk takes about 8 hours. **70 E3**

Cairn Gorm High Circuit *Aviemore, Highland* A 7 mile circular route from the ski-area car park at Aviemore up to the summit of Cairn Gorm and back, via the rim of coire an t-Sneachda, Cairn Lochan and the ridge via Lurcher's Gully back to the car park. **72 A3**

Cape Wrath Trail *Fort William, Highland* This 300 mile route runs almost parallel to the 'North to the Cape' route. However, leads via Kintail, Torridon, Dundonnel and Assynt, including Beinne Eighe and Lurg Mór on the way. **70 E3**

Great Glen Cycle Route *Fort William, Highland* This 50 mile route is mainly off road and links Fort William and Inverness, going through a variety of spectacular scenery and forestry. **70 E3**

Great Glen Way *Fort William, Highland* This 73 mile walking route, like the cycle route, runs from Fort William to Inverness, but follows a slightly different path. It goes along Glen Mor, follows the north-west shores of Loch Lochy and Loch Ness and then the course of the Caledonian Canal. Much of the walk is along towpaths and broad forest paths, with a few more challenging sections. **70 E3**

Lairig Ghru trail *Aviemore, Highland* A demanding 24 mile hike from Aviemore, over the Lairig Ghru Pass to Braemar **72 A3**

North to the Cape *Fort William, Highland* This trail leads 200 miles from Fort William to Cape Wrath, via Knoydart, Eas a Chùluinn and some of the Munros of Beinn Eighe National Nature Reserve. It is extremely challenging in places. **70 E3**

Bottlenose dolphins breaching in the Moray Firth Charlie Phillips / Alamy

Edinburgh and East Central

Edinburgh Butterfly and Insect World *Dobbies Garden World, Lasswade, Midlothian.* Breeding butterflies from around the world, in enclosures that visitors may walk through. The smaller animals include, leaf-cutting ants, beetles, scorpions, locusts, spiders, and grasshoppers, while among the larger specimens are terrapins, snakes, an iguana and some quail.
🖥 www.edinburgh-butterfly-world.co.uk **32 A2**

Edinburgh Zoo *134 Corstorphine Road, Edinburgh, City of Edinburgh.* The collection holds more than 1500 animals, including endangered species such as snow leopards, white rhinos and pygmy hippos. Not forgetting the two most famous residents, Tian Tian and Yuan Guang, a pair of giant pandas on loan from China.
🖥 www.edinburghzoo.org.uk **41 F8**

Scottish Seabird Centre *North Berwick, East Lothian.* The chief feature of this centre is the close-up views of the birdlife of nearby Bass Rock, obtained via a live link to cameras there. There are also games for children and exhibits on Scotland's different seabirds. 🖥 www.seabird.org **43 C7**

Perth, Angus, Dundee and Fife

Deep Sea World *Forthside Terrace, North Queensferry, Fife.* Attractions include sharks, piranhas, an underwater tunnel, touch pools with rays and snake-handling sessions. 🖥 www.deepseaworld.com **41 D6**

St Andrews Aquarium *The Scores, St Andrews, Fife.* This popular attraction holds seals, sharks, exotic fish, crustaceans, rays, octopuses, seahorses and touchpools.
🖥 www.standrewsaquarium.co.uk **67 F5**

Scottish Deer Centre *Rankeilour, Cupar, Fife.* The centre has red, fallow and sika deer, as well as reindeer, wolves and falconry displays, strenuous guided nature trails and a play area. 🖥 www.tsdc.co.uk **57 A8**

The Highlands

Cairngorm Reindeer Centre *Glenmore, Highland.* Scotland's only free-roaming herd of reindeer.
🖥 www.cairngormreindeer.co.uk **72 A4**

Chanonry Point *Fortrose, Highland.* This spit is an excellent site for seeing some of the Moray Firth's dolphins chasing fish at high tide. 🖥 www.moraydolphins.co.uk/chanonry-point.html **80 C2**

Craig Highland Farm *Woodside, Plockton, Highland.* Set on the shore of Loch Carron, this farm has rare and traditional breeds of sheep and chickens, as well as rabbits, pigs, geese and ponies on the farm. In the surrounding area there is a chance of seeing seals, otters and pine martens.
🖥 http://craighighlandfarm.co.uk **77 E8**

Dolphins and seals of the Moray Firth *North Kessock, Highland.* More than 100 bottle-nosed dolphins live in the Moray Firth. At the visitor centre in North Kessock, visitors can listen in to the dolphins' calls. Among the best viewing points is nearby Kessock Bridge 🖥 www.moraydolphins.co.uk/north-kessock.html **80 D1**

Eilean Bàn *Kyle of Lochalsh, Highland.* Island wildlife sanctuary under the Skye Bridge. Once the home of Gavin Maxwell, author of 'Ring of Bright Water', this sanctuary is particularly associated with otters. Guided tours must be prebooked at the Bright Water Visitor Centre in Kyleakin (01599 530040). 🖥 www.eileanban.org **77 F7**

Highland Wildlife Park *Kincraig, Highland.* This extensive park is devoted to the native fauna of the Highlands, from the whole range of habitats. Forest specialities include polecat, wildcat, red squirrel and capercaillie, while arctic fox and snowy owl prefer tundra; otters and beavers are wetland species and tawny owls, badgers and black grouse inhabit the woodlands. Some species are extinct in the wild, or have only been reintroduced in limited areas: these include lynx, white-tailed sea eagle, wolf and chough. In the reserve, exotic but rare, animals such as moufflon, Przewalski's horse, Soay sheep and European bison are held. 🖥 www.highlandwildlifepark.org.uk **72 B3**

Loch Ness Exhibition Centre *Drumnadrochit, Highland.* This exhibition explores the history of Nessie through eyewitness accounts and the research of various expeditions to locate the monster.
🖥 www.lochness.com **79 F7**

Beaches and resorts

Aberdeen and Moray

Cullen *Moray.* The sands of Cullen Bay are sheltered from the wind and benefit from the warm waters of the Gulf Stream, which finishes its journey in the Moray Firth. **82 B2**

Fraserburgh Bay *Fraserburgh, Aberdeenshire.* The bay, with good sandy beaches, lies to the east of the fishing town and is relatively sheltered. **83 B6**

Argyll, Bute, Stirling, Trossachs

Rothesay *Bute, Argyll and Bute.* A handsome Victorian resort with a pier, palm-tree lined promenade and 1920s Winter Gardens. Attractions include Rothesay Castle, Bute Museum, St Mary's Chapel, Ardencraig Gardens and Ascog Fernery and Gardens. **54 F3**

Edinburgh and East Central

North Berwick *East Lothian.* An attractive Victorian seaside resort, with long sandy beaches, golf courses and a small harbour. The beach of Milsey Bay is particularly good. Local attractions include boat trips to Bass Rock, The Scottish Seabird Centre, the Auld Kirk and Dirleton Castle. **43 C7**

Perth, Angus, Dundee and Fife

Anstruther Easter *Fife.* This summer resort used to be an important centre of the herring-fishing industry. Among the best of the beaches is Billow Ness beach. Attractions and excursions include the tiny village of Cellardyke, with traditional stone houses and an old harbour, 'The Scottish Fisheries Museum', and boat trips on the 'May Princess' to the Isle of May **58 B3**

Arbroath *Angus.* A busy resort, once an important hub of the haddock fishing and smoking industries. The long, sandy beach is south of the town. Other attractions include the ruins of Arbroath Abbey, the Signal Tower, in the old shore station of the Bell Rock lighthouse, housing a local history museum, and the red sandstone church of St Vigeans about a mile north of the town. There are good walks along the clifftops north of the town. **67 C6**

Broughty Ferry *Dundee, Dundee City.* Set against the backdrop of an attractive suburb of Dundee, this stretch of sandy beach looks across the Firth of Tay to Tentsmuir Forest. **66 D4**

Crail *Fife.* As well as many beaches, natural bathing facilities are available at Roome Bay. Lobster and crab boats still work from the harbour, which is surrounded by old fishing cottages, many of which are lived in by members of the thriving artists' colony. Great views of the harbour can be obtained from Castle Walk. There is also a Crail Museum and Heritage Centre **58 B4**

Earlsferry and Elie beaches *Earlsferry, Fife.* A series of beautiful golden-brown sandy beaches and sheltered coves overlooking the outer Firth of Forth. **58 C2**

Lunan Bay *Angus.* Almost two miles of fine, sandy beaches overlook Lunan Bay a few miles from Montrose. **67 B6**

Montrose *Angus.* A wide expanse of golden sand, backed by sand dunes, stretches along the coast north of the town. **67 B7**

St Andrews *Fife.* The West Sands lie north of the city centre, backed by a series of some of the most famous golf courses in the world. **67 F5**

South of Scotland

Coldingham Bay *Coldingham, Scottish Borders.* This tiny, sandy beach has a thriving surfing community and some of the best cold-water diving in Europe. **35 A7**

The Highlands

Achmelvich *Highland.* A semicircular bay with brilliant white sands and blue water,

St Andrews Chris Wallard Photography / iStock

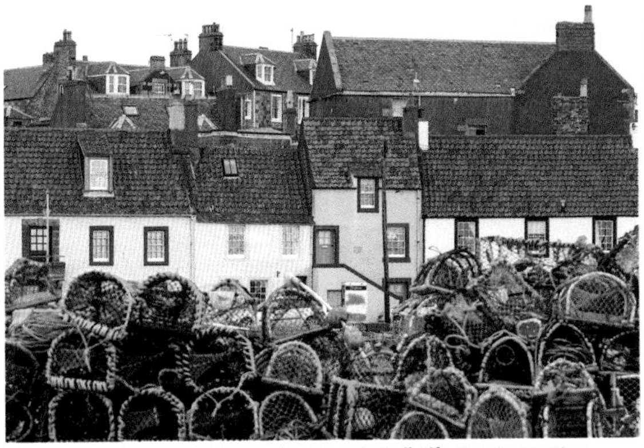

▲ Lobster pots in front of fisherman's cottages in Crail, Fife Marianthi Lainas / Alamy

looking out towards the distant Isle of Lewis. **84 A4**

Brora Beach *Brora, Highland.* North of the little village of the same name on the east coast lies a two-mile stretch of good, sandy beach. **87 C6**

Dornoch *Highland.* A pleasant seaside resort, famous for its golf course, Dornoch's beaches overlook Dornoch Firth. Dornoch Cathedral is also worth a visit. Seals can sometimes be seen lounging on the sandbars beyond the south beach. **86 E4**

Embo Beach *Embo, Highland.* Facing onto the North Sea, the sands of Embo Beach are a good area for envigorating walks. **86 D5**

Gairloch *Highland.* There are several good beaches near this small resort, of which Big Sand is best sheltered fom the wind. There are also some excellent coastal walks. The Gairloch Museum has a range of displays about aspects of life here. **84 F2**

Gruinard Beach *Little Gruinard, Highland.* A sheltered beach overlooking the bay of the same name and looking over Gruinard Isle towards the Summer Islands. **84 E3**

Morar beach *Morar, Highland.* Part of the stretch of beaches known as the Silver Sands of Morar that circle a narrow bay. **69 C6**

Portmahomack *Highland.* A broad area of sand stretches west of the town. The Tarbat Discovery Centre, in Tarbat church, has Pictish and early Christian archaeological finds from the area. To the north-east of the town, Tarbat Ness provides good walks to the lighthouse. **87 E6**

Towns and villages

Aberdeen and Moray

Fordyce *Aberdeenshire.* A well-preserved historic village. There are rich canopied tombs in the medieval St Tarquin's church. **82 B2**

Argyll, Bute, Stirling, Trossachs

Blairlogie *Stirling.* An attractive little village with a ruined 17th-century church, Logie Auld Kirk, surrounded by orchards. **39 A7**

Inveraray *Argyll and Bute.* An 18th-century planned town in a stunning setting overlooking Loch Fyne. It is stuffed with Georgian buildings, a Neoclassical church and a Georgian Jail. Excellent views can be obtained from the bell tower of All Saints Church **54 B3**

Luss *Argyll and Bute.* Attractive conservation village with lovely views over Loch Lomond. The church has some good Victorian stained glass. **37 B6**

Port Charlotte *Islay, Argyll and Bute.* Founded in 1828 by Walter Frederick Campbell, Port Charlotte is Islay's prettiest village, with white-washed cottages overlooking Loch Indaal. Islay Nature Centre is a good source of information about the island's flora and fauna. **49 A2**

Tarbert *Argyll and Bute.* The pretty harbour front of this fishing village is best seen from the ruins of Robert the Bruce's castle. **54 F1**

Tobermory *Mull, Argyll and Bute.* An attractive fishing village at the northern tip of the island, with brightly coloured houses perched between the bay and the steep cliffs. Among the attractions are the Mull Museum and the Tobermory Distillery. **61 B8**

Edinburgh and East Central

Aberlady *East Lothian.* Pretty conservation village with Gothic-style cottages, fine medieval glass in the church and a small nature reserve on the silted-up site of the old harbour. **43 D5**

Cramond *City of Edinburgh.* A pretty village in the western outskirts of Edinburgh, overlooking the Forth. It also has a Roman fort, a medieval bridge and tower house and a 17th-century church. Depending on the tide, Cramond Island can be reached across a causeway. **41 E7**

Dirleton *East Lothian.* Reputed to be the prettiest village in Scotland. Castle and garden. **43 D6**

Haddington *East Lothian.* A compact country town, with some fine architecture from the 17th–19th centuries. In Court Street, the Town House was built by William Adam in 1748 and there are other stylish buildings in this area of the town. St Mary's Church, in Church Street, is an architectural mixture with several interesting tombs. **43 F6**

North Berwick *East Lothian.* A charming seaside town set in an attractive coastal setting, looking out on Bass Rock. There are fragments of the Auld Kirk near the harbour and the Coastal Communities Museum is in School Road. **43 C7**

Glasgow and the Clyde

Biggar *South Lanarkshire.* A pleasant town in a rural setting, and dominated by Tinto Hill. Attractions include Biggar Puppet Theatre and museums including Brownsbank Cottage the home of Poet Hugh MacDiarmid, Biggar and Upper Clydesdale Museum, Greenhill Covenanters' House, and Biggar Gasworks Museum. **20 B4**

Perth, Angus, Dundee and Fife

Comrie *Perth and Kinross.* This pretty conservation village suffers more earth tremors than anywhere else in the British Isles because it is sited directly above the Highland Boundary Fault. **40 C4**

Crail *Fife.* An attractive fishing village, with cobbled streets, grander merchants' houses and the 12th-century St Mary's Church. **58 B4**

Culross *Fife.* A former royal burgh maintained by the National Trust for Scotland. Many of the houses are 17th century. Attractions include Culross Palace, Culross Abbey, the Town House and the Study. **40 C3**

Dunfermline *Fife.* The centre of the town has quaint narrow cobbled streets and some fine late 19th-century Gothic Revival buildings. The dominant abbey ruins include a palace, Abbot House, built into them at a later date. **41 C5**

Falkland *Fife.* The village of Falkland grew up around Falkland Palace and has many well-preserved 17th- and 18th-century buildings. **57 B7**

Kirriemuir *Angus.* The centre of town is a maze of narrow, winding passages with picturesque shopping streets. Attractions include JM Barrie's Birthplace and a small aviation museum that also houses a camera obscura. **66 B3**

South of Scotland

Dumfries *Dumfries and Galloway.* One of the towns associated with the poet Robert Burns, who spent the last 3 years of his life here. As well as the Burns sites, Mid Steeple is worth a look as is the Devorgilla Bridge, built in 1341. **48 B3**

Jedburgh *Scottish Borders.* The most prominent feature of this pleasant old market town is the ruined abbey. The 19th-century Jedburgh Castle Jail is built on the site of the 12th-century castle and has displays on the history of prison life. **24 E2**

Kirkcudbright *Dumfries and Galloway.* An attractive small town on the river Dee with colourful houses, and a thriving artistic colony. MacLellan's Castle is a 16th-century tower house at the end of the high street. **47 D8**

Melrose *Scottish Borders.* Dominated by the ruined abbey, this pretty little town also has a tiny ecclesiastical museum in the Commendator's House, an archaeological museum in the Trimontium Exhibition off Market Square and the charming Priorwood Garden. **23 C6**

Peebles *Scottish Borders.* A handsome town on the River Tweed. The Old Parish Church on the High Street has some interesting features. On the same street there is a small museum, the Tweeddale Museum and Gallery. **21 A9**

The Highlands

Dornoch *Highland.* Cathedral, fortified 16th-century Bishop's Palace, Witch's Stone commemorating the last witch burned in Scotland, in 1722. **86 E4**

Plockton *Highland.* A picturesque village overlooking Loch Carron, it was transformed from a sleepy hamlet to a fishing village in the late 18th century. **77 E8**

Rosemarkie *Highland.* A pretty village on the coast of the Black Isle. The Groam House Museum has a good collection of carved Pictish standing stones. **80 C2**

Buildings

Castles and palaces

Aberdeen and Moray

Braemar Castle *Braemar, Aberdeenshire.* This romantic castle dates from 1628. After being requisitioned as a government garrison after the 1745 rebellion, it became a family residence. Highlights include the dungeon and the remarkable, star-shaped defensive walls. It has now been leased to the local community. www.braemarcastle.co.uk **73 C6**

Brodie Castle *Brodie, Forres, Moray.* The oldest part of the building is a typical 'Z'-shaped Scottish tower house, which dates from 1567 with additions from the 17th and 19th centuries. The collection includes a good range of paintings, fine furniture and porcelain. The rooms are known for their panelling and beautiful plasterwork. The parkland includes a woodland walk and a wild garden. www.nts.org.uk/visit/places/brodie-castle **81 C4**

Castle Fraser, Garden and Estate *Sauchen, Inverurie, Aberdeenshire.* This impressive castle, although looking like a medieval French chateau, is one of the fortress-like Castles of Mar. It was built between c.1575 and 1636. The interior was remodelled in 1838 and some rooms still have decoration and furnishings dating from that period. The extensive grounds include an 18th-century walled garden that has been remodelled to create a formal area. www.nts.org.uk/visit/places/castle-fraser **74 A4**

Craigievar Castle *Alford, Aberdeenshire.* A beautiful pink tower house, lavishly decorated with turrets and substantially as it was on its completion in 1626. Nearly all of its rooms have contemporary decorative plaster ceilings, and there is a good collection of furniture collected over the centuries. Guided tours of castle. Gardens open. www.nts.org.uk/visit/places/craigievar **74 B2**

Crathes Castle, Garden and Estate *Banchory, Aberdeenshire.* In fact a late 16th-century tower house with a number of 'medieval features' added, Crathes castle has several remarkable painted ceilings of that date as well as family portraits and vernacular furniture. The walled garden is made up of eight areas and the yew hedge dates to 1702. There are several nature trails in the grounds. www.nts.org.uk/visit/places/crathes-castle **74 C4**

Drum Castle, Garden and Estate *Banchory, Aberdeenshire.* The massive square keep of Drum Castle is one of the three oldest tower houses in Scotland, dating from the late 13th century and was given by Robert the Bruce to his armour bearer, William de Irvine, in 1323. The Jacobean mansion was added in 1619 and further extensions made in the 19th century. The house remained in the hands of the Irvines until 1976 when the National Trust for Scotland took over and contains a collection of portraits and good Georgian furniture. The grounds contain the woods of Drum – remnant oak and pine woodland – and a garden of historic roses. www.nts.org.uk/visit/places/crathes-castle **75 B4**

Dunnottar Castle *Stonehaven, Aberdeenshire.* Set high on a 160ft cliff above the sea, the ruins of this castle include a chapel from 1392. The original fortress was built in the 9th century and bloody episodes in the past include William Wallace's slaughter of the whole English Plantagenet garrison in 1297 and the torture of 165 Covenanters in 1685. The drawing room was restored in 1926. www.dunnottarcastle.co.uk **75 D5**

Fyvie Castle *Fyvie, Aberdeenshire.* The oldest of the five towers dates from the 13th century and the castle is a fine example of Scottish baronial architecture. The 17th-century morning room has beautiful contemporary panelling and a fine plaster ceiling, while later Edwardian remodelling includes a beautiful dining room. The collection includes 16th-century tapestries, paintings by Gainsborough, Raeburn and Romney and antique arms and armour. The grounds and Fyvie Loch were designed as a landscaped parkland around the beginning of the 19th century, replacing the original hunting grounds. The grounds include a restored racquets court, an ice house and a bird hide. www.nts.org.uk/visit/places/fyvie-castle **82 E4**

Argyll, Bute, Stirling, Trossachs

Duart Castle *Craignure, Mull, Argyll and Bute.* Perched on a spit of rock, this was the home of the MacLeans from the 13th century. Having been burned down by the Campbells, it was confiscated by the government after the rebellion of 1745. It was brought back and restored by Fitzroy MacLean early in the 20th century. Highlights include the dungeons and ramparts. www.duartcastle.com **62 D2**

Dunstaffnage Castle *Dunbeg, Argyll and Bute.* The 13th-century castle lies on the site of the Scots court until Kenneth MacAlpin unified Scotland and moved the seat of power to Scone in the 10th century. It was captured by Robert the Bruce in 1309, then handed over to the Campbells in 1470. Flora

Caerlaverock Castle, Dumfries & Galloway Gary Cook / Alamy

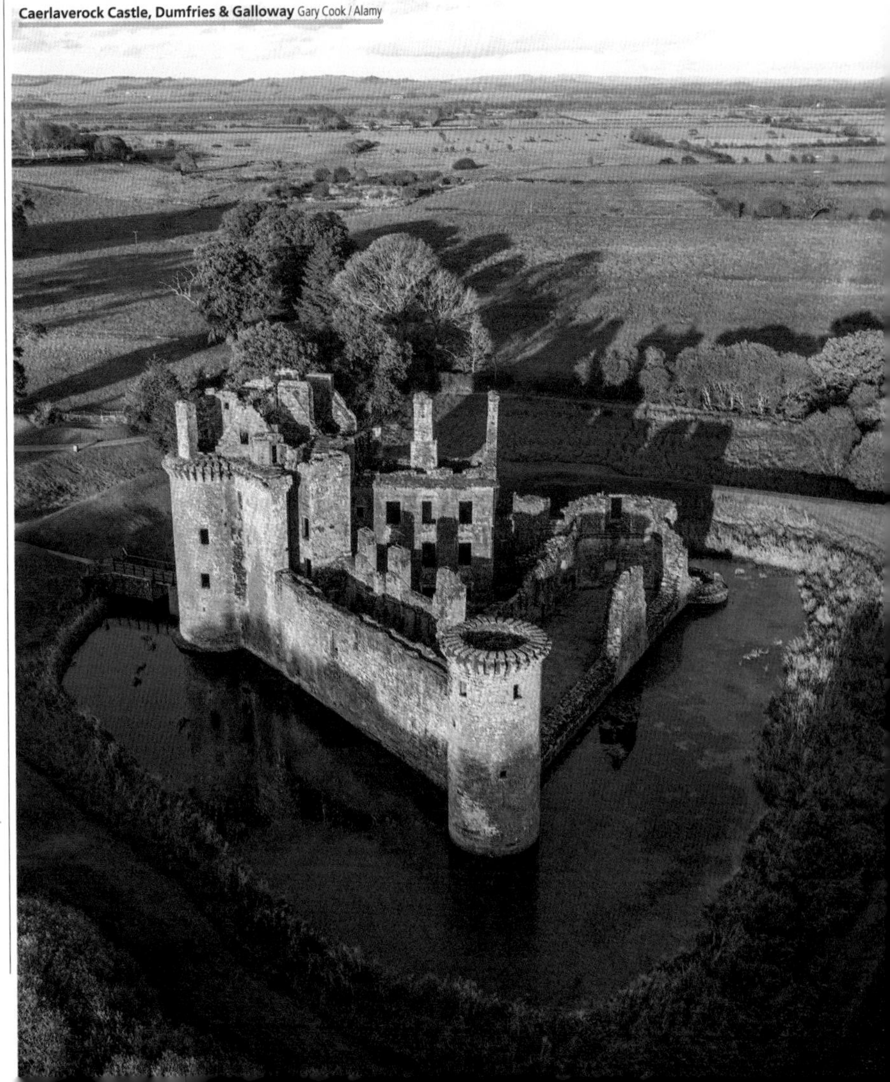

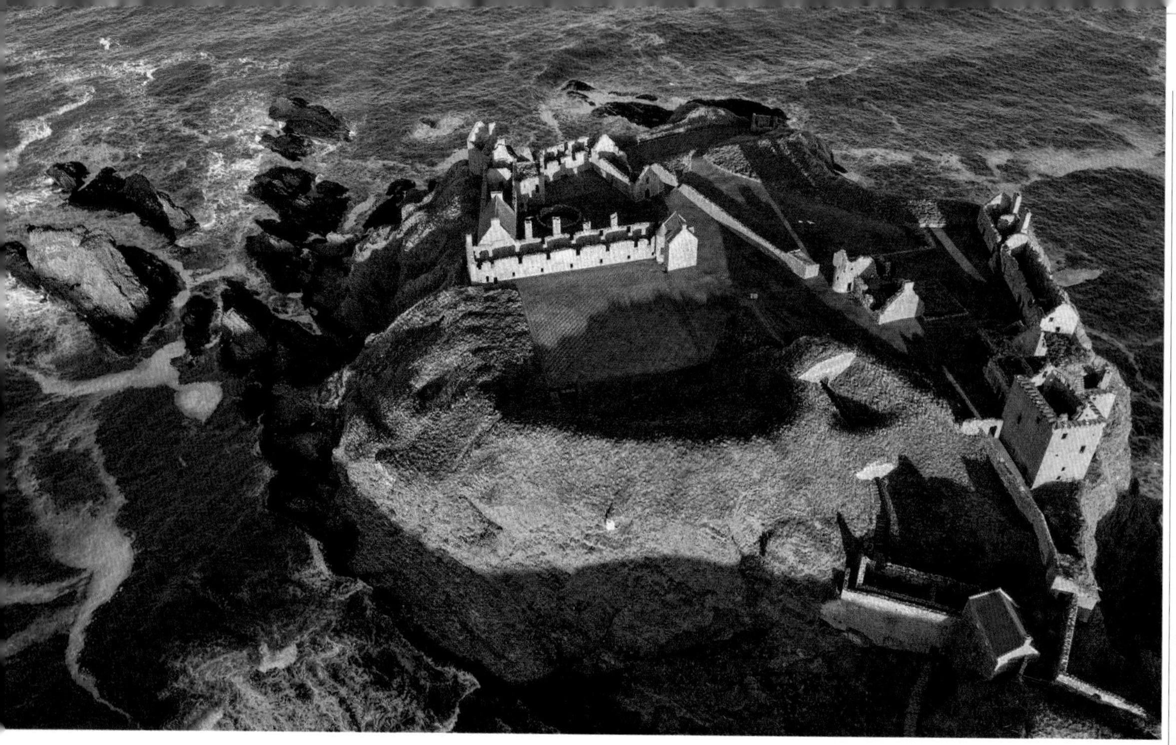

▲ **Dunnottar Castle** Andy Thompson / Alamy

MacDonald was held here temporarily, and the castle burned down in 1810. The curtain walls and battlements are substantially intact, making it fun for children to explore. 💻www.historicenvironment.scot/visit-a-place/places/dunstaffnage-castle-and-chapel **62 D3**

Inveraray Castle *Inveraray, Argyll and Bute.* This greenish-grey castle is an early example of Gothic Revival building and contains pictures, 18th-century French furniture and a vast collection of arms and armour. 💻www.inveraray-castle.com **54 B3**

Skipness Castle and Chapel *Skipness, Argyll and Bute.* The castle, of which a five-storey tower remains, once controlled shipping through Loch Fyne. The surrounding hamlet was originally a Norse settlement. Open Apr–Sep. 💻www.historicenvironment.scot/visit-a-place/places/skipness-castle-and-chapel **51 A5**

Stirling Castle *Upper Castle Hill, Stirling, Stirling.* This strategically placed castle had its heyday in the first half of the 16th century during the reigns of James IV and V, the latter of whom made the Renaissance-style additions to the medieval building. It later became the headquarters of the Argyll and Sutherland Highlanders, with pipe banners, regimental colours and silver. Some of the medals date as far back as the Battle of Waterloo. 💻www.stirlingcastle.gov.uk 💻www.argylls.co.uk/museum **39 B6**

Edinburgh and East Central

Craigmillar Castle *Craigmillar, City of Edinburgh.* Guarding the southern approach to Edinburgh, the first part of this now ruined, but extensive, castle was built in the late 14th century and enclosing walls were added during the early 15th century. The outer wall and moat were added in the 16th century. Most of the castle can be explored, including the tower and cellars. Mary Queen of Scots' brother and Lord Bothwell met here to plan her second husband's murder. 💻www.historicenvironment.scot **42 F1**

Dirleton Castle *Dirleton, East Lothian.* This rose-tinted, fairy-tale castle dates back to the 13th century. Sacked by Cromwell's forces in 1650 and then further pulled down by the owners of the land to create a pretty folly. 💻www.historicenvironment.scot/visit-a-place/places/dirleton-castle **43 D6**

Edinburgh Castle *Castlehill, Edinburgh, City of Edinburgh.* Attractions in this 800-year-old castle, perched high above the city on the plug of an extinct volcano, include the royal palace, the castle museum, the Scottish crown jewels, the Stone of Destiny, the Great Hall, the 12th-century St Margaret's chapel and the castle vaults. 💻www.edinburghcastle.scot **41 F8**

Lauriston Castle *2a Cramond Road South, Davidson's Mains, Edinburgh, City of Edinburgh.* The centre of this mansion, which is set in its own parkland, is a 16th-century tower house. The rest of the building is neo-Jacobean. The collection includes fine furniture and Flemish tapestries. 💻www.edinburghmuseums.org.uk/venue/lauriston-castle **41 F8**

Linlithgow Palace *Linlithgow, West Lothian.* Once one of the favourite palaces of Scotland's kings, this building was begun under James I in 1425 and continued for more than a century. Mary Queen of Scots was born here in 1542. Cromwell's troops were billeted here in the 1650s. Although it burned down in 1746, the pink walls still stand to as much as five storeys and much of the interior layout can still be seen. There is a small exhibition of architectural finds in the great hall. 💻www.historicenvironment.scot/visit-a-place/places/linlithgow-palace **40 E4**

Palace of Holyroodhouse *Canongate, Edinburgh, City of Edinburgh.* A royal palace built for James IV in 1498, remodelled in the 1560s and renovated in early 17th century for James VI. The tour includes Mary Queen of Scots' apartments. 💻www.rct.uk/visit/palace-of-holyroodhouse **42 F1**

Tantallon Castle *Near North Berwick, East Lothian.* Ruined 14th-century castle, the ancient stronghold of the Douglases. It was destroyed by Cromwell in 1651 after a 12-day siege. The setting on the cliffs facing Bass Rock is dramatic, especially in windy weather. 💻www.historicenvironment.scot/visit-a-place/places/tantallon-castle **43 C7**

Glasgow and the Clyde

Bothwell Castle *Bothwell, Uddingston, South Lanarkshire.* The strategically located fortress is widely thought of as Scotland's finest 13th-century castle. The massive red sandstone ruins include the main keep. The walls are up to 16ft thick, which is why substantial parts of the building remain, despite its near 800-year history of sieges. 💻www.historicenvironment.scot/visit-a-place/places/bothwell-castle **28 C4**

Craignethan Castle *Crossford, South Lanarkshire.* Rebuilt as the last great medieval castle in Scotland in 1530 for James V, this building has a feature unique in Scotland – a caponier – a vault wedged into the moat between the two sections of the castle allowing defenders to fire on attackers from behind 5ft thick walls. The tower house and its cellars are virtually intact. 💻www.historicenvironment.scot/visit-a-place/places/craignethan-castle **29 E7**

Perth, Angus, Dundee and Fife

Aberdour Castle *Aberdour, Burntisland, Fife.* The earliest part of the castle, the tower, dates from the 14th century, while the other parts were added in the 16th and 17th centuries, including the fine dovecot. 💻www.historicenvironment.scot/visit-a-place/places/aberdour-castle-and-gardens **41 C7**

Balhousie Castle *Hay Street, Perth, Perth and Kinross.* See Black Watch Regimental Museum **66 E1**

Blair Castle *Blair Atholl, Pitlochry, Perth and Kinross.* Almost the archetypical Scottish castle, with whitewashed walls and turrets, Blair Castle dates originally from 1269. The contents are magnificent, including paintings, furniture, beautiful plasterwork. The military aspect is most obvious in the entrance hall where a wide range of weapons is on display, while the ballroom holds family portraits and a vast display of antlers and tapestry room contains rich Brussels tapestries and an ornate four-poster. The grounds are impressive, with woodland walks, as well as Highland cattle and peacocks that add to the overall impression of grandeur. 💻www.blair-castle.co.uk **65 B7**

Broughty Castle *Castle Green, Broughty Ferry, Dundee City.* This fort protected the ferry crossing over the Tay estuary and was built in the 15th century. It was besieged by the English in the 16th century and attacked by Cromwell's troops in the 17th. In the mid-19th century it was restored as part of Britain's coastal defences. The museum now housed within it has displays on arms and armour, local history and whaling. Fine views over the Tay estuary and Fife can be obtained from the observation tower. 💻www.leisureandculturedundee.com/culture/broughty-castle 💻www.historicenvironment.scot/visit-a-place/places/broughty-castle **66 D4**

Castle Menzies *Aberfeldy, Perth and Kinross.* Until the middle of the last century, this 16th-century Z-plan tower house was the seat of the Clan Menzies. It has now been restored by the Menzies Clan Society to what it would have looked like when first built. 💻www.castlemenzies.org **65 C6**

Castle of St Andrews *The Scores, St Andrews, Fife.* Founded in 1200 as the palace of the bishops and archbishops of St Andrews, most of the remains date from the 14th and 16th centuries. Its history is full of betrayals, murders and sieges, especially at the time of the Reformation, including burnings at the stake. The secret passage dates from this period. 💻www.historicenvironment.scot/visit-a-place/places/st-andrews-castle **67 F5**

Culross Palace *Culross, Fife.* The interior walls of this palace, built between 1597 and 1611 for Sir George Bruce, are covered in wooden panelling, painted with moral scenes and passages of both Scots and Latin. The house is set within peaceful walled gardens. 💻www.nts.org.uk/visit/places/culross **40 C3**

Falkland Palace, Garden and Old Burgh *Falkland, Fife.* A country residence of the Stuart kings and queens when on hunting trips in the Fife forest. The palace was built between 1501 and 1541 by James IV and his son, James V, who died here after his defeat by the English at the battle of Solway Firth in 1542. Mary Queen of Scots spent time here, and Charles II stayed here before his coronation by the Covananters at Scone in 1651. It was abandoned after the uprising of 1715 and not restored until the late 19th century. Externally, it is a beautiful example of early Renaissance architecture. Guided tours include the drawing room, the tapestry gallery and the chapel royal, which is still in use and the keeper's apartments in the gatehouse are also on display. The real (royal) tennis court – the oldest in Britain – was built in 1539. 💻www.nts.org.uk/visit/places/falkland-palace **57 B7**

Glamis Castle *Glamis, Angus.* Best known as the childhood home of the late Queen Mother, Glamis was given to the Lyon family in 1372. Originally, it was a five-storey L-shaped castle and one of the settings for Macbeth. Features on the guided tour include the Victorian dining room with a fine plaster ceiling, the drawing room with beautiful early 17th-century plasterwork, the chapel, with idiosyncratic late 17th-century paintings, King Malcolm's Room, with leather panelling and an ornate carved wooden chimneypiece, the royal apartments, Duncan's Hall and a 15th-century crypt. The grounds include a formal Italian Garden and woodland walks. 💻www.glamis-castle.co.uk **66 C3**

Kellie Castle and Garden *Pittenweem, Fife.* The oldest part of the castle is believed to date from 1360, but the building was enlarged to its present form in about 1606, then deserted for more than two centuries. Sympathetically restored in around 1878, its plaster ceilings, painted panelling and furniture form a harmonious whole. The walled garden has been laid out to a late Victorian plan. 💻www.nts.org.uk/visit/places/kellie-castle **58 B3**

Loch Leven Castle *Castle Island, Kinross, Fife.* A fortress dating from the 14th century that belonged to the Douglas family. Mary Queen of Scots was imprisoned, and signed her abdication here before escaping and finally being captured in England. The tower is 14th-century and the curtain wall dates from the 16th century. Access is by ferry from Kinross. 💻www.historicenvironment.scot/visit-a-place/places/lochleven-castle **57 B6**

Scone Palace *Scone, Perth and Kinross.* The site of the first capital of United Scotland. The earliest part of the current palace dates to 1580 and the additions to 1803–8. Its contents include French furniture, 16th-century needlework including hangings embroidered by Mary Queen of Scots, china and ivories and good paintings. David Douglas, after whom the Douglas fir was named, was born here and there is a fine collection of rare conifers in the pinetum, including one Douglas fir grown from a seed he sent back from California. Highland cows and peacocks roam in the gardens. 💻www.scone-palace.co.uk **66 E1**

South of Scotland

Brodick Castle, Garden and Country Park *Brodick, Arran, North Ayrshire.* This red sandstone castle dates from the 13th century, on the site of an earlier Viking fortress, with 17th- and 19th-century additions The collections include paintings, silver and antiques. The gardens were laid out in the 1920s and include specimens from the Himalayas, Chile, New Zealand and Tasmania. The woodland garden contains a fine collection of rhododendrons and the formal garden, which was originally laid out in 1710, has been restored as a Victorian garden. 💻www.nts.org.uk/visit/places/brodick-castle-garden-country-park **51 C6**

Caerlaverock Castle *Dumfries, Dumfries and Galloway.* This unusual castle was built in the late 13th century, and first saw action during the Wars of Independence when it

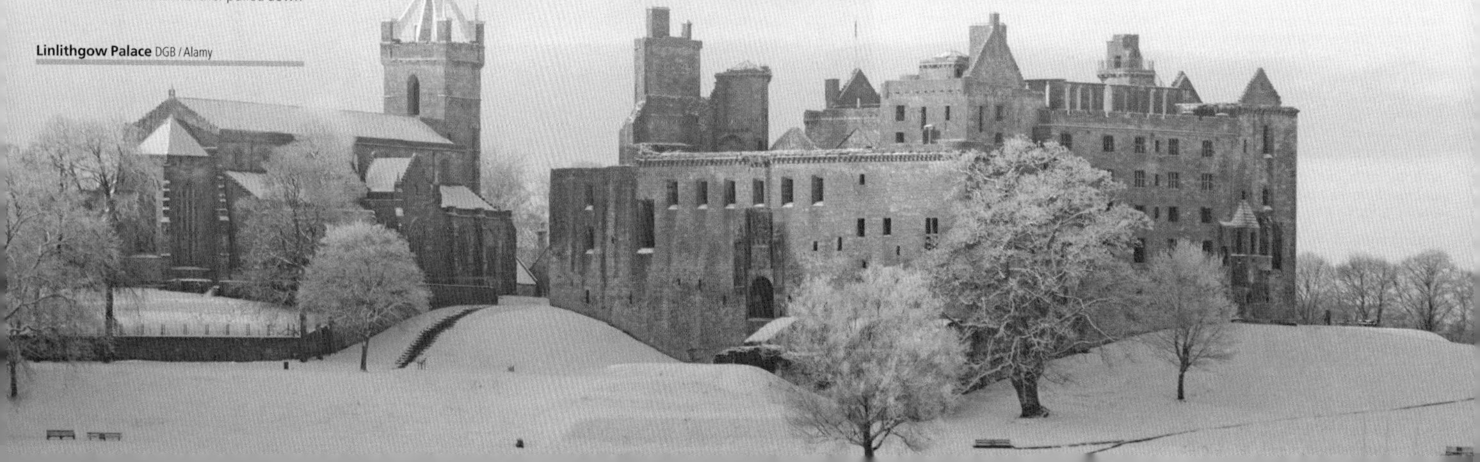

Linlithgow Palace DGB / Alamy

was besieged by Edward I in 1300. In 1312, it was attacked by the Scots and in 1356–7 by the English again. Its triangular form, with defensive towers, was strong: during the Civil War it was besieged for 13 weeks before being forced to surrender. Inside is an unexpected building, the Nithsdale Lodging, a Renaissance façade with mythological and heraldic scenes. Sadly it was destroyed by the Covenanters within a few years. www.historicenvironment.scot/visit-a-place/places/caerlaverock-castle/ **48 C4**

Culzean Castle and Country Park *Maybole, South Ayrshire.* One of Scotland's most impressive stately homes. Its strategic site, looking over the Firth of Clyde towards Arran, has been associated with the Kennedy family since the 12th century. Although the current castle suits its position by looking defensive on the outside, inside it is a grand neoclassical house. It was built by Robert Adam between 1772 and 1790 and is notable for the oval staircase, some of the plasterwork, the saloon, family portraits and furniture. Guided tours are available. The extensive country park includes woodland trails, a camellia house, lakes, clifftop views and a walled garden. The Gas House has an exhibition on coal gas lighting. www.nts.org.uk/visit/places/culzean **6 B3**

Drumlanrig Castle *Thornhill, Dumfries and Galloway.* The home of the dukes of Buccleuch and Queensberry, Drumlanrig was built between 1679 and 1689. The collection includes paintings by Leonardo da Vinci, Rembrandt and Holbein, among others, and relics of Bonnie Prince Charlie. Outdoor activities include an adventure playground, marked walking, hiking and cycling routes as well as field sports. www.drumlanrigcastle.co.uk **9 E8**

Dundonald Castle *Dundonald, South Ayrshire.* Robert II built this castle in the 1370s, incorporating part of an earlier building, making it the first home of a Stuart king. He used the castle as a summer residence until his death in 1390. It has an unpleasant dungeon, and the commanding views over Kilmarnock show the importance of this strategic location. www.dundonaldcastle.org.uk **17 C6**

Floors Castle *Kelso, Scottish Borders.* Designed by William Adam in 1721 and remodelled in the 19th century by William Playfair. Substantial collection of French and English furniture, porcelain, paintings by Canaletto, Reynolds and Gainsborough. Walled garden and garden centre. www.floorscastle.com **24 C3**

Thirlestane Castle *Lauder, Scottish Borders.* Country house with a late 16th-century keep, beautiful late 17th-century plaster ceilings, historic toy collection and exhibition of life in the Scottish Borders from prehistoric times onwards. www.thirlestanecastle.co.uk **33 E6**

The Highlands

Castle Moil *Kyleakin, Skye, Highland.* A small ruined medieval castle, perched on a jagged knoll overlooking Loch Alsh. **77 F7**

Cawdor Castle *Cawdor, Highland.* Although built two centuries too late, Cawdor will always be associated with the Shakespearian story of Macbeth's murder of Duncan, it represents the idea of a perfect medieval castle, with turrets, dungeons, gargoyles, a drawbridge, fortified walls and hidden passageways. The interior contains a great deal of fine furniture. The grounds include a woodland and nature trails. www.cawdorcastle.com **80 D3**

Dunrobin Castle *Golspie, Highland.* The home of the Earls of Sutherland, this 'castle' was remodelled in 1845 by Charles Barry in the Scottish Baronial style. The French feel extends to the extensive gardens, which are loosely based on the designs for those at Versailles. There are 189 rooms, which were created by the Scottish architect Robert Lorimer after a fire in 1915. www.dunrobincastle.co.uk **87 C5**

Dunvegan Castle and Garden *Dunvegan, Skye, Highland.* Dunvegan has been the main stronghold of the Macleod chiefs for almost eight centuries, but this mock fortress dates from the 1840s. It includes several relics, including the 'fairy flag' thought to protect Macleods from harm. The dining room has a display of old silver, while the dungeon is unpleasant. The castle lies on a rocky outcrop between the sea and several acres of beautiful gardens. www.dunvegancastle.com **76 D2**

Eilean Donan Castle *Dornie, Skye, Highland.* Built on an offshore island in 1214 as a defence against the Danes, Eilean Donan was ruined in 1719 after Spanish Jacobite forces were defeated at the Battle of Glenshiel. It was restored by a member of the Clan MacRae and among its contents are Jacobite relics and a museum of clan warfare, as well as furniture from the 1650s and impressive interiors. www.eileandonancastle.com **77 F8**

Kinloch Castle *Kinloch, Rùm, Highland.* Guided tours of the castle are timed to coincide with ferry arrivals. Despite the appearance of the turreted exterior, it was complete in 1900 as part of a sporting estate. It has an Edwardian interior and furnishings appropriate to the upper-class life of the time. www.isleofrum.com/isleofrumheritag.php **68 C3**

Urquhart Castle *Drumnadrochit, Highland.* Standing above Loch Ness, this is one of the largest castles in Scotland. It was fought over for centuries, with parts being rebuilt as necessary. By 1600 it had been abandoned and was finally blown up in 1689 to prevent it being used by the Jacobites. Most of the existing buildings date from after the 16th century. www.historicenvironment.scot/visit-a-place/places/urquhart-castle **79 F7**

The Outer Islands

Bishop's Palace *Broad Street, Kirkwall, Mainland, Orkney.* The 12th-century palace was built for Bishop William the Old and the round tower was added in the 16th century. www.historicenvironment.scot/visit-a-place/places/bishop-s-and-earl-s-palaces-kirkwall **99 B5**

Earl's Palace *Watergate, Kirkwall, Mainland, Orkney.* Started in 1607 for Earl Patrick Stewart, the son of Mary Queen of Scots' illegitimate half-brother, the palace was the most accomplished example of Renaissance architecture in Scotland at the time. Even though he was using forced labour, he ran out of money and it was never completed. Although roofless, many details remain, including ornate windows, the grand entrance, and the magnificent central hall. The Earl was imprisoned in 1609 and executed in 1615. www.historicenvironment.scot/visit-a-place/places/bishop-s-and-earl-s-palaces-kirkwall **99 B5**

Houses

Aberdeen and Moray

Haddo House *Ellon, Aberdeenshire.* A magnificent Palladian mansion, designed in 1732 by William Adam for William, 2nd Earl of Aberdeen. The interior is predominantly 'Adam Revival': this refurbishment was carried out in about 1880 for John, 7th Earl and 1st Marquess of Aberdeen. The contents include fine paintings, furniture and objets d'art. The extensive grounds were created in the early 19th century and hold deer, otters and red squirrels. www.nts.org.uk/visit/places/haddo-house **83 E5**

Argyll, Bute, Stirling, Trossachs

Argyll's Lodging *Upper Castle Wynd, Stirling, Stirling.* This romantic building has served as both a home and a military hospital. The kitchen is the oldest part of the building, and dates to the early 16th century, while the rest of this impressive, turreted town house has been restored to look as it did when new in the 1680s. The drawing room still has the 9th Duke of Argyll's chair of state and is hung with antique tapestries. Combined tickets with Stirling Castle, from where they should be purchased. Guided tours available. www.historicenvironment.scot/visit-a-place/places/argyll-s-lodging/ **39 B6**

The Hill House *Upper Colquhoun Street, Helensburgh, Argyll and Bute.* The best-preserved, and very popular, example of Charles Rennie Mackintosh's domestic architecture. It was commissioned in 1902 by the publisher Walter Blackie to include all the decorative schemes and furniture. Some of the fabric designs and one of the overmantels were by Mackintosh's wife, Margaret. www.nts.org.uk/visit/places/the-hill-house **36 D4**

Edinburgh and East Central

Dalmeny House *Queensferry, Edinburgh, City of Edinburgh.* The first neo-Gothic stately home in Scotland, Dalmeny House was built in 1815 by William Wilkins for the fourth Earl of Rosebery. Portraits include examples by Gainsborough, Lawrence, Raeburn, Millais and Reynolds. The collection includes important 18th-century French furniture and some memorabilia of Napoleon. Guided tours by prearrangement only, in June and July. https://roseberyestates.co.uk/dalmeny-house **41 E7**

The Georgian House *7 Charlotte Square, Edinburgh, City of Edinburgh.* Robert and James Adam, furniture 18th century, Hepplewhite, Chippendale and Sheraton. It is laid out as it may have been when it was newly built. A working barrel organ plays a selection of Scottish airs. In the basement are the original wine cellar and a kitchen. www.nts.org.uk/visit/places/georgian-house **41 F8**

Gladstone's Land *477B Lawnmarket, Edinburgh, City of Edinburgh.* A 17th-century Edinburgh tenement building, which would have been occupied by several merchant families. Completed in 1620, the six-storey building's ground floor has been restored to its original form as an arcaded booth. Inside, rooms have been redecorated and furnished in late 17th-century style and several have painted ceilings. www.nts.org.uk/visit/places/gladstones-land **41 F8**

Hopetoun House *Old Philipstoun, West Lothian.* A Robert Adam-designed, 18th century masterpiece, notable for its gardens based on those at Versailles. The interior is filled with paintings and statues and 18th-century furniture. Formal gardens, nature trail, deer parks, stables museum. www.hopetoun.co.uk **40 E5**

John Knox House *43–45 High Street, Edinburgh, City of Edinburgh.* Home of the first Moderator of the Presbyterian Church of Scotland, John Knox, contains memorabilia and 15th-century interiors. www.visitscotland.com/info/see-do/scottish-storytelling-centre-john-knox-house-p254581 **41 F8**

Glasgow and the Clyde

David Livingstone Centre *165 Station Rd, Blantyre, South Lanarkshire.* The explorer and missionary David Livingstone was born in this tenement in 1813. The Livingstone family's rooms show the harshness of life for mill-workers while the other 23 tenements have displays on his missionary work and his adventures. www.david-livingstone-trust.org **28 A2**

Holmwood *63 Netherlee Road, Cathcart, Glasgow, City of Glasgow.* A rare classical building by the Glasgow architect Alexander 'Greek' Thomson in 1857–8 for James Couper, a paper mill owner. The dining room has a frieze with scenes from the Iliad. The original highly imaginative decorative scheme for the house has been revealed by a recent renovation. www.nts.org.uk/visit/places/holmwood **28 A2**

Perth, Angus, Dundee and Fife

Alloa Tower *Alloa Park, Alloa, Clackmannanshire.* The mid 15th-century tower remains from the ancestral home of the earls of Mar and Kellie. The 6th earl partially restored and updated it before his exile after the 1715 Jacobite uprising. Among the rare medieval survivals are the timber roof structure and groin vaulting. The collection includes paintings by Jamesone, David Allan and Raeburn. www.nts.org.uk/visit/places/alloa-tower **40 B1**

House of Dun *Montrose, Angus.* A Palladian mansion designed by Robert Adam for the Laird of Dun in 1730. The ornate relief plasterwork in the main rooms is full of Jacobite symbolism, and the restored interior has an extensive collection of period furniture and objects. Among the attractions in the courtyard is a gamekeeper's workshop. The grounds border the Montrose Basin and include woodland walks and a bird hide. See also Montrose Basin Nature Reserve. www.nts.org.uk/visit/places/house-of-dun **67 B6**

JM Barrie's Birthplace *9 Brechin Road, Kirriemuir, Angus.* JM Barrie (1860–1937), the author of 'Peter Pan', was born here. The upper floors are furnished as they may have been at that time. The adjacent house, No 11, houses an exhibition about Barrie's literary and theatrical works. www.nts.org.uk/visit/places/j-m-barries-birthplace **66 B3**

South of Scotland

Abbotsford House *Melrose, Scottish Borders.* Built in 1822, this is the house Sir Walter Scott lived in for the last 10 years of his life. Contains relics associated with the poet and some of his collections, including Napoleon's pen case, Rob Roy's sword and a lock of Bonnie Prince Charlie's hair. The library contains more than 9000 of his books. Gardens, grounds and private chapel. www.scottsabbotsford.com **23 C6**

Bowhill House *Selkirk, Scottish Borders.* Built in the 18th to 19th centuries, this country house contains antique French furniture, works of art by painters including Gainsborough, Reynolds, Canaletto and Claude. Among other exhibits is the shirt that the Duke of Monmouth, an illegitimate son of Charles II, wore to his execution. Activities in the estate grounds include an adventure playground, fishing, walking and hiking. www.bowhillhouse.co.uk **22 D4**

Broughton House and Garden *12 High Street, Kirkcudbright, Dumfries and Galloway.* An 18th-century town house, to which the Glasgow School of Art painter E A Hornel added an art gallery, a library, a studio and a sheltered Japanese garden. An extensive collection of paintings includes Hornel's own bright, colourful depictions of his native Galloway. www.nts.org.uk/visit/places/broughton-house **47 D8**

Burns House *Burns Street, Dumfries, Dumfries and Galloway.* The poet's home for the last three years of his life, with some of his possessions and furniture. www.visitscotland.com/info/see-do/robert-burns-house-p250471 **48 B3**

Ellisland Farm *Dumfries, Dumfries and Galloway.* Built by Robert Burns in 1788 as a working farm, Ellisland also houses a small museum dedicated to the poet with such personal effects as his pistol, sword, flute and fishing rod, as well as 18th-century farming implements. While here, Burns composed well over 100 songs and poems, including Auld Lang Syne. www.ellislandfarm.co.uk **48 A3**

Manderston House *Duns, Scottish Borders.* Originally a Georgian building, but expanded between 1871 and 1905 into a large country house partly in the earlier, Neoclassical style of Robert Adam. The interior is lavishly decorated and furnished and includes decorative plaster ceilings and a silver staircase. Other features of interest are the biscuit-tin museum, the extravagant marble dairy (complete with cloisters), the tower house folly and 50 acres of gardens and woodland. www.manderston.co.uk **34 D5**

Mellerstain *Gordon, Scottish Borders.* Thought by many to be Scotland's finest mansion, Mellerstain was started by William Adam, who built two wings and completed by his son, Robert in 1778. It has collections of antique furniture, paintings and impressive classical interior. www.mellerstain.com **24 B1**

Paxton House *Berwick-upon-Tweed, Northumbria.* Designed by John and James Adam, Paxton is a Palladian mansion with a classicly serene exterior and simple interior with plasterwork by Robert Adam. The picture gallery houses paintings on loan from the National Gallery of Scotland. The grounds are extensive and were designed by an assistant of Capability Brown. Other attractions include a Victorian boathouse with a salmon-netting museum, an adventure playground, Highland cattle, Shetland ponies, woodland walks and a hide from where red squirrels can be watched. www.paxtonhouse.co.uk **35 D7**

Thomas Carlyle's Birthplace *The Arched House, Ecclefechan, Dumfries and Galloway.* The tiny house where the historian and essayist Thomas Carlyle was born in 1795 holds a collection of his belongings and letters. Built by his father and uncle in about 1791, the house, with its central passage, is representative of the local artisan dwelling of that period. www.nts.org.uk/visit/places/thomas-carlyles-birthplace **2 D4**

Traquair House *Innerleithen, Scottish Borders.* The oldest continually inhabited house in Scotland, home to a branch of the Stuart family since 1491. At least 27 monarchs are said to have visited and the family have particular associations with the Jacobite uprisings. The collections on display include paintings, manuscripts, glass, embroidery and silver. There is also a priest's hole and a hidden priest's room, as well as a bedspread said to have been embroidered by Mary Queen of Scots. The grounds include woodland walks, a maze, a brewery and craft workshops. The Bear Gates were last used by Bonnie Prince Charlie and the then owner swore they would never be opened again until there was another Stuart on the throne. www.traquair.co.uk **22 B2**

Monuments and ancient sites

Argyll, Bute, Stirling, Trossachs

Campbeltown Cross *Off Main Street, Campbeltown, Argyll and Bute.* A 14th-century carved cross, brought from Kilkivan in the 17th century. Among the carvings are figures of saints, including St Michael slaying the dragon. **50 D3**

Kildalton Cross *Kildalton, Kintour, Islay, Argyll and Bute.* One of the finest Celtic crosses in Scotland, carved in the late 8th century, stands in the churchyard of the ruined medieval church. It has representations of the Virgin and Child, saints and biblical scenes. **49 A4**

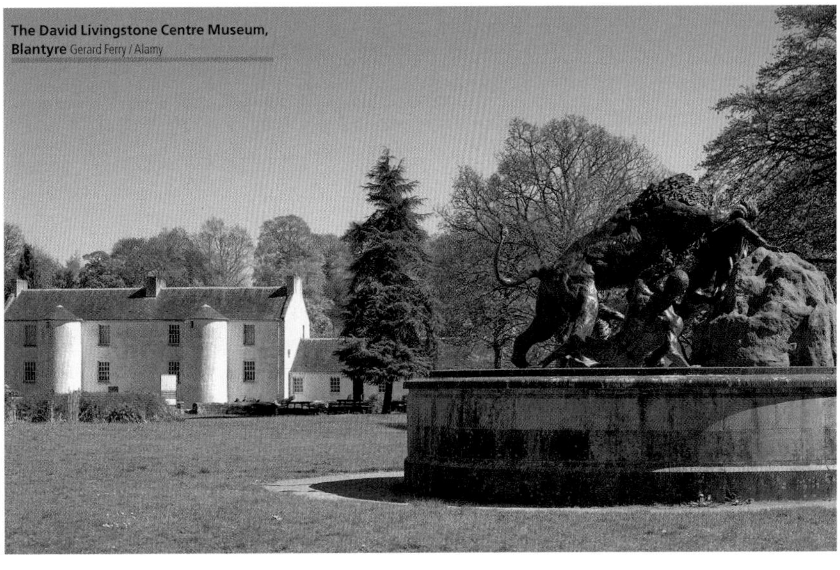
The David Livingstone Centre Museum, Blantyre Gerard Ferry / Alamy

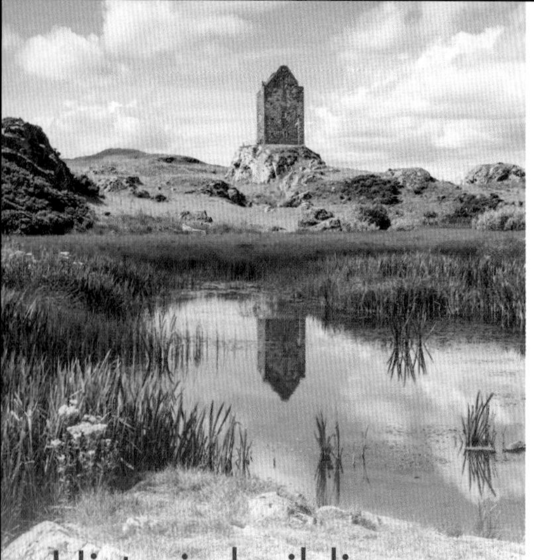

Historic buildings

Argyll, Bute, Stirling, Trossachs

Bonawe Iron Furnace (industrial) *Taynuilt, Argyll and Bute* The best preserved 18th-century charcoal-fired ironworks in Scotland with an exhibition. At its height this site employed more than 600 people. www.historicenvironment.scot/visit-a-place/places/bonawe-historic-iron-furnace/ **63 D5**

Cruachan power station *Dalmally, Argyll and Bute* At the northern end of Loch Awe, Cruachan is one of Scotland's first hydroelectric powerstations and has been operational since 1966. Guided tours (advance booking recommended) and visitor centre with interactive displays. www.visitcruachan.co.uk **63 E6**

McCaig's Tower *Pulpit Hill, Oban, Argyll and Bute* A replica of the Colosseum in Rome, built by John Stuart McCaig between 1897 and 1900. It served both as a memorial to his family and a means of creating work during an economic downturn. Although it is not finished, its walls reach as much as 40 feet and it provides excellent views. www.visitscotland.com/info/see-do/mccaigs-tower-p255141 **62 E3**

Edinburgh and East Central

Falkirk Wheel *Lime Road, Tamfourhill, Falkirk* Built to reconnect the Forth and Clyde and Union canals, the Falkirk Wheel is the world's first rotating boat lift. It rises to 115ft, a height that would have required 11 locks, moving 600 tonnes of water to that height in 4 minutes. The visitor centre has an interactive exhibition and a viewing gallery. Boat trips on the wheel can be prebooked. www.scottishcanals.co.uk/falkirk-wheel **39 D8**

Outlook Tower and Camera Obscura *Castlehill, Edinburgh, City of Edinburgh* The camera obscura at the top of this tower uses a series of mirrors and lenses to throw images of nearby streets and buildings and the people in them onto a horizontal circular screen. www.camera-obscura.co.uk **41 F8**

The Pineapple *Dunmore, Airth, Falkirk* Folly, garden of Dunmore House, near Falkirk 1761, 45 feet-high summer house heated with hot air circulated through cavities in the wall (just like the Romans). www.nts.org.uk/visit/places/the-pineapple **40 C1**

Scottish Parliament Visitor Centre *George IV Bridge, Edinburgh, City of Edinburgh* This centre explains the way the new Scottish parliament works. The debating chamber is open to the public when parliament is not sitting. www.visitparliament.scot **41 F8**

Perth, Angus, Dundee and Fife

Camera Obscura *Kirrie Hill, Kirriemuir, Angus* J M Barrie presented his home town with this cricket pavilion and the Camera Obscura within it in 1930. It offers views of Strathmore and the surrounding glens. www.kirriemuircameraobscura.com **66 B3**

Earthquake House *Comrie, Perth and Kinross* Britain's first seismometer was set up in Comrie in 1840 and moved here in 1874 to record the incidence of tremors that still occur on the Highland Boundary Fault. There are now modern seismometers installed as well as a model of the original and they can all be viewed from outside. www.undiscoveredscotland.co.uk/comrie/earthquakehouse **65 C5**

Secret Bunker *Underground Nuclear Command Centre, Crown Buildings, near Anstruther Easter, Fife* A labyrinth of tunnels that would have become Scotland's administrative centre in the wake of a nuclear attack. Rooms open include dormitories, canteen, communications, the chapel and the command centre. There are also guided tours and two cinemas. www.secretbunker.co.uk **58 B3**

South of Scotland

Smailholm Tower *Gordon, Scottish Borders* A restored 16th-century peel tower that provides excellent views over the countryside and contains a display on the ballads and legends of the borders. www.historicenvironment.scot/visit-a-place/places/smailholm-tower **24 C1**

The Outer Islands

Barony Mills *Birsay, The Barony, Mainland, Orkney* A working watermill dating from 1873, with its integral kiln for drying bere, the type of barley grown in the region. www.birsay.org.uk/baronymill.htm **98 A3**

Churchill Barriers (military/maritime) *St Mary's, Mainland, Orkney* The four concrete and stone barriers were built between Mainland, Lamb Holm, Glims Holm, Burray and South Ronaldsay during World War II to protect the Royal Navy's ships in Scapa Flow, after HMS 'Royal Oak' was torpedoed in 1939. https://www.orkney.com/listings/churchill-barriers **99 C5**

Click Mill *Dounby, Mainland, Orkney* A horizontal watermill that provided a means of grinding enough flour for 2–3 families. The functioning mechanism can be seen beneath the building. www.historicenvironment.scot/visit-a-place/places/click-mill **98 A4**

◀ **Smailholm Tower** David Kilpatrick / Alamy

▼ **The Pineapple** Phil Seale / Alamy

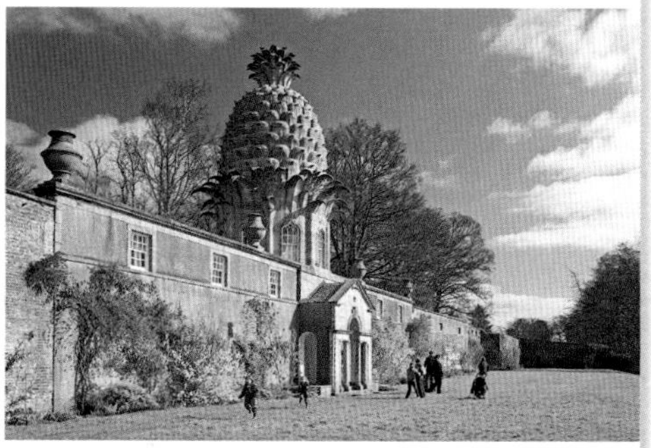

Kilmartin valley *Kilmartin, Argyll and Bute.* More than 150 ancient sites in Kilmartin valley include Temple Wood stone circle, cairns at Ballymeanoch, Ri Cruin, Nether Largie and Dunchraigaig, an Iron Age hillfort at Dunadd, standing stones at Nether Largie, Ballymeanoch, where there is also a henge as well as numerous carved stones. Some of the finds from the area are on view in Kilmartin House Museum. www.kilmartin.org **53 C8**

Wallace Monument *Manor Powis, Stirling.* A 216ft high monument, built in the Scots baronial style in the form of a medieval tower. Abbey Craig is where Wallace surveyed the ground before the battle of Stirling Bridge. At the tower's top is a representation of the Crown Royal of Scotland. A 16ft tall bronze statue of William Wallace is set about 32ft up on one corner of the building. Highlights inside include the Wallace Sword, a 700-year-old two-handed broadsword. At the top of the tower is a parapet offering views across the Forth valley and to Stirling. www.nationalwallacemonument.com **39 A7**

Edinburgh and East Central

Caiy Stane *Caiystane View, Oxgangs Road, Edinburgh, City of Edinburgh.* A 10ft high prehistoric stone, also known as the Kel Stone or General Kay's Monument, with markings known as cup-marks carved into it, is thought to mark the site of an ancient battle. **41 F8**

Rough Castle *Bonnybridge, Falkirk.* One of the forts that were built at 2-mile intervals along the entire length of the Antonine Wall, built by the Emperor Antonious Pius in AD 142 between the firths of Clyde and Forth. Rough Castle is the best-preserved part of the wall. www.historicenvironment.scot/visit-a-place/places/antonine-wall-rough-castle **39 D7**

Scott Monument *East Princes St Gardens, Edinburgh, City of Edinburgh.* Gothic monument to Sir Walter Scott. At its centre is a statue of the poet and his dog, Maida, with his heroes carved as small figures. Visitors can climb 287 steps to the top of the 200ft monument for amazing views. www.edinburghmuseums.org.uk/venue/scott-monument **41 F8**

South of Scotland

Auchagallon stone circle *Auchagallon, North Ayrshire.* A Bronze Age cairn surrounded by a ring of 15 standing stones, overlooking Machrie Bay. www.historicenvironment.scot/visit-a-place/places/auchagallon-cairn **50 C4**

Burns Monument and Gardens *Alloway, South Ayrshire.* A Greek-style monument containing manuscripts, books and relics associated with Robert Burns. The gardens are full of rare shrubs from the Himalayas. www.nts.org.uk/visit/places/robert-burns-birthplace-museum **17 F5**

Machrie Moor Standing Stones *Balmichael, Arran, North Ayrshire.* A complex of six stone circles of different sizes and architecture, cairns, ruined huts and isolated standing stones. The different styles of the circles suggest that they were built at different times. Among the theories about their construction is that four of them align with the midsummer sunrise so they may be a form of calendar for agricultural purposes. www.historicenvironment.scot/visit-a-place/places/machrie-moor-standing-stones **51 C5**

The Highlands

Clava Cairns *Newlands, Highland.* One of the best-preserved Bronze Age burial sites in Britain, the complex consists of two passage graves, both aligned with the midwinter sunset, a ring cairn and other smaller circles. Each monument is surrounded by a stone circle and they all date to about 3000 BCE. www.historicenvironment.scot/visit-a-place/places/clava-cairns **80 D2**

Glenfinnan Monument *Glenfinnan, Highland.* Set at the head of Loch Shiel in superb Highland scenery, this monument was erected in 1815 by Alexander Macdonald of Glenaladale in tribute to the clansmen who fought and died in the cause of Bonnie Prince Charlie in the 1740s. www.nts.org.uk/visit/places/glenfinnan-monument **70 D1**

Grey Cairns of Camster *Camster, Highland.* A series of burial chambers under long burial mounds set within bleak moorland. The chamber of the Round Cairn has a corbelled ceiling and the main chamber of the Long Cairn can also be entered. The mounds were built between 6000 and 4500 years ago. www.historicenvironment.scot/visit-a-place/places/grey-cairns-of-camster **91 D6**

Monument to the Massacre of Glencoe *Carnoch, Highland.* The monument commemorates the night in February 1692. Robert Campbell of the Argyll Campbells gave the order to kill all members of the Clan MacDonald because of their failure to swear an oath of allegiance to William III. Even in an age where murder was common, this was against the Highland rules of hospitality. **63 B6**

The Outer Islands

Blackhammer Cairn *Brinian, Rousay, Orkney.* A restored Neolithic burial cairn, similar in shape and layout to the contemporary houses at the Knap of Howar site. www.historicenvironment.scot/visit-a-place/places/blackhammer-chambered-cairn/ **100 D2**

Broch of Burroughston *Edmonstone, Shapinsay, Orkney.* This Iron Age broch is one of the best preserved on Orkney and was occupied until Viking times. www.orkney.com/listings/burroughston-broch **99 A6**

Broch of Gurness *Aikerness, Westray, Orkney.* The best-preserved broch in Orkney. Built in the first century AD, this tower was originally 30ft high. The remains of small dwellings cluster between the broch and the outer defences, which consist of three ramparts and ditches. It is thought that as many as 40 families may have lived in these houses. www.historicenvironment.scot/visit-a-place/places/broch-of-gurness/ **100 A2**

Broch of Mousa *Mousa, Shetland.* The walls of this large 2000-year-old broch stand to a height of more than 42ft, and are substantially intact. The broch is double-skinned, with passages and galleries between the two skins giving access to all levels. www.historicenvironment.scot/visit-a-place/places/mousa-broch/ **101 D3**

Brough of Birsay *The Barony, Mainland, Orkney.* The remains of Pictish and Norse settlements including farms, domestic buildings and a Norse cathedral from the early 12th century. Archaeologists have found evidence of metalworking on the site, and items are on display in the small museum. www.historicenvironment.scot/visit-a-place/places/brough-of-birsay **98 A3**

Calanais Standing Stones and Visitor Centre *Calanais, Lewis, Western Isles.* A complex of standing stones. The main circle (Calanais) and the central megalith were erected about 5000 years ago and a chambered cairn inserted within the circle. The other rows and avenue were added over the following 2000 years. Callanish II is the remains of another circle with a cairn, Callanish III is another ring or ellipse and Callanish IV is another ring on the other side of the loch. There are also other settings of stones in the area. www.historicenvironment.scot/visit-a-place/places/calanais-standing-stones www.callanishvisitorcentre.co.uk **96 D5**

Clickhimin Broch *Lerwick, Mainland, Shetland.* The hugh circular broch, which was partially reconstructed in the 19th century, dominates the remains of the fort and houses. The site was a farm in the late Bronze Age and later developed into, first, a blockhouse fort and, second, a broch. Up to 60 people are thought to have lived in this settlement at its height. www.historicenvironment.scot/visit-a-place/places/clickimin-broch **101 B3**

Cuween Hill Cairn *Finstown, Mainland, Orkney.* A Neolithic burial chamber, probably associated with the Stonehall settlement and thought to date to about 3000 BCE, cut into solid rock at the top of Cuween hill. It has one main chamber with smaller chambers running off the walls. Visitors gain entrance to the tomb via a narrow passage that appears to be astronomically aligned. Excavations in the early 20th century revealed eight human

The Glenfinnan Monument and Loch Shiel robertharding / Alamy

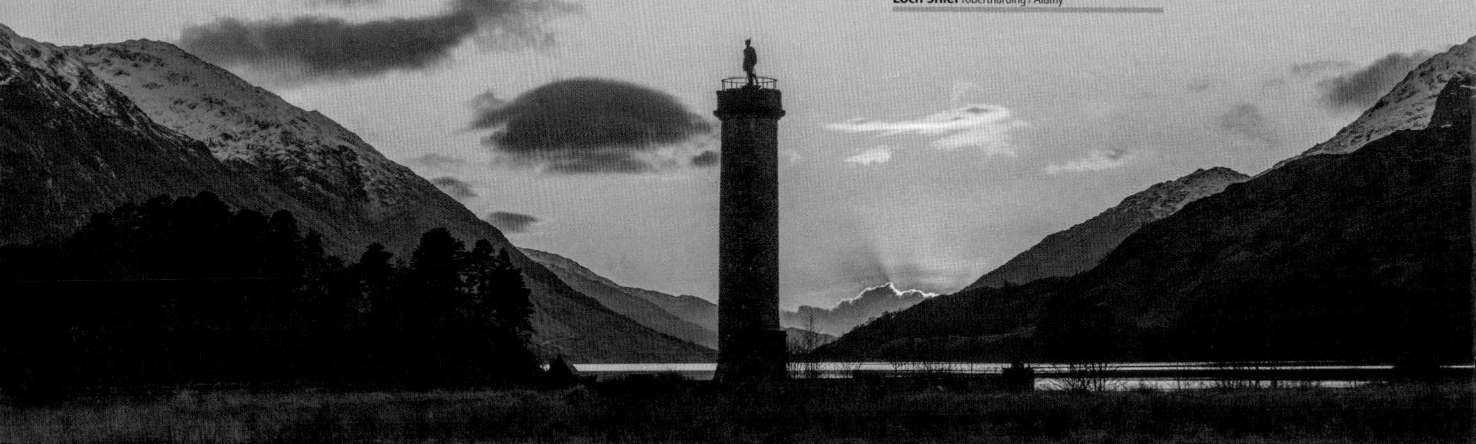

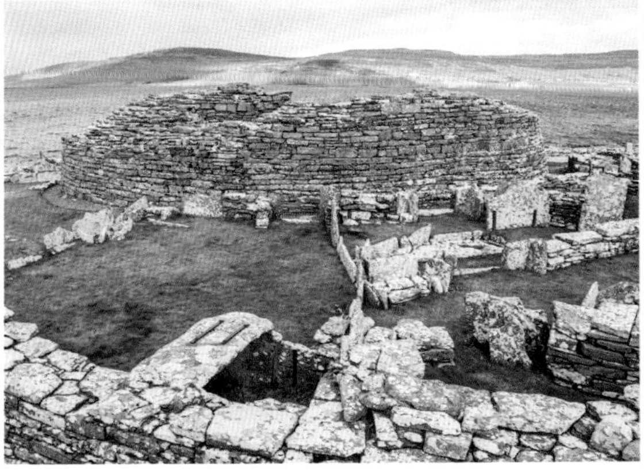

and 24 dog skulls as well as ox bones. www.historicenvironment.scot/visit-a-place/places/cuween-hill-chambered-cairn/ **98 B4**

Dun Carloway Broch *Dun Charlabhaig, Lewis, Western Isles.* One of the best preserved brochs in the Western Isles, with parts of the wall standing to nearly 32ft. It was built in the 1st century BCE. It is in a strong defensive position at the top of a steep hill, which would also have given the occupants a good view of anyone approaching. Several rooms on the ground floor and part of the stairway within the walls, which are 13ft thick at the base, can be explored. www.historicenvironment.scot www.callanishvisitorcentre.co.uk/dunebroch.html **96 C4**

Dwarfie Stane *Whaness, Hoy, Orkney.* Unique in Britain, the Dwarfie Stane is a tomb carved into a large red sandstone block. It is thought to be Neolithic. The 3ft square entrance passage leads to two 'bed' spaces. www.historicenvironment.scot/visit-a-place/places/dwarfie-stane/ **98 C3**

Jarlshof *Sumburgh, Mainland, Shetland.* This large archaeological site, has remains dating back to the Stone Age, including a Bronze Age smithy, Iron Age houses, a broch, Pictish wheelhouses, Viking longhouses, and a ruined 16th-century laird's house. The buildings are open for visitors to explore inside. www.historicenvironment.scot/visit-a-place/places/jarlshof-prehistoric-and-norse-settlement/ **101 F3**

Maes Howe *Finstown, Mainland, Orkney.* Built about 3000 BCE, this beautiful chambered tomb is covered by a 114ft earth mound. The entrance passage is in line with the midwinter sunset. Vikings raided the tomb in the 12th century and left a variety of graffiti on the walls. Guided tours, advance booking required. www.historicenvironment.scot/visit-a-place/places/maeshowe-chambered-cairn **98 B4**

Midhowe Broch *Trumland, Westness, Rousay, Orkney.* An Iron Age broch perched on a small promontary and protected from the land side by two ditches and a stone wall. Parts of the tower stand to head height and there are remnants of later outbuildings. The interior divisions within the broch are of a later date. www.historicenvironment.scot/visit-a-place/places/midhowe-broch **100 C1**

Midhowe Chambered Cairn *Trumland, Westness, Rousay, Orkney.* Protected under a large shed, this chambered tomb has been stripped of its soil so that visitors can see its complex structure from the walkways above. The main chamber is 75ft long and

▲ **Broch of Gurness Iron Age village, Orkney** Giulia Hetherington

subdivided into 12 compartments with flat stones. www.historicenvironment.scot/visit-a-place/places/midhowe-chambered-cairn **100 C1**

Mine Howe *Kirkwall, Mainland, Orkney.* Originally discovered in 1946, sealed, and then re-excavated in 2000, Mine Howe consists of a series of underground passages and chambers sunk into the top of a hill. There is also evidence of a surrounding ditch and nearby later settlement. The site has been dated to the Iron Age, but its function remains a mystery. There is a small-scale reconstruction of part of the cairn nearby. **99 B5**

Quoyness Cairn *Els Ness, Kettlehoft, Sanday, Orkney.* Constructed in about 2900 BCE and enclosed by an arc of 11 linked Bronze Age mounds, this Neolithic cairn appears to have been the heart of a sacred area. The central chamber is about 13ft high and reached through a 30ft long low entrance passage. The bones of at least 10 adults and five children, as well as animal bones, stone and bone tools and carved stones were found in the main chamber and four of the six smaller chambers that open off it. www.historicenvironment.scot/visit-a-place/places/quoyness-chambered-cairn/ **100 C4**

Ring of Brodgar *Hestwall, Mainland, Orkney.* A 328ft stone circle, raised about 2500 BCE, with 36 of the original 60 massive stones still in situ, and surrounded by a massive ditch. www.historicenvironment.scot/visit-a-place/places/ring-of-brodgar-stone-circle-and-henge **98 B3**

Skara Brae *Skaill, Mainland, Orkney.* This is one of the best-preserved prehistoric villages in Europe. Some of its fixtures, such as beds, have survived for 5000 years since it was abandoned. www.historicenvironment.scot/visit-a-place/places/skara-brae **98 B3**

Standing Stones of Stenness *Finstown, Mainland, Orkney.* A prehistoric stone circle, dating to about 2500 BCE. Four of the 12 stones are still standing. www.historicenvironment.scot/visit-a-place/places/stones-of-stenness-circle-and-henge **98 B4**

Stone o' Setter *Calfsound, Eday, Orkney.* A standing stone roughly 16ft high, set in a spectacular landscape. Weathering has made it resemble a giant hand. www.visitscotland.com/info/see-do/stone-of-setter-p986461 **100 C3**

Tomb of the Eagles *Liddel, South Ronaldsay, Orkney.* A small stone cairn, in a dramatic setting, with a subdivided main chamber and three side chambers. Built in around 3000 BCE, it contained the remains of at least 340 people. Among the animal bones were those from white-tailed sea eagles and it is thought that the bird may have been significant to the people who built the tomb. There is a small 'hands-on' museum in the farmhouse. www.tomboftheeagles.co.uk **99 E5**

Wideford Hill Cairn *Kirkwall, Mainland, Orkney.* A large chambered cairn, with three concentric walls and three large cells running off the main chamber. The entrance passage is more than 16ft long. www.historicenvironment.scot/visit-a-place/places/wideford-hill-chambered-cairn **99 B5**

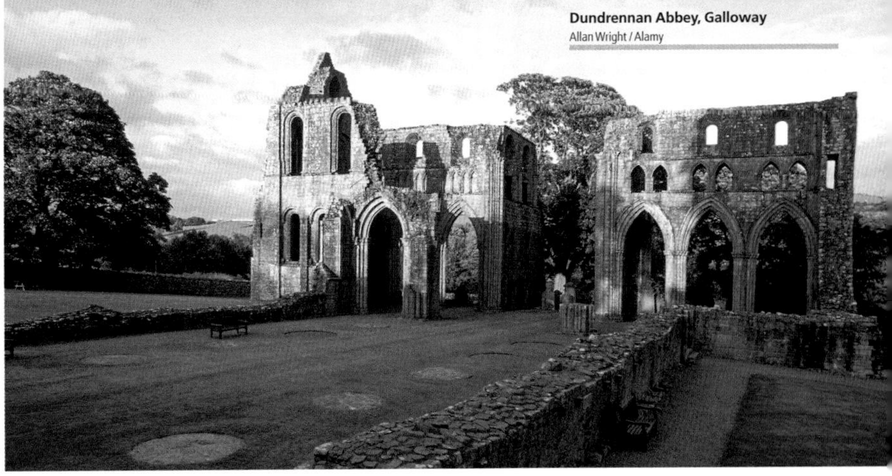

Dundrennan Abbey, Galloway
Allan Wright / Alamy

Religious buildings

Aberdeen and Moray

Cathedral Church of St Machar *Church Square, Aberdeen, Aberdeen City.* This site was founded by St Machar, a follower of St Columba, in 580, although this fortified granite cathedral dates from the 15th century. The nave ceiling dates from 1520 and almost 50 different coats of arms from Scotland's nobles and bishops as well as Europe's royal houses make up its heraldic scheme. www.stmachar.com **75 B6**

Elgin Cathedral *North College Street, Elgin, Moray.* This lovely ruin is the remains of a 13th-century building, which was burned down by the Wolf of Badenoch in 1390 as revenge for his excommunication for leaving his wife. There are several unusual medieval gravestones and a rare Pictish cross slab remains within the shell of the building. www.historicenvironment.scot/visit-a-place/places/elgin-cathedral **81 B7**

King's College Chapel *College Bounds, Aberdeen, Aberdeen City.* Finished in 1495, the chapel retains much of its original fittings and furniture, in particular the screens, stalls and ceiling are rare surviving examples of Scottish medieval wood carving. The stained glass is particularly fine. www.abdn.ac.uk/about/campus/kings-college-chapel-380.php **75 B6**

Pluscarden Abbey *Kellas, Elgin, Moray.* One of only two working monasteries in Scotland, this Benedictine house was originally founded for a French order in 1230. The site includes the partially restored abbey, monastic buildings and church choir. Stained-glass workshops are also run by the monks. www.pluscardenabbey.org **81 C6**

St Machar's Cathedral *Aberdeen, Aberdeen City.* See Cathedral Church of St Machar **75 B6**

Argyll, Bute, Stirling, Trossachs

Balquhidder Church *Balquhidder, Callander, Stirling.* A small church that holds an 8th-century stone called the St Angus' Stone, a 17th-century bell and some Gaelic bibles. Its chief claim to fame is the grave of Rob Roy, which lies in the churchyard. https://scotlandschurchestrust.org.uk/church/balquhidder-parish-church **56 B1**

Cambuskenneth Abbey *Cambuskenneth, Stirling.* The ruins of an abbey founded by David I in 1147. The only substantial remains are the 14th-century bell tower. King James III and his wife, Queen Margaret of Denmark are buried here, marked by a 19th-century monument. www.historicenvironment.scot/visit-a-place/places/cambuskenneth-abbey **39 B7**

Church of the Holy Rude *St John Street, Stirling, Stirling.* This simple church is the site of the last coronation in Scotland, that of James VI in 1567. The stained glass is 19th-century. www.holyrude.org **39 B6**

Dunblane Cathedral *Cathedral Square, Dunblane, Stirling.* A superb, mainly 13th-century, Gothic church, with carved choir stalls, pews and screens, a hermit's cell, smart tombs and a Jesse Tree window. www.dunblanecathedral.org.uk **56 B2**

Holy Trinity Church *12 Keir Street, Bridge of Allan, Stirling.* Built in 1860, this small church is interesting for its Charles Rennie Mackintosh designs and its stained glass windows. **39 A6**

Inchmahome Priory *Port of Menteith, Stirling.* In spring and summer a ferry runs from Port of Menteith to the isle of Inchmahome, a beautiful ruined Augustinian priory in a lovely setting, with impressive tombs of important families from the surrounding area. www.historicenvironment.scot/visit-a-place/places/inchmahome-priory **55 B8**

Iona Abbey *Baile Mor, Iona, Argyll and Bute.* A 13th-century Benedictine abbey, damaged during the Reformation but restored in the early 20th century and now home to a thriving religious community. Within the site are other structures, including the ruins of the Augustinian nunnery, St Martin and St John's crosses both from the 8th century, St Oran's chapel, and the infirmary museum. To the left of the abbey's entrance is St Columba's shrine, where the saint who founded the community in 563 may be buried. The island's cemetery surrounds St Oran's chapel and among the 60 kings said to be buried here are both Duncan and Macbeth. Many of the old grave slabs have been moved to the museum and the abbey's cloisters for safekeeping. www.iona.org.uk www.historicenvironment.scot/visit-a-place/places/iona-abbey-and-nunnery **61 E5**

Macquarie Mausoleum *Salen, Mull, Argyll and Bute.* The simple tomb, set in a clearing, of Lachlan Macquarie, governor of New South Wales from 1809–20. His predecessor Captain William Bligh had been unpopular because of his despotism, and the more liberal Macquarie is remembered by some as 'The father of Australia'. It is owned by the National Trust of Australia and managed by National Trust for Scotland. www.undiscoveredscotland.co.uk/mull/macquarie **61 C8**

Edinburgh and East Central

Holyrood Abbey *Holyrood Palace grounds, Canongate, Edinburgh, City of Edinburgh.* The ruins of the old royal foundation include one of the west towers and the elaborate west doorway and one Romanesque doorway. It was sacked by the English in 1547, the whole eastern part of the building was pulled down during the reformation and Charles I's attempts at repair included a stone roof that collapsed in 1768, taking most of the rest of the building with it. www.historicenvironment.scot/visit-a-place/places/holyrood-abbey **41 F8**

Rosslyn Chapel *Roslin, Midlothian.* Properly known as the Collegiate Church of St Matthew, this is one of Scotland's most beautiful churches. It was built in the mid-15th century for William St Clair, 3rd Earl of Orkney. The interior is richly carved with vines and flowers, biblical figures, green men, moral tales and figures associated with Freemasonry and the Knights Templar, as well as cacti and corn, which were not known in Europe at that time, leading some people to speculate that St Clair's grandfather Prince Henry of Orkney had reached America a century before Columbus. A pair of carvings in the Lady Chapel ceiling is supposed to represent the apprentice who carved the beautiful apprentice pillar in the southeast corner and his master who murdered him in a fit of jealousy. www.rosslynchapel.com **32 B1**

St Cuthbert's Kirk *Dalmeny, Edinburgh, City of Edinburgh.* This Romanesque church has survived virtually intact. Of particular note are the beasts carved on the south doorway and the grotesques inside on the chancel arch and corbels. **41 F8**

St Giles Cathedral *High Street, Edinburgh, City of Edinburgh.* Gothic cathedral. Contents include the early 20th-century Thistle Chapel, which is dedicated to Scotland's highest order of chivalry and holds lovely stalls and heraldic stained-glass windows. www.stgilescathedral.org.uk **41 F8**

Glasgow and the Clyde

Cathedral of St Kentigern *Cathedral Square, Glasgow, City of Glasgow.* Glasgow's Cathedral, also known as St Mungo's, is the only pre-Reformation cathedral in mainland Scotland to have survived virtually intact. St Kentigern (St Mungo) founded a monastic community here in the 5th century. The first stone church was consecrated in 1136, but burned down at the end of the 12th century. It was rebuilt as what is today known as the lower church. This was a medieval pilgrimage centre, focused on the shrine of St Kentigern. The upper church is a beautiful Gothic building, dating from the 15th century. The late 15th-century choir screen is a rare survival, and is decorated with figures depicting the seven deadly sins. www.glasgowcathedral.org/history **28 A2**

Glasgow Cathedral *Glasgow, City of Glasgow.* See Cathedral of St Kentigern. **28 A2**

Paisley Abbey *Abbey Close, Paisley, Renfrewshire.* Not particularly prepossessing from the outside, the abbey has a surprisingly pleasing interior. First built in 1163, rebuilt in the 14th-15th centuries and then restored in the 19th century, it is

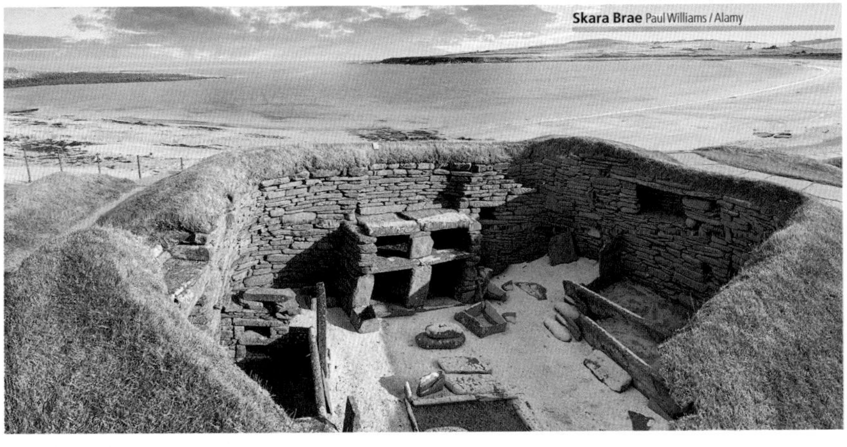

Skara Brae Paul Williams / Alamy

spacious and elaborately decorated. The stained glass, of various periods and styles, is particularly beautiful. The oldest item in the abbey is the 10th-century Celtic cross of St Barrochan. www.paisleyabbey.org.uk **27 B8**

St Mungo's Cathedral, Glasgow *Glasgow, City of Glasgow.* See Cathedral of St Kentigern. **28 A2**

Perth, Angus, Dundee and Fife

Arbroath Abbey *Abbey Street, Arbroath, Angus.* William the Lion founded this monastery in 1178 and parts of the church and the domestic range remain. The church is chiefly famous as being the site where the Declaration of Arbroath was written in 1320. The declaration was a letter from eight earls and 31 barons to the pope, asking for support in their fight for Scottish independence from England. www.historicenvironment.scot/visit-a-place/places/arbroath-abbey **67 C6**

Balmerino Abbey *Balmerino, Fife.* A Cistercian monastery, founded in 1229 and destroyed by the English in 1547. The ruined building may be viewed from the grounds, which contain many ancient trees, including a Spanish chestnut tree, which is more than 400 years old and one of the oldest in the country. www.visitscotland.com/info/see-do/balmerino-abbey-p247561 **66 E3**

Brechin Cathedral *Church Square, Brechin, Angus.* Although the building is mainly the result of an early 20th-century reconstruction, the oldest part is the 104ft free-standing round tower, which was built in around 1000 and is one of only two of this type in Scotland and thought to be a place of sanctuary from Viking raids. The main door is set 6ft above the ground for the same reason. It has some lovely carvings including animals and saints, while there are several Pictish stones inside the church. www.brechincathedral.org.uk **67 A5**

Culross Abbey *Culross, Fife.* Founded in 1217 by Malcolm, Earl of Fife. Although the Gothic nave is ruinous, the choir is still used as the town's parish church. www.historicenvironment.scot/visit-a-place/places/culross-abbey **40 C3**

Dunfermline Abbey and Palace *St Margaret's Street, Dunfermline, Fife.* The nave of this culturally important abbey remains from the mid-12th-century Romanesque building, while the flying buttresses, the shrine to the saint and the baptismal porch at the northwest end are Gothic additions. Traces of the Celtic and 11th-century Culdee church can be seen through gratings in the nave floor. Of the many royal burials in the abbey, only those of St Margaret and Robert the Bruce have been located. A small part of the ruins of the royal palace lies next door. www.dunfermlineabbey.co.uk **41 C5**

Dunkeld Cathedral *High Street, Dunkeld, Perth and Kinross.* The nave and clocktower of this partly ruined Gothic cathedral date from the 15th century while the choir, which is still in use as the parish church, was built in the previous century. Features of interest include an effigy of the Wolf of Badenoch and a 'lepers' peep' in the north wall, which allowed them to receive the sacrament without contaminating the rest of the congregation. The building suffered extensive damage during the Reformation and was restored in about 1600, but was burned during the battle of Dunkeld in 1689. www.dunkeldcathedral.org.uk **65 C8**

Holy Trinity Church *Off South Street, St Andrews, Fife.* The town church (or kirk), this medieval building was moved from its original site near the cathedral in 1410. Since then it suffered from alterations after the Reformation and an early 20th-century restoration, but the stained glass and carvings are well worth a visit. https://scotlandschurchestrust.org.uk/church/parish-church-of-the-holy-trinity-st-andrews **67 F5**

Kirk of St John the Baptist *31 St John Place, Perth, Perth and Kinross.* Founded in 1126, the present church dates from the 15th century. An attractive building nestling in the middle of a network of cobbled streets, it was the venue in 1559 for John Knox's diatribe on idolatry, which helped to lead to the Reformation and the wholesale destruction of monasteries and religious art in Scotland. It was restored as a war memorial in the 1920s. https://scotlandschurchestrust.org.uk/church/st-johns-kirk-of-perth **66 E1**

St Andrews Cathedral and Priory *Off Pends Road, St Andrews, Fife.* Once the most important religious building in Scotland, this medieval cathedral took more than 150 years to build. There is a display of artefacts discovered within the building and grounds, as well as some early Christian and medieval monuments. www.historicenvironment.scot/visit-a-place/places/st-andrews-cathedral **67 F5**

South of Scotland

Crossraguel Abbey *Maybole, South Ayrshire.* Substantial remains of a 13th-century Cluniac monastery. Some ornate carving remains in the apse of the abbey church, giving an indication of the richness of the building. More sculpture remains in the sacristy, including animals, humans and a green man. The chapter house, where the monks would meet to discuss abbey business, is substantially intact, as are the gatehouse and dovecote. The late 15th-century tower house was the abbot's residence www.historicenvironment.scot/visit-a-place/places/crossraguel-abbey **6 C4**

Dryburgh Abbey *Dryburgh, Scottish Borders.* A lovely ruined abbey set in a loop of the River Tweed. Its architecture is 'Transitional', with elements of Romanesque and Early Gothic. The poet, Sir Walter Scott is buried here. www.historicenvironment.scot/visit-a-place/places/dryburgh-abbey **23 C7**

Dundrennan Abbey *Kirkcudbright, Dumfries and Galloway.* The ruins of a beautiful Cistercian monastery, where Mary Queen of Scots spent her last night in Scotland before fleeing to England. www.historicenvironment.scot/visit-a-place/places/dundrennan-abbey **47 D8**

Glenluce Abbey *Glenluce, Dumfries and Galloway.* The ruins of this Cistercian abbey include a 15th-century chapter house with carved bosses and corbels including green men, cloisters and part of the complex water-supply system. www.historicenvironment.scot/visit-a-place/places/glenluce-abbey **46 D3**

Jedburgh Abbey *Abbey Place, Jedburgh, Scottish Borders.* Partially restored ruined abbey, founded by King David I in 1138 and built in the Romanesque style. Visitor centre. www.historicenvironment.scot/visit-a-place/places/jedburgh-abbey/ **24 E2**

Kelso Abbey *Bridge Street, Kelso, Scottish Borders.* The earliest and probably the largest abbey in the Scottish Borders, Kelso was founded in 1128. It was repeatedly attacked by the English in the 16th century, but what does remain is some of the best Romanesque architecture in Scotland. www.historicenvironment.scot/visit-a-place/places/kelso-abbey **24 C3**

Melrose Abbey *Abbey Street, Melrose, Scottish Borders.* Ruined Cistercian abbey, built in the Perpendicular Gothic style. It was founded in 1136 and rebuilt by Robert the Bruce in the 14th century. A number of famous Scots are buried in the chancel. According to legend, the heart of Robert the Bruce was buried here and in 1997 a cask with a heart was excavated. It has since been reburied in the chapter house. Decorative, and often humorous, carvings survive in the chancel, including a gargoyle of a pig playing bagpipes on the roof. Fine stonework also survives in some of the window tracery, the pulpitum screen. www.historicenvironment.scot/visit-a-place/places/melrose-abbey **23 C7**

St Michael's Parish Church *Linlithgow, Scottish Borders.* One of Scotland's best examples of a parish church, despite severe damage in both the Reformation and Commonwealth periods. www.undiscoveredscotland.co.uk/linlithgow/stmichaels/index.html **40 E4**

Sweetheart Abbey *New Abbey, Dumfries and Galloway.* The remains of a Cistercian abbey, founded in 1273. The roofless church survives but the monastic buildings have gone. There are traces of elaborate carving in some of the windows. The abbey's name comes from its founder, Devorgilla de Balliol, Lady of Galloway, who carried her husband's heart around in a casket for the last 22 years of her life. Her tomb is in the south transept. www.historicenvironment.scot/visit-a-place/places/sweetheart-abbey **48 C3**

The Highlands

Beauly Priory *Beauly, Highland.* The ruins of this priory, one of only three built for the Valliscaulian order, date to 1230. The chapel of the holy cross, next to the north side of the nave, was added in the early 15th century. www.historicenvironment.scot/visit-a-place/places/beauly-priory **79 D7**

Croick Church *Croick, Highland.* This small chapel and its windswept churchyard sheltered 92 Highlanders in 1845 after their eviction from Glen Calvie to make way for the Duke of Sutherland's sheep. The chapel windows have graffiti scratched into them by the villagers. www.croickchurch.com **86 D1**

Dornoch Cathedral *Castle Street, Dornoch, Highland.* Originally founded in 1224, restored in the 19th century and returned to something approaching its original glory in the 20th century. The stained glass was donated by Andrew Carnegie. www.dornoch-cathedral.com **86 E4**

Fortrose Cathedral *Fortrose, Highland.* The ruins of a beautiful early 13th-century cathedral, founded by King David I, situated in the middle of the pretty village green. www.historicenvironment.scot/visit-a-place/places/fortrose-cathedral **80 C2**

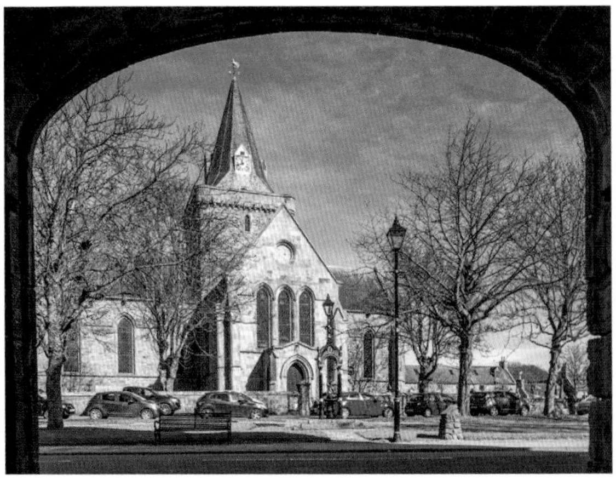

▲ **Dornoch Cathedral** Sebastian Wasek / Alamy

The Outer Islands

Italian Chapel *St. Mary's, Mainland, Orkney.* A tiny chapel, adapted from two Nissen huts, created by Italian prisoners of war who were held here during World War II while working on the Churchill Barriers (see page X). The facade and trompe-l'oeil interior were restored in 1960 and the chapel is still regularly used for Mass. www.orkney.com/listings/the-italian-chapel **99 C5**

St Magnus Cathedral *Broad Street, Kirkwall, Mainland, Orkney.* Begun in 1137 by Earl Rognvald in honour of his uncle, St Magnus, the earliest part of Orkney's cathedral was built by masons who had previously worked on Durham Cathedral and is Romanesque in style. Later additions, such as the extended nave, are Gothic. There are interesting 17th-century tombs with skull-and-crossbones motifs and moralising texts. Among the monuments is that dedicated to the sailors who died when the Royal Oak was torpedoed in Scapa Flow in 1939. www.stmagnus.org **99 B5**

Museums and galleries

Art and crafts

Aberdeen and Moray

Aberdeen Art Gallery *Schoolhill, Aberdeen, Aberdeen City.* As well as a collection featuring the work of contemporary painters and a large number of portraits by Pre-Raphaelite artists, this gallery has a selection of modern ceramics, textiles and jewellery. www.aagm.co.uk **75 B6**

Duff House *Banff, Aberdeenshire.* An elegant Georgian Baroque mansion, designed by William Adam and completed in 1737. It houses a collection of paintings on permanent loan from the National Gallery of Scotland and temporary exhibitions. www.nationalgalleries.org/visit/duff-house **82 B3**

Edinburgh and East Central

Scottish National Gallery *2 The Mound, Edinburgh, City of Edinburgh.* This gallery holds an extensive collection of paintings, including works by Botticelli, Raphael, Titian, El Greco, Velázquez, Rembrandt, Cézanne, Degas, van Gogh, Monet, Gauguin, Seurat and Renoir. www.nationalgalleries.org/visit/scottish-national-gallery **41 F8**

Scottish National Gallery of Modern Art *Belford Road, Edinburgh, City of Edinburgh.* The main building, Modern One, holds the national collection of 20th-century art, including works by Pablo Picasso, Georges Braque, Henry Moore, Barbara Hepworth, Henri Matisse, Joan Miró, Max Ernst, Balthus, Roy Lichtenstein and David Hockney. Across the road, Modern Two houses an extensive collection of items donated by Sir Eduardo Paolozzi including works by Alberto Giacometti and Paolozzi himself. There are also sculptures in the grounds. www.nationalgalleries.org/visit/scottish-national-gallery-modern-art **41 F8**

Scottish National Portrait Gallery *1 Queen Street, Edinburgh, City of Edinburgh.* The collection includes portraits of famous people from the last four centuries of Scottish life, from the royal families to traditional heroes and modern actors. www.nationalgalleries.org/visit/scottish-national-portrait-gallery **41 F8**

Talbot Rice Gallery *Old College, University of Edinburgh, Chambers Street, Edinburgh, City of Edinburgh.* Items from the university's art collection are housed here, including some old masters and works by 20th-century Scottish artists. There are also regular exhibitions of contemporary art. www.ed.ac.uk/talbot-rice **41 F8**

Glasgow and the Clyde

Burrell Collection *2060 Pollokshaws Road, Glasgow, City of Glasgow.* Set within Pollok Country Park, this museum holds the fruits of more than 80 years collecting by Sir William Burrell, a wealthy ship owner. The broad range of artefacts includes, 19th-century French paintings, stained glass, Chinese ceramics, one of the original casts of Rodin's 'The Thinker', as well as furniture, textiles, 'objets d'art' and silver. www.glasgowlife.org.uk/museums/venues/the-burrell-collection **28 B2**

▼ **Our Dynamic Earth** Jui-Chi Chan / Alamy

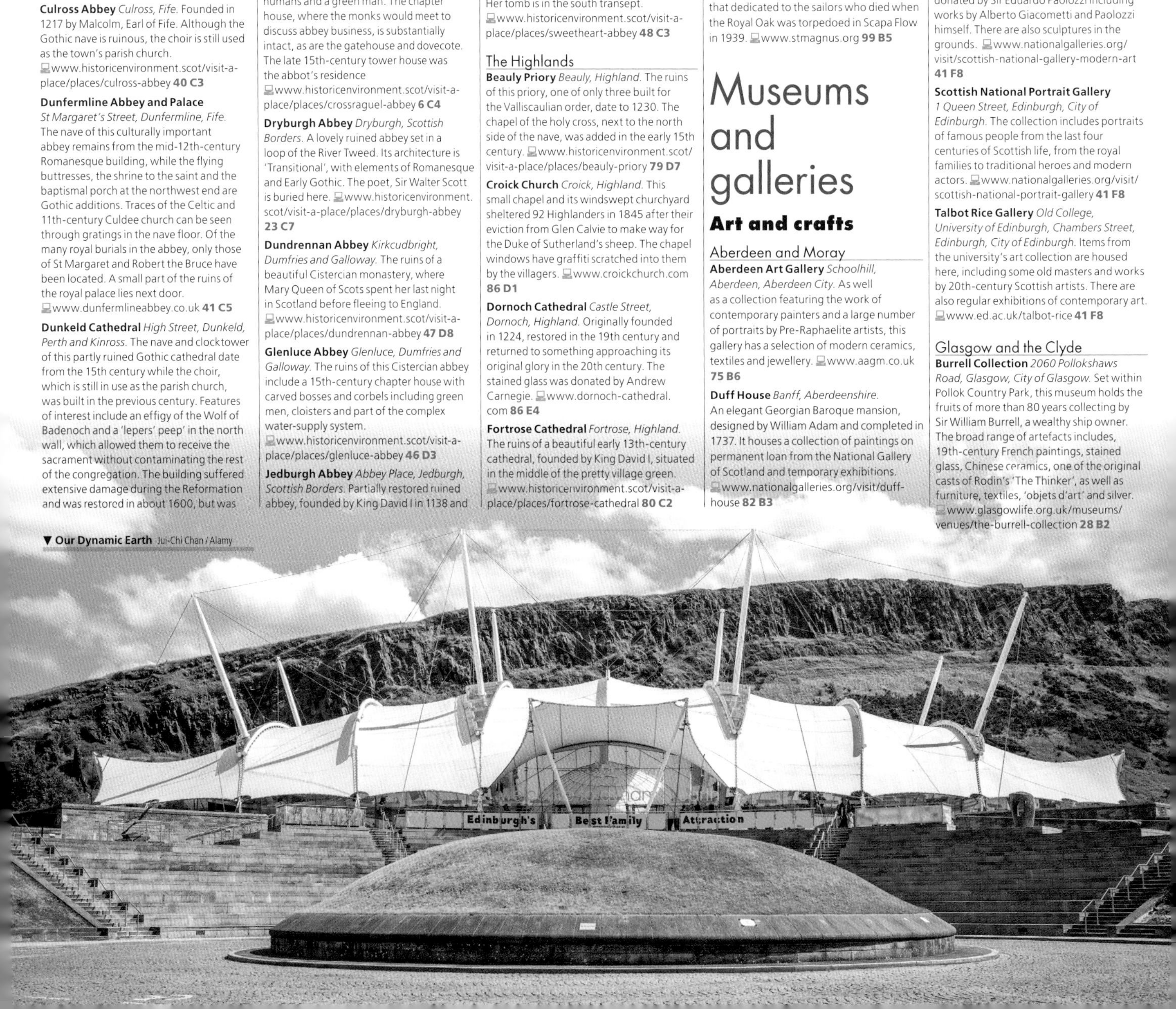

▲ **Glasgow Science Centre**
John Graham / Bassline Images / Alamy

◄ **Fort George** David Gowans / Alamy

Hunterian Art Gallery *22 Hillhead Street, Glasgow, City of Glasgow.* Part of the University of Glasgow, this gallery contains the second largest collection of works by James McNeill Whistler – some 60 in all – as well as works by Rembrandt, Rubens and 19th- and 20th-century Scottish artists. A reconstruction of Charles Rennie Mackintosh's house is reached through an extension and contains more than sixty original pieces of Mackintosh furniture and displays about the artist's home. 🖳www.gla.ac.uk/hunterian **28 A2**

The Lighthouse *11 Mitchell Lane, Glasgow, City of Glasgow.* State of the art exhibition centre that includes a Mackintosh Interpretation Centre, in which the artist's output is examined, and an IT area. 🖳https://glasgow.gov.uk/index.aspx?articleid=17717 **28 A2**

South of Scotland
Maclaurin Art Gallery and Rozelle House *Monument Road, Rozelle Park, Ayr, South Ayrshire.* Good collection of contemporary art. Nature trail. 🖳www.themaclaurin.org.uk **17 E5**

Science and technology
Aberdeen and Moray
Aberdeen Science Centre *The Tramsheds, 179 Constitution Street, Aberdeen, Aberdeen City.* A series of hands-on science exhibits that will occupy children of all ages. 🖳www.aberdeensciencecentre.org **75 B6**

Argyll, Bute, Stirling, Trossachs
Denny Tank *Castle Street, Dumbarton, West Dunbartonshire.* This outpost of the Scottish Maritime Museum holds the world's oldest ship model experiment tank, where ship designers test models of ships before construction. The entire process is explained in a series of explanatory panels. 🖳www.scottishmaritimemuseum.org **37 E7**

Edinburgh and East Central
Dental Museum *Edinburgh, City of Edinburgh.* See Surgeons' Hall Museums **41 F8**

Our Dynamic Earth *107 Holyrood Road, Edinburgh, City of Edinburgh.* A fully interactive exploration of the geological and biological history of the Earth, including aquaria, audiovisual clips, simulations of different climates on Earth from tundra to rain forests 🖳www.dynamicearth.co.uk **41 F9**

Surgeons' Hall Museums *Nicolson Street, Edinburgh, City of Edinburgh.* Incorporating the Wohl Museum of Pathology, The Exhibition of the History of Surgery and Dental Museums, this specialist collection explores the development of surgical techniques over 500 years and houses wide collections of dental instruments and medical specimens. 🖳https://museum.rcsed.ac.uk/ **41 F8**

Glasgow and the Clyde
Glasgow Science Centre *50 Pacific Quay, Glasgow, City of Glasgow.* A science centre with interactive displays and a planetarium. 🖳www.glasgowsciencecentre.org **28 A2**

Perth, Angus, Dundee and Fife
Mills Observatory *Glamis Road, Dundee, City of Dundee.* Britain's only full-time public observatory, it features a refracting telescope, small planetarium and displays of historic and modern equipment, pictures and models. 🖳www.leisureandculturedundee.com/mills-home **66 D3**

The Outer Islands
Orkney Wireless Museum *Kiln Corner, Junction Road, Kirkwall, Mainland, Orkney.* This museum is devoted to the wartime communications that operated at Scapa Flow in World War II. 🖳www.orkneywirelessmuseum.org.uk **99 B5**

Transport
Aberdeen and Moray
Grampian Transport Museum *Main Street, Alford, Aberdeenshire.* This museum houses a wide collection of transport-related items, including cars, steam engines, trams and buses. 🖳www.gtm.org.uk **74 A2**

Edinburgh and East Central
National Museum of Flight *East Fortune, East Lothian.* The old World War II aircraft hangars hold more than 50 vintage aircraft, among them a Tiger Moth, a Spitfire and a Vulcan, as well as a Concorde with an accompanying exhibition. 🖳www.nms.ac.uk/national-museum-of-flight/ **43 E6**

Myreton Motor Museum *Aberlady, East Lothian.* A collection of vintage cars, military vehicles and motorbikes, as well as motoring memorabilia. 🖳www.myretonmotormuseum.co.uk **43 E5**

Glasgow and the Clyde
Riverside Museum *100 Pointhouse Place, Finnieston, Glasgow* An enormous collection of cars, trains, trams and other transport memorabilia. The Tall Ship is berthed alongside. 🖳www.glasgowlife.org.uk/museums/venues/riverside-museum **28 A2**

Military history
Aberdeen and Moray
Gordon Highlanders Museum *St Luke's Viewfield Road, Aberdeen, Aberdeen City.* A museum devoted to one of Scotland's most famous regiments. 🖳www.gordonhighlanders.com **75 B6**

Argyll, Bute, Stirling, Trossachs
Museum of the Argyll and Sutherland Highlanders *Stirling, Stirling.* See Stirling Castle **39 B6**

Edinburgh and East Central
National War Museum *Castlehill, Edinburgh, City of Edinburgh.* Set within Edinburgh Castle, this museum explores the last 400 years of war and military service, both within Scotland and as experienced by Scots serving abroad. 🖳www.nms.ac.uk/national-war-museum **41 F8**

Perth, Angus, Dundee and Fife
Black Watch Regimental Museum *Balhousie Castle, Hay Street, Perth, Perth and Kinross.* This 16th-century castle houses weapons, uniforms, documents and medals showing the story of this famous regiment throughout their history. 🖳www.theblackwatch.co.uk **66 E1**

The Highlands
Culloden *Culloden Moor, Inverness, Highland.* The site of the end of the last Jacobite uprising. On 16 April, 1746, the army of Prince Charles Edward Stuart (Bonnie Prince Charlie) was crushed by the the Duke of Cumberland's forces, led by the Duke of Cumberland. The battlefield is being restored to how it was at the time and flags show the positions of the two armies. Features include the Graves of the Clans, the Well of the Dead, the Memorial Cairn, the Cumberland Stone and the Field of the English. Leanach Cottage, which survived the battle being fought around it, and outside which 30 Jacobites were burned alive, is open to the public. Guided tours of the battlefield are available and the visitor centre provides a background to the battle. 🖳www.nts.org.uk/visit/places/culloden **80 D2**

Fort George/Queen's Own Highlanders Regimental Museum *Fort George, Inverness, Highland.* Set within the ramparts of Fort George, which was built after the battle of Culloden and which is still an active army base, this museum contains regimental exhibits from 1778 onwards. 🖳www.thehighlandersmuseum.com 🖳www.historicenvironment.scot/visit-a-place/places/fort-george/ **80 C2**

Queen's Own Highlanders Regimental Museum *Inverness, Highland.* See Fort George **80 C2**

Local history
Aberdeen and Moray
Elgin Museum *High Street, Elgin, Moray.* This museum of local history also houses an assortment of anthropological items from around the world, Pictish exhibits and a good collection of fossils. 🖳www.elginmuseum.org.uk **81 B7**

Whisky
Aberdeen and Moray
Glenfarclas Distillery *Ballindalloch, near Marypark, Moray* A small, independent distillery, founded in 1836 and still run by members of the same family. 🖳https://glenfarclas.com **81 E7**

Glenfiddich Distillery *Dufftown, Moray* Pre-booked guided tours of one of Scotland's most famous distilleries. 🖳www.glenfiddich.com/uk/distillery **81 D8**

Glenlivet Distillery *Tomintoul, Moray* One of Scotland's most famous distilleries. 🖳www.maltwhiskydistilleries.com/theglenlivet **81 F6**

Macallan Distillery *Near Craigellachie, Moray* Prebooked guided tours around one of Speyside's best-known distilleries. 🖳www.themacallan.com/en/distillery **81 D7**

Strathisla Distillery *Seafield Avenue, Keith, Moray* Tours of the oldest working distillery in the Highlands, where Chivas Regal is made. 🖳www.maltwhiskydistilleries.com **82 C1**

Argyll, Bute, Stirling, Trossachs
Ardbeg Distillery *Ardbeg, Isle of Islay, Argyll and Bute* Prebooked guided tours around one of Islay's whisky distilleries. 🖳www.ardbeg.com/en-gb/visit-us **49 B4**

Bowmore Distillery *School Street, Bowmore, Isle of Islay, Argyll and Bute* Guided tours of one of Islay's best-known distilleries. 🖳www.bowmore.com/distillery-tours/experiences **49 A3**

Bunnahabhain Distillery *Port Askaig, Isle of Islay, Argyll and Bute* Prebooked guided tours of one of Islay's distilleries. 🖳https://bunnahabhain.com/visit-us/ **52 F4**

Caol Ila Distillery *Port Askaig, Isle of Islay, Argyll and Bute* Prebooked tours of one of Islay's distilleries. 🖳www.malts.com/en-gb/visit-our-distilleries/caol-ila **52 F4**

Lagavulin Distillery *Port Ellen, Isle of Islay, Argyll and Bute* Pre-booked, guided tours of one of Islay's whisky distilleries. 🖳www.malts.com/en-row/distilleries/lagavulin/tours **49 B4**

Laphroaig Distillery *Laphroaig, Isle of Islay, Argyll and Bute* Guided tours around one of Scotland's most famous distilleries. Advance booking is required. 🖳www.laphroaig.com/en/tours-laphroaig **49 B3**

Oban Distillery *Stafford Street, Oban, Argyll and Bute* Guided tours and exhibition around a distillery that has been producing single-malt whisky since 1794. 🖳www.malts.com/en-gb/visit-our-distilleries/oban **62 E3**

Tobermory Distillery *Tobermory, Isle of Mull, Argyll and Bute* Prebooked tours around one of the oldest distilleries. 🖳https://tobermorydistillery.com/tours/ **61 B8**

Edinburgh and East Central
The Scotch Whisky Experience *354 Castlehill, Edinburgh, City of Edinburgh* Dedicated to the history of Scotch whisky, exhibits in the centre explain how it is manufactured. Guided tours include tastings. 🖳www.scotchwhiskyexperience.co.uk **41 F8**

Perth, Angus, Dundee and Fife
Blair Athol Distillery *Perth Road, Pitlochry, Perth and Kinross* Tours of one of Scotland's best known distilleries. Visitor centre. 🖳www.discovering-distilleries.com/blairathol **65 B7**

Glenturret Distillery *The Hosh, Crieff, Perth and Kinross* Guided tours are available around Scotland's oldest distillery, which was founded in 1775. Museum of whisky. 🖳https://theglenturret.com **65 E6**

South of Scotland
Isle of Arran Distillers *Lochranza, Isle of Arran, North Ayrshire* Guided tours around Scotland's youngest distillery, which opened in 1995. 🖳www.arranwhisky.com **51 A5**

The Highlands
Ben Nevis Distillery *Lochy Bridge, Fort William, Highland* Visitor centre and tours around a small distillery at the foot of Ben Nevis. 🖳www.bennevisdistillery.com **70 E3**

Clynelish Distillery *Brora, Highland* The northernmost distillery in mainland Scotland. Guided tours. 🖳www.malts.com/en-row/distilleries/clynelish/ **87 C6**

Glenmorangie Distillery *Tain, Highland* Guided tours and visitor centre located in one of the most famous distilleries. 🖳www.glenmorangie.com **86 E4**

Talisker Distillery *Carbost, Isle of Skye, Highland* Prebooked visits to Skye's only distillery, which produces a peaty single malt. 🖳www.malts.com/en-row/distilleries/talisker **76 E3**

The Outer Islands
Highland Park Distillery *The Hosh, Kirkwall, Mainland, Orkney* Tours around the world's northernmost distillery, showing the complete whisky-making process. 🖳www.highlandpark.co.uk **99 C5**

Fraserburgh Heritage Centre *Quarry Road, Fraserburgh, Aberdeenshire.* Exhibits include the history of the town, small boats and experiments into wireless communication conducted by Guglielmo Marconi in the town in 1904. 🖳www.fraserburghheritage.com **83 B6**

The Joiner's Workshop and Visitor Centre *Fordyce, Aberdeenshire.* A small museum housing a collection of woodworking tools and machinery. Demonstrations. 🖳www.visitabdn.com/listing/fordyce-joiners-workshop-and-visitor-centre **82 B2**

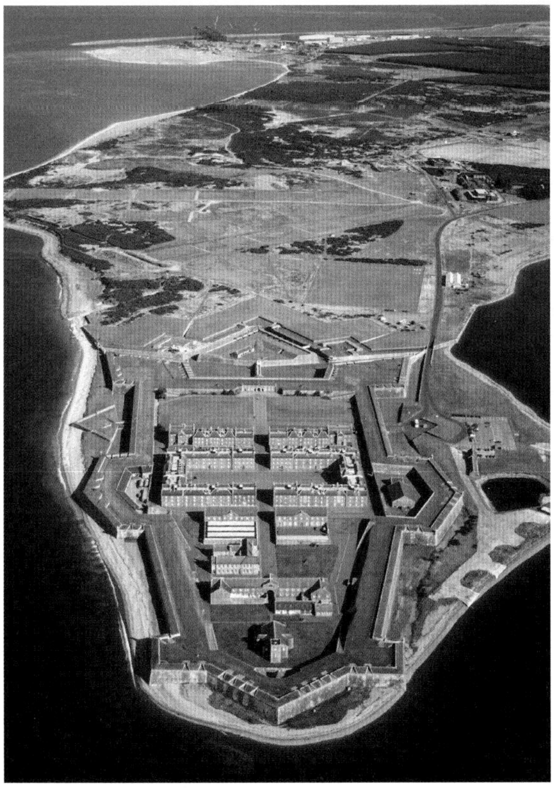

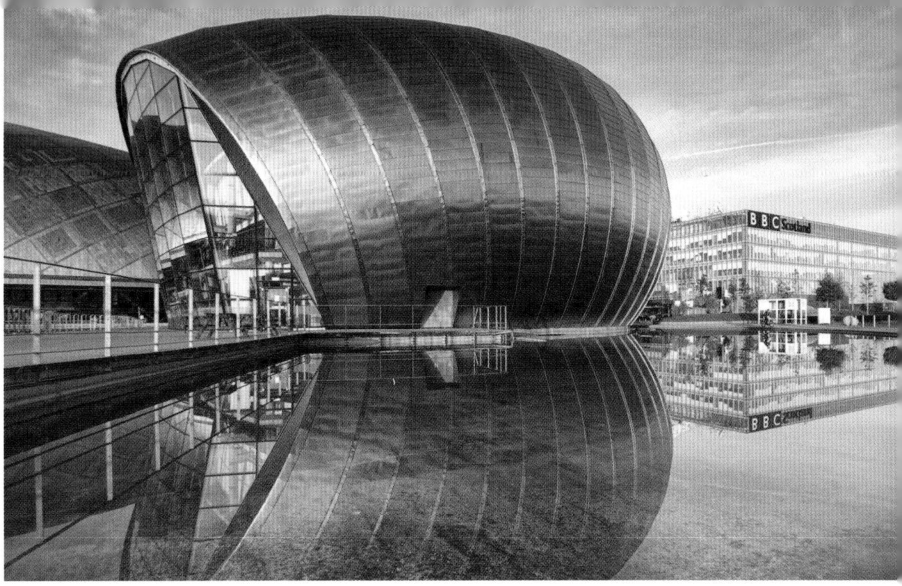

▲ **Glasgow Science Centre** John Graham / Bassline Images / Alamy

◀ **Fort George** David Gowans / Alamy

Hunterian Art Gallery *22 Hillhead Street, Glasgow, City of Glasgow.* Part of the University of Glasgow, this gallery contains the second largest collection of works by James McNeill Whistler – some 60 in all – as well as works by Rembrandt, Rubens and 19th- and 20th-century Scottish artists. A reconstruction of Charles Rennie Mackintosh's house is reached through an extension and contains more than sixty original pieces of Mackintosh furniture and displays about the artist's home. www.gla.ac.uk/hunterian **28 A2**

The Lighthouse *11 Mitchell Lane, Glasgow, City of Glasgow.* State of the art exhibition centre that includes a Mackintosh Interpretation Centre, in which the artist's output is examined, and an IT area. https://glasgow.gov.uk/index.aspx?articleid=17717 **28 A2**

South of Scotland

Maclaurin Art Gallery and Rozelle House *Monument Road, Rozelle Park, Ayr, South Ayrshire.* Good collection of contemporary art. Nature trail. www.themaclaurin.org.uk **17 E5**

Science and technology

Aberdeen and Moray

Aberdeen Science Centre *The Tramsheds, 179 Constitution Street, Aberdeen, Aberdeen City.* A series of hands-on science exhibits that will occupy children of all ages. www.aberdeensciencecentre.org **75 B6**

Argyll, Bute, Stirling, Trossachs

Denny Tank *Castle Street, Dumbarton, West Dunbartonshire.* This outpost of the Scottish Maritime Museum holds the world's oldest ship model experiment tank, where ship designers test models of ships before construction. The entire process is explained in a series of explanatory panels. www.scottishmaritimemuseum.org **37 E7**

Edinburgh and East Central

Dental Museum *Edinburgh, City of Edinburgh.* See Surgeons' Hall Museums **41 F8**

Our Dynamic Earth *107 Holyrood Road, Edinburgh, City of Edinburgh.* A fully interactive exploration of the geological and biological history of the Earth, including aquaria, audiovisual clips, simulations of different climates on Earth from tundra to rain forests. www.dynamicearth.co.uk **41 F9**

Surgeons' Hall Museums *Nicolson Street, Edinburgh, City of Edinburgh.* Incorporating the Wohl Museum of Pathology, The Exhibition of the History of Surgery and Dental Museums, this specialist collection explores the development of surgical techniques over 500 years and houses wide collections of dental instruments and medical specimens. https://museum.rcsed.ac.uk/ **41 F8**

Glasgow and the Clyde

Glasgow Science Centre *50 Pacific Quay, Glasgow, City of Glasgow.* A science centre with interactive displays and a planetarium. www.glasgowsciencecentre.org **28 A2**

Perth, Angus, Dundee and Fife

Mills Observatory *Glamis Road, Dundee, City of Dundee* . Britain's only full-time public observatory, it features a refracting telescope, small planetarium and displays of historic and modern equipment, pictures and models. www.leisureandculturedundee.com/mills-home **66 D3**

The Outer Islands

Orkney Wireless Museum *Kiln Corner, Junction Road, Kirkwall, Mainland, Orkney.* This museum is devoted to the wartime communications that operated at Scapa Flow in World War II. www.orkneywirelessmuseum.org.uk **99 B5**

Transport

Aberdeen and Moray

Grampian Transport Museum *Main Street, Alford, Aberdeenshire.* This museum houses a wide collection of transport-related items, including cars, steam engines, trams and buses. www.gtm.org.uk **74 A2**

Edinburgh and East Central

National Museum of Flight *East Fortune, East Lothian.* The old World War II aircraft hangars hold more than 50 vintage aircraft, among them a Tiger Moth, a Spitfire and a Vulcan, as well as a Concorde with an accompanying exhibition. www.nms.ac.uk/national-museum-of-flight/ **43 E6**

Myreton Motor Museum *Aberlady, East Lothian.* A collection of vintage cars, military vehicles and motorbikes, as well as motoring memorabilia. www.myretonmotormuseum.co.uk **43 E5**

Glasgow and the Clyde

Riverside Museum *100 Pointhouse Place, Finnieston, Glasgow.* An enormous collection of cars, trains, trams, and other transport memorabilia. The Tall Ship is berthed alongside. www.glasgowlife.org.uk/museums/venues/riverside-museum **28 A2**

Military history

Aberdeen and Moray

Gordon Highlanders Museum *St Luke's Viewfield Road, Aberdeen, Aberdeen City.* A museum devoted to one of Scotland's most famous regiments. www.gordonhighlanders.com **75 B6**

Argyll, Bute, Stirling, Trossachs

Museum of the Argyll and Sutherland Highlanders *Stirling, Stirling.* See Stirling Castle **39 B6**

Edinburgh and East Central

National War Museum *Castlehill, Edinburgh, City of Edinburgh.* Set within Edinburgh Castle, this museum explores the last 400 years of war and military service, both within Scotland and as experienced by Scots serving abroad. www.nms.ac.uk/national-war-museum **41 F8**

Perth, Angus, Dundee and Fife

Black Watch Regimental Museum *Balhousie Castle, Hay Street, Perth, Perth and Kinross.* This 16th-century castle houses weapons, uniforms, documents and medals showing the story of this famous regiment throughout their history. www.theblackwatch.co.uk **66 E1**

The Highlands

Culloden *Culloden Moor, Inverness, Highland.* The site of the end of the last Jacobite uprising. On 16 April, 1746, the army of Prince Charles Edward Stuart (Bonnie Prince Charlie) was crushed by the the Duke of Cumberland's forces, led by the Duke of Cumberland. The battlefield is being restored to how it was at the time and flags show the positions of the two armies. Features include the Graves of the Clans, the Well of the Dead, the Memorial Cairn, the Cumberland Stone and the Field of the English. Leanach Cottage, which survived the battle being fought around it, and outside which 30 Jacobites were burned alive, is open to the public. Guided tours of the battlefield are available and the visitor centre provides a background to the battle. www.nts.org.uk/visit/places/culloden **80 D2**

Fort George/Queen's Own Highlanders Regimental Museum *Fort George, Inverness, Highland.* Set within the ramparts of Fort George, which was built after the battle of Culloden and which is still an active army base, this museum contains regimental exhibits from 1778 onwards. www.thehighlandersmuseum.com www.historicenvironment.scot/visit-a-place/places/fort-george/ **80 C2**

Queen's Own Highlanders Regimental Museum *Inverness, Highland.* See Fort George **80 C2**

Local history

Aberdeen and Moray

Elgin Museum *High Street, Elgin, Moray.* This museum of local history also houses an assortment of anthropological items from around the world, Pictish exhibits and a good collection of fossils. www.elginmuseum.org.uk **81 B7**

Fraserburgh Heritage Centre *Quarry Road, Fraserburgh, Aberdeenshire.* Exhibits include the history of the town, small boats and experiments into wireless communication conducted by Guglielmo Marconi in the town in 1904. www.fraserburghheritage.com **83 B6**

The Joiner's Workshop and Visitor Centre *Fordyce, Aberdeenshire.* A small museum housing a collection of woodworking tools and machinery. Demonstrations. www.visitabdn.com/listing/fordyce-joiners-workshop-and-visitor-centre **82 B2**

Whisky

Aberdeen and Moray

Glenfarclas Distillery *Ballindaloch, near Marypark, Moray* A small, independent distillery, founded in 1836 and still run by members of the same family. https://glenfarclas.com **81 E7**

Glenfiddich Distillery *Dufftown, Moray* Pre-booked guided tours of one of Scotland's most famous distilleries. www.glenfiddich.com/uk/distillery **81 D8**

Glenlivet Distillery *Tomintoul, Moray* One of Scotland's most famous distilleries. www.maltwhiskydistilleries.com/theglenlivet **81 F6**

Macallan Distillery *Near Craigellachie, Moray* Prebooked guided tours around one of Speyside's best-known distilleries. www.themacallan.com/en/distillery **81 D7**

Strathisla Distillery *Seafield Avenue, Keith, Moray* Tours of the oldest working distillery in the Highlands, where Chivas Regal is made. www.maltwhiskydistilleries.com **82 C1**

Argyll, Bute, Stirling, Trossachs

Ardbeg Distillery *Ardbeg, Isle of Islay, Argyll and Bute* Prebooked guided tours around one of Islay's whisky distilleries. www.ardbeg.com/en-gb/visit-us **49 B4**

Bowmore Distillery *School Street, Bowmore, Isle of Islay, Argyll and Bute* Guided tours of one of Islay's best-known distilleries. www.bowmore.com/distillery-tours/experiences **49 A3**

Bunnahabhain Distillery *Port Askaig, Isle of Islay, Argyll and Bute* Prebooked guided tours of one of Islay's distilleries. https://bunnahabhain.com/visit-us/ **52 F4**

Caol Ila Distillery *Port Askaig, Isle of Islay, Argyll and Bute* Prebooked tours of one of Islay's distilleries. www.malts.com/en-gb/visit-our-distilleries/caol-ila **52 F4**

Lagavulin Distillery *Port Ellen, Isle of Islay, Argyll and Bute* Pre-booked, guided tours of one of Islay's whisky distilleries. www.malts.com/en-row/distilleries/lagavulin/tours **49 B4**

Laphroaig Distillery *Laphroaig, Isle of Islay, Argyll and Bute* Guided tours around one of Scotland's most famous distilleries. Advance booking is required. www.laphroaig.com/en/tours-laphroaig **49 B3**

Oban Distillery *Stafford Street, Oban, Argyll and Bute* Guided tours and exhibition around a distillery that has been producing single-malt whisky since 1794. www.malts.com/en-gb/visit-our-distilleries/oban **62 E3**

Tobermory Distillery *Tobermory, Isle of Mull, Argyll and Bute* Prebooked tours around one of the oldest distilleries. https://tobermorydistillery.com/tours/ **61 B8**

Edinburgh and East Central

The Scotch Whisky Experience *354 Castlehill, Edinburgh, City of Edinburgh* Dedicated to the history of Scotch whisky, exhibits in the centre explain how it is manufactured. Guided tours include tastings. www.scotchwhiskyexperience.co.uk **41 F8**

Perth, Angus, Dundee and Fife

Blair Athol Distillery *Perth Road, Pitlochry, Perth and Kinross* Tours of one of Scotland's best known distilleries. Visitor centre. www.discovering-distilleries.com/blairathol **65 B7**

Glenturret Distillery *The Hosh, Crieff, Perth and Kinross* Guided tours are available around Scotland's oldest distillery, which was founded in 1775. Museum of whisky. https://theglenturret.com **65 E6**

South of Scotland

Isle of Arran Distillers *Lochranza, Isle of Arran, North Ayrshire* Guided tours around Scotland's youngest distillery, which opened in 1995. www.arranwhisky.com **51 A5**

The Highlands

Ben Nevis Distillery *Lochy Bridge, Fort William, Highland* Visitor centre and tours around a small distillery at the foot of Ben Nevis. www.bennevisdistillery.com **70 E3**

Clynelish Distillery *Brora, Highland* The northernmost distillery in mainland Scotland. Guided tours. www.malts.com/en-row/distilleries/clynelish/ **87 C6**

Glenmorangie Distillery *Tain, Highland* Guided tours and visitor centre located in one of the most famous distilleries. www.glenmorangie.com **86 E4**

Talisker Distillery *Carbost, Isle of Skye, Highland* Prebooked visits to Skye's only distillery, which produces a peaty single malt. www.malts.com/en-row/distilleries/talisker **76 E3**

The Outer Islands

Highland Park Distillery *The Hosh, Kirkwall, Mainland, Orkney* Tours around the world's northernmost distillery, showing the complete whisky-making process. www.highlandpark.co.uk **99 C5**

Argyll, Bute, Stirling, Trossachs

Auchindrain Folk Museum *Auchindrain, Argyll and Bute.* A collection of about 20 thatched cottages furnished and decorated to show what life was like before the Highland Clearances. www.auchindrain.org.uk **54 B3**

Battle of Bannockburn Visitor Centre *Glasgow Road, Whins of Milton, Stirling.* At the battle of Bannockburn, in 1314, Robert the Bruce of Scotland defeated the forces of Edward II of England, one in a series of battles that eventually led to Scottish independence. Audiovisual presentations and exhibits tell the story of the relationship between the two countries between the 13th and 17th centuries. www.nts.org.uk/visit/places/bannockburn **39 B6**

Bute Museum *Rothesay, Bute, Argyll and Bute.* A good collection covering the geology, natural history and archaeology of the island, including a lignite necklace thought to be more than 3500 years old. www.butemuseum.org.uk **54 F3**

Dunblane Museum *The Cross, Dunblane, Stirling.* A tiny museum, housed in a 17th-century building, with exhibits on both the history of the nearby cathedral and local archaeology. www.dunblanemuseum.org.uk **56 B2**

Iona Heritage Centre *Baile Mor, Iona. Argyll and Bute.* A small museum on the social history of the last 200 years of life on the island, including the effects of the clearances in the 19th century, which halved the population of the island at a stroke. www.ionaheritage.co.uk **61 E5**

Kilmartin House Museum *Kilmartin, Argyll and Bute.* A small museum, housed in the old Manse, with explanations on the nature and use of crannogs (dwellings in lochs), henges and cairns, as well as axe-polishing and other activities. www.kilmartin.org **53 C8**

Mull Museum *Main Street, Mull, Tobermory, Argyll and Bute.* This small museum houses exhibits relating to the history of the town and island, especially its fishing heritage. www.mullmuseum.org.uk **61 B8**

Museum of Islay Life *Port Charlotte, Islay, Argyll and Bute.* A local museum that explores life on Islay from prehistoric times to the present. http://islaymuseum.org **49 A2**

Smith Art Gallery and Museum *Dumbarton Road, Stirling, Stirling.* The history of Stirling, both royal and social, is explored in this museum, which was founded in 1874. Among its exhibits is the world's oldest known football, which is thought to date from the 1540s. www.smithartgalleryandmusem.co.uk **39 B6**

Edinburgh and East Central

Museum of Edinburgh *Huntly House, 142 Canongate, Edinburgh, City of Edinburgh.* Exhibits in this museum devoted to the history of Edinburgh include an original copy of the National Covenant, dating to 1638, and the bowl and collar of Greyfriars Bobby. www.edinburghmuseums.org.uk/venue/museum-edinburgh **41 F8**

The People's Story *163 Canongate, Edinburgh, City of Edinburgh.* This museum, housed in the late 16th-century Canongate Tolbooth, celebrates the social history of the inhabitants of Edinburgh from the late 18th century to the present, with an emphasis on the cultural displacements of the Industrial Revolution. www.edinburghmuseums.org.uk/venue/peoples-story-museum **41 F8**

Glasgow and the Clyde

North Lanarkshire Heritage Centre *High Road, Motherwell, North Lanarkshire.* Multimedia exhibition on the history of Motherwell and the surrounding area. https://culturenl.co.uk/museums/visiting-us/north-lanarkshire-heritage-centre **29 C5**

Perth, Angus, Dundee and Fife

Arbroath Signal Tower Museum *Ladyloan, Arbroath, Angus.* Housed in the old signal tower from where messages were sent to the lighthouse on Bass Rock, this museum of local history covers subjects including textiles and fishing. www.angusalive.scot/museums-galleries/visit-a-museum-gallery/arbroath-signal-tower-museum **67 C6**

Crail Museum and Heritage Centre *62 Marketgate, Crail, Fife.* A small local museum with artefacts relating to the fishing and trading history of the East Neuk area of Fife. www.crailmuseum.org.uk **58 B4**

Kirkcaldy Galleries *War Memorial Gardens, Kirkcaldy, Fife.* An exploration of the history of the town and the surrounding area, together with an art gallery. www.onfife.com/venues/kirkcaldy-galleries **42 B1**

Meigle Sculptured Stone Museum *Meigle, Perth and Kinross.* A small museum with a comprehensive collection of Pictish carved stones from the region. www.historicenvironment.scot/visit-a-place/places/meigle-sculptured-stone-museum/ **66 C2**

Perth Art Gallery and Museum *George Street, Perth, Perth and Kinross.* This museum illustrates the town's history and has a good range of archaeological artefacts. A large section is devoted to the local whisky industry. www.culturepk.org.uk/museums-and-galleries/perth-museum-and-art-gallery **66 E1**

Scottish Crannog Centre *Kenmore, Perth and Kinross.* A museum devoted to the history of crannogs (loch-dwellings) with archaeological items from a nearby example, tours of a recreated crannog and demonstrations of Iron Age technology and crafts that visitors may try for themselves. www.crannog.co.uk **65 C5**

The Scottish Fisheries Museum *Anstruther, Fife* A museum covering the history of Scottish fishing industry and communities at sea and on shore. Exhibits range from important paintings in the art gallery to a working boatyard and the historic vessel 'Reaper' in Anstruther harbour. www.scotfishmuseum.org **58 B3**

South of Scotland

Dumfries Museum and Camera Obscura *Church Street, Dumfries, Dumfries and Galloway.* This museum is devoted to southwestern Scotland's geology, archaeology and history. It is set in a converted 18th-century windmill and its camera obscura provides panoramic views of the town and countryside around. www.dumgal.gov.uk/article/15737/Dumfries-Museum-and-Camera-Obscura **48 B3**

Isle of Arran Heritage Museum *Brodick, Arran, North Ayrshire.* A museum of local history located in the former outbuildings of Brodick Castle and providing a good overview of life here since prehistoric times. Exhibits include a working kitchen, geological finds, a blacksmith's forge and 19th-century memorabilia. www.arranmuseum.co.uk **51 C6**

Jedburgh Castle Jail and Museum *Castlegate, Jedburgh, Scottish Borders.* A Georgian prison, now a museum with displays about prison life through the ages. For a 19th-century building, the conditions are very comfortable, reflecting the influence of John Howard, the penal reformer, in the design. www.liveborders.org.uk/culture/museums/our-museums/jedburgh-castle-jail-and-museum **24 E2**

Moffat Museum *Church Gate, Moffat, Dumfries and Galloway.* Housed in a former bakery, this museum traces the history of Moffat and the surrounding region. www.moffatmuseum.co.uk **11 C5**

Stewartry Museum *St Mary Street, Kirkcudbright, Dumfries and Galloway.* An idiosyncratic collection showing the history and culture of this part of Galloway. www.dgculture.co.uk/venue/the-stewartry-museum-kirkcudbright **47 D8**

The Highlands

Caithness Broch Centre *The Old School House, Auckengill, Highland.* Small museum exploring the brochs of this part of Scotland and their long influence on the lives of the people of the region. www.undiscoveredscotland.co.uk/keiss/brochcentre www.thebrochproject.co.uk **91 B7**

Gairloch Museum *Auchtercairn, Gairloch, Highland.* Arranged in a number of buildings this museum shows details of West Highland life from the time of the Picts to the present day. There are displays of activities such as butter-making and corn-grinding. www.gairlochmuseum.org **84 F2**

Highland Folk Museum *Kingussie Road, Newtonmore, Highland.* An 80-acre museum housed in several historic buildings that covers all the aspects of Highland life from the 1700s to the mid 19th century. www.highlifehighland.com **72 C2**

Laidhay Croft Museum *Latheronwheel, Highland.* A small museum exploring the harsh life of crofters and clansmen in the area before the Highland Clearances. http://laidhay.co.uk **91 E5**

Timespan Heritage Centre *Dunrobin Street, Helmsdale, Highland.* A heritage centre devoted to the history and people of this part of Sutherland, including crofting, the Vikings, the Highland clearances, witches, 19th- century sporting pursuits and the Kildonan gold rush. https://timespan.org.uk/museum/ **87 B7**

West Highland Museum *Cameron Square, Fort William, Highland.* This museum covers all aspects of local history, including the Jacobite Rising of 1745, the development of tartan, and social history. www.westhighlandmuseum.org.uk **70 E3**

Wick Heritage Museum *19 Bank Row, Pultneytown, Wick, Highland.* The items in this museum include those from all aspects of the local fishing industry, with model boats, part of the old Noss Head lighthouse and hundreds of photographs from the 1880s. www.wickheritage.org **91 C7**

The Outer Islands

Blackhouse Museum *Arnol, Lewis, Western Isles.* A restored black house, showing how crofters lived in turf-roofed cottages, with people in one part and the animals in the other. www.historicenvironment.scot/visit-a-place/places/the-blackhouse-arnol **97 C6**

Orkney Museum *Tankerness House, Broad Street, Kirkwall, Mainland, Orkney.* Housed in a refurbished 16th-century merchant laird's house, this local museum shows life in the Orkneys over the last 5000 years. www.orkney.gov.uk/Service-Directory/S/orkney-museum.htm **99 B5**

Shetland Crofthouse Museum *Boddam, Mainland, Shetland.* This museum, housed in a 19th-century croft, portrays crofting life of the time with traditional furniture and fittings. www.shetlandheritageassociation.com/members/south-mainland/the-croft-house-museum **101 E2**

Shetland Museum and Archives *Hay's Dock, Lerwick, Mainland, Shetland.* Explores the geology and history of the islands, with displays on the whaling, fishing and knitting industries. www.shetlandmuseumandarchives.org.uk **101 B3**

Tankerness House *Kirkwall, Mainland, Orkney.* See Orkney Museum **99 B5**

Unst Heritage Centre *Haroldswick, Unst, Shetland.* This small museum, which is housed in the old school, concentrates on the history of the island, especially the herring-fishing industry. www.unstheritage.com/web/unst-heritage-centre **102 B6**

Factories, mills and mines

Edinburgh and East Central

National Mining Museum Scotland *Lady Victoria Colliery, Newtongrange, Midlothian.* Tours of a pithead, a mock-up of a working pitface and the winding engine, as well as displays on the history of coal-mining in Scotland. www.nationalminingmuseum.com **32 B2**

Glasgow and the Clyde

New Lanark World Heritage Village *New Lanark Mills, Lanark, South Lanarkshire.* Restored warehouses and mill buildings house what was once the largest cotton-spinning complex in Britain with exhibitions on the work and workers at this model establishment. www.newlanark.org **29 F8**

Perth, Angus, Dundee and Fife

Barry Mill *Barry, Angus.* There has been a mill on this site since at least 1539, but the present meal mill dates from 1814. It operated until 1982, when it ceased production, but has since been restored to working order. www.nts.org.uk/visit/places/barry-mill **67 D5**

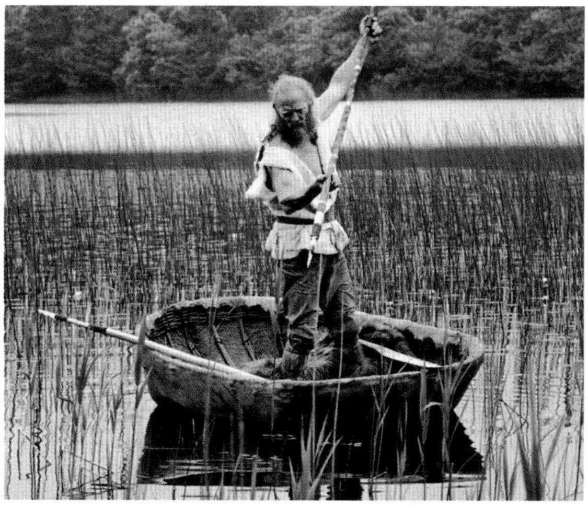

▲ **A re-enactment of Neolithic spear fishing from a coracle, Kilmartin House Museum, Argyll and Bute**
David Lyons / Alamy

South of Scotland

Mill on the Fleet *Gatehouse of Fleet, Dumfries and Galloway.* Local museum tracing the history of the cotton milling, shipbuilding, brewing and social history of this area of Dumfries and Galloway, set in a restored bobbin mill. www.millonthefleet.co.uk **47 D8**

The Highlands

Aluminium Story Visitor Centre *Linnhe Road, Kinlochleven, Highland.* Displays on how aluminium has been produced in the area for more than 90 years using hydro-electric power. **63 A6**

The Outer Islands

Lewis Loom Centre *3 Bayhead, Stornoway, Lewis, Western Isles.* Housed in a building known as the Old Grainstore, this weaving centre has demonstrations of the manufacture of Harris Tweed included in guided tours. www.visitscotland.com/info/see-do/lewis-loom-centre-p247911 **97 D7**

General museums

Aberdeen and Moray

Provost Skene's House *Broad Street, Aberdeen, Aberdeen City.* Housed in a 16th-century private home, the oldest-surviving one in Aberdeen, this museum has archaeological exhibits, a costume gallery and a series of rooms showing changing interiors through the 17th, 18th and 19th centuries. The painted gallery has a cycle of 17th-century paintings depicting the life of Christ. www.aagm.co.uk **75 B6**

Edinburgh and East Central

Museum of Childhood *42 High Street, Edinburgh, City of Edinburgh.* The collection includes antique toys and games, clothing, health and education. Video presentations and activity area. www.edinburghmuseums.org.uk/venue/museum-childhood **41 F9**

National Flag Heritage Centre *Athelstaneford, East Lothian.* The exhibition in this redundant church traces the history of the Scottish flag, the saltire or flag of St Andrew, which originated near here. http://scottishflagtrust.com **43 E6**

National Museum of Scotland *Chambers Street, Edinburgh, City of Edinburgh.* Exhibits include the decorative arts, geology, natural history, archaeology, ethnography, technology and science. The history of Scotland over the last 2.9 billion years is explored in modern galleries, including its role as an independent state before Union with England in the early 18th century and the Industrial Revolution. The collections of the former Royal Museum include an extraordinary range of items from all over the world: reliefs from the Assyrian royal palace of Nimrud, Buddhas from the far east, silverware, porcelain, fossils, classical Greek and Roman sculpture, scientific instruments, stuffed animals, a James Watt beam engine and Egyptian mummies. www.nms.ac.uk **41 F9**

Writers' Museum *Lady's Stair's House, off Lawnmarket, Edinburgh, City of Edinburgh.* Collections of manuscripts, letters and

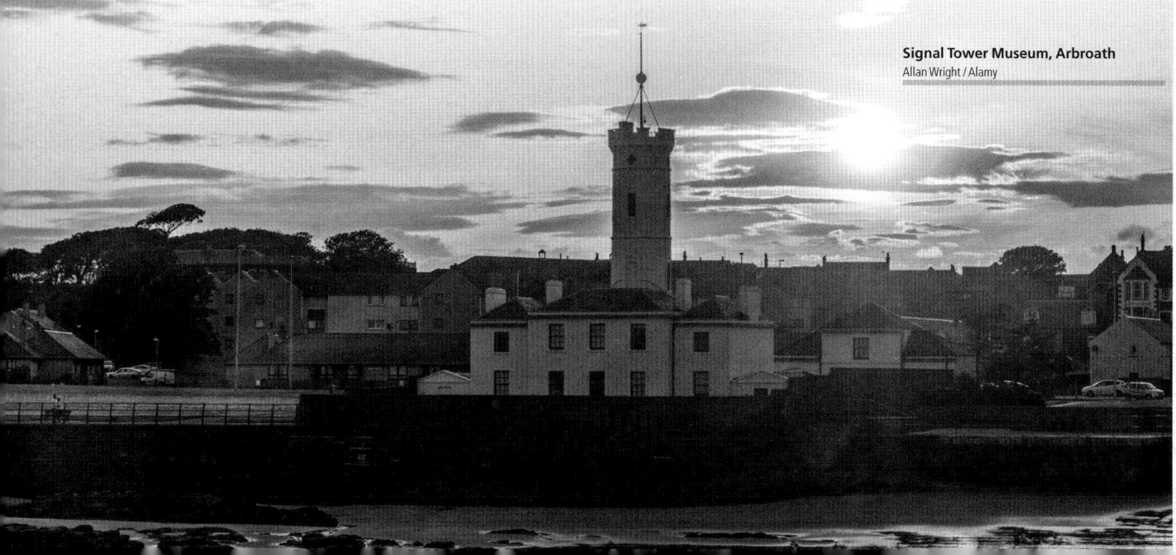

Signal Tower Museum, Arbroath
Allan Wright / Alamy

possessions of Robert Burns, Sir Walter Scott and Robert Louis Stevenson. ⌨www.edinburghmuseums.org.uk/venue/writers-museum **41 F8**

Glasgow and the Clyde

Hunterian Museum *University of Glasgow, Main/Gilbert-Scott building, University Avenue, Glasgow, City of Glasgow.* Contains a wide range of zoological and archaeological specimens, including a dinosaur, large numbers of coins and an exploration of the Romans and Vikings in Scotland. The ethnographic part of the collection includes an exhibit on Captain Cook's voyages. ⌨www.gla.ac.uk/hunterian **28 A2**

Kelvingrove Art Gallery and Museum *Kelvingrove Park, Glasgow, City of Glasgow.* The museum holds extensive collections on the natural history of Scotland, prehistoric and Roman Scotland, arms and armour, as well as antique musical instruments. ⌨www.glasgowlife.org.uk/museums/venues/kelvingrove-art-gallery-and-museum **28 A2**

National Museum of Rural Life *Kittochside, East Kilbride, South Lanarkshire.* An exhibition based within a working farm that continues to use traditional agricultural methods, this museum is divided into three principal sections: the Land Gallery, which explores how the Scots have used the land over the centuries and the effect of this on the landscape; the People's Gallery, which looks at the changing lives of farmers and their families over the last 400 years; and the Tools Gallery, which has an extensive collection of farming implements, ranging from early ploughs to a combine harvester. There is also an extensive collection of vintage agricultural machines. Visitors are encouraged to visit the 18th-century farmhouse where the cows are still milked by hand. Seasonal farming activities. ⌨www.nms.ac.uk/national-museum-of-rural-life/⌨www.nts.org.uk/visit/places/national-museum-of-rural-life **28 C3**

St Mungo's Museum of Religious Life *2 Castle Street, Glasgow, City of Glasgow.* This gallery has a collection of artworks representing figures from most of the world's major religions, including a controversial painting by Salvador Dalí – Christ of St John of the Cross – as well as statues of the Buddha and Hindu deities such as Ganesh. ⌨www.glasgowlife.org.uk/museums/venues/st-mungo-museum-of-religious-life-and-art **28 A2**

▶ **The Hunterian Museum in the University of Glasgow** Monica Wells / Alamy

Perth, Angus, Dundee and Fife

Andrew Carnegie Birthplace Museum *Moodie Street, Dunfermline, Fife.* The small weaver's cottage where the 19th-century philanthropist was born has been converted into a museum, with an attached memorial hall. ⌨www.carnegiebirthplace.com **41 C5**

McManus Art Galleries and Museum *Albert Square, Dundee, Dundee City.* Housed in an imposing, recently refurbished, Victorian building designed by Gilbert Scott, this museum explores Dundee's history, as well as holding collections of musical instruments, precious metalwork, sculpture, furniture and an extensive collection of 19th- and 20th-century paintings. ⌨www.mcmanus.co.uk **66 D4**

South of Scotland

Mary Queen of Scots Visitor Centre *Queen Street, Jedburgh, Scottish Borders.* The house where Mary Queen of Scots rested after an infamous visit to her lover, the Earl of Bothwell while still married to Henry, Lord Darnley. Contains paintings, engravings and articles relating to Mary's life. ⌨www.liveborders.org.uk/culture/museums/our-museums/mary-queen-of-scots-visitor-centre **24 E2**

Old Bridge House Museum *Mill Road, Dumfries, Dumfries and Galloway.* Built in 1660, this house has been restored and furnished as it would have been in the second half of the 19th century, and is filled with an eclectic range of Victorian domestic articles. ⌨www.dgculture.co.uk/venue/old-bridge-house-museum **48 B3**

Robert Burns Birthplace Museum *Murdoch's Lone, Alloway, South Ayrshire.* Museum and visitor centre based around the cottage in which the poet was born. ⌨www.nts.org.uk/visit/places/robert-burns-birthplace-museum **17 F5**

Robert Burns Centre *Mill Road, Dumfries, Dumfries and Galloway.* A converted 18th-century watermill with exhibits about Robert Burns and the town of Dumfries. ⌨www.visitscotland.com/info/see-do/robert-burns-centre-p251171 **48 B3**

The Highlands

Inverness Museum and Art Gallery *Castle Wynd, Inverness, Highland.* Exhibits on varied subjects including geology, wildlife and the history of weaponry. ⌨https://www.highlifehighland.com/inverness-museum-and-art-gallery **80 D1**

Family Attractions

Aberdeen and Moray
Alford Valley Railway
Main Street, Alford, Aberdeenshire
A narrow-gauge train runs for about a mile from Alford Station to Murray Park, through the valley's wooded landscape. ⌨www.facebook.com/AlfordValleyRailway **74 A2**

Keith and Dufftown Railway
Dufftown Station, Dufftown, Moray
Also known as the Whisky Line, this is an 11-mile route through beautiful countryside, providing views of wildlife, spectacular scenery. The diesel trains operate during summer weekends. ⌨www.keith-dufftown-railway.co.uk **81 E8**

Edinburgh and East Central
Bo'ness and Kinneil Railway
Bo'ness Station, Union Street, Bo'ness, Falkirk
Steam trains run in the summer months. Railway exhibition at Bo'ness station. ⌨www.bkrailway.co.uk **40 D3**

Edinburgh Dungeon
31 Market Street, Edinburgh, City of Edinburgh
Horror theme park exploring the more grisly side of Edinburgh's history. ⌨www.thedungeons.com/edinburgh **41 F8**

The Real Mary King's Close
Writer's Court, Edinburgh, City of Edinburgh Visitor attraction reconstructing life in 17th-century Edinburgh, including a range of houses. ⌨www.realmarykingsclose.com **41 F8**

Glasgow and the Clyde
Leadhills and Wanlockhead Railway *The Station, Leadhills, South Lanarkshire* Diesel trains operate on this tourist railway between Leadhills and the disused lead mine at Wanlockhead, where there is a small museum and a beam engine. ⌨www.leadhillsrailway.co.uk **9 A8**

M&D's Scotland's Theme Park *Strathclyde Country Park, 366 Hamilton Road, Motherwell, North Lanarkshire* The largest theme park in Scotland, with rides for both children and thrill-seekers, set among a large complex of attractions. ⌨https://scotlandsthemepark.com **29 C5**

The Highlands
Jacobite Steam Train
Fort William Railway Station, Fort William, Highland
Return trips along the West Highland Railway between Fort William and Mallaig by steam train, through scenery incuding Loch Shiel, over the 21 arches of the Glenfinnan viaduct and past the beautiful beaches of Morar. ⌨https://westcoastrailways.co.uk/jacobite/steam-train-trip **70 E3**

Strathspey Steam Railway
Dalfaber Road, Aviemore, Highland This restored railway runs through Highland scenery between Aviemore and Broomhill via Boat of Garten. ⌨www.strathspeyrailway.co.uk **72 A4**

Treasures of the Earth *Corpach, Fort William, Highland* A centre dedicated to crystals, rocks and gemstones, their properties, where they come from and how they are mined. Exhibits include a recreated mine which shows the conditions under which the miners work. ⌨www.treasuresoftheearth.co.uk **70 E2**

The Strathspey Railway alongside the River Spey with the Cairngorms in the distance Phil Metcalfe / Alamy

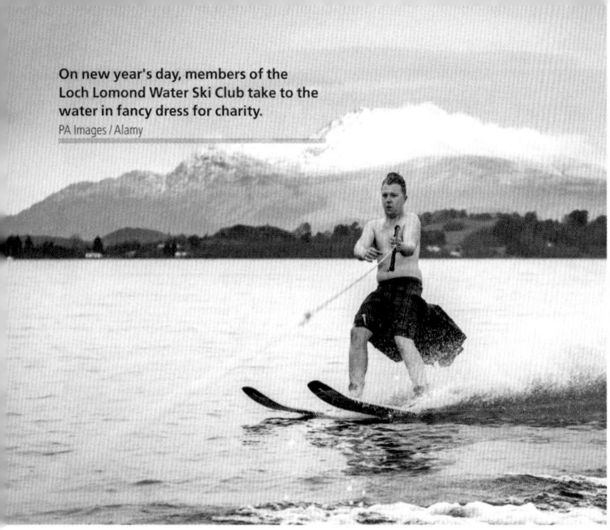

On new year's day, members of the Loch Lomond Water Ski Club take to the water in fancy dress for charity.
PA Images / Alamy

Sport

Activity centres

Edinburgh and East Central

Beecraigs Country Park *The Park Centre, Linlithgow, West Lothian.* Outdoor pursuits include, target and field archery, orienteering, canoeing and climbing, climbing and hillcraft, skiing and skiboarding. There is also a working deer farm with a red deer herd and a fishery. www.westlothian.gov.uk/beecraigs **40 F3**

Glasgow and the Clyde

Strathclyde Country Park *336 Hamilton Road, Motherwell, North Lanarkshire.* Activities available include: rowing, windsurfing, water skiing, dinghy sailing and canoeing (instruction provided on request), wayfaring and competitive orienteering. Mountain bikes can be rented. www.northlanarkshire.gov.uk/index.aspx?articleid=6760 **29 C5**

South of Scotland

Galloway Activity Centre *Parton, Castle Douglas, Dumfries and Galloway.* Offers courses in sailing, windsurfing, canoeing and powerboating, as well as such activities as quad biking, mountain biking, climbing and abseiling. www.lochken.co.uk **48 C1**

The Highlands

Monster Activities *Fort Augustus, Highland.* In summer a wide range of outdoor activities is offered including mountain biking, abseiling, trekking, archery and knife throwing, as well as sailing, canoeing, kayaking, waterskiing, wakeboarding and white-water rafting. www.monsteractivities.com **71 B5**

Vertical Descents *Inchree Falls, Onich, Highland.* Activities offered include canyoning, white-water rafting, rock climbing and abseiling, mountain biking, go-karting, archery and paintballing. www.verticaldescents.com **70 E3**

Climbing and caving

Perth, Angus, Dundee and Fife

The Mountaineering Council of Scotland *The Old Granary, West Mill Street, Perth, Perth and Kinross.* Details of mountaineering clubs in Scotland. Publishes booklets on climbs and safety, and a newsletter. www.mcofs.org.uk **66 E1**

Cycling

Argyll, Bute, Stirling, Trossachs

Finlay Ross General Store *Baile Mor, Iona, Argyll and Bute.* Cycling is a good way to get around this small island to see the spectacular scenery. **61 E5**

Killin Outdoor Centre and Mountain Shop *Main Street, Killin, Stirling.* Easy access to the area around Loch Tay as well as Glen Lochay and Glen Dochart. www.killinoutdoor.co.uk/hire-info **64 D3**

Edinburgh and East Central

Bike Trax *13 Lochiun Place, Tollcross, Edinburgh, City of Edinburgh.* A convenient place on the outskirts of Edinburgh for hiring bicycles to explore the surrounding regions. www.biketrax.co.uk/hire **41 F8**

South of Scotland

Alpine Bikes *Unit 2 Glentress Peel, Glentress Forest, Peebles* Cycle hire in the beautiful surroundings of the Tweed Valley with a mixture of easy and more challenging places to cycle. www.tiso.com/shops/glentress **22 B1**

The Highlands

Alpine Bikes *117 High Street, Fort William, Highland.* Ideally placed for cycling in both the flat areas around Loch Linnhe and more challenging areas in the hills. www.tiso.com **70 E3**

Bothy Bikes *Aviemore Shopping Centre, Grampian Road, Aviemore, Highland.* Hires out mountain bikes well suited to the challenging rides available in the Cairngorm National Park. www.bothybikes.co.uk/bike-hire-aviemore-in-the-scottish-highlands **72 A3**

Inverness Bike Hire *12 Church Street, Inverness* Inverness is a good base for cycling as it is close to Loch Ness, the Black Isle, the Moray Firth and the foothills of the mountains to the west. www.invernessbikehire.co.uk **80 D1**

Skye Bicycle Hire *Uig Campsite, Uig, Isle of Skye.* In the north of the island, Uig is located close to the stunning landscapes of both northern and western Skye. www.uig-camping-skye.co.uk **76 B3**

Skye Bike Shack *.The Old Croft House, 6 Carbost, Skeabost Bridge, By Portree* Cycle hire within easy reach of Skye's scenic coastal roads. A short bus ride from Portree. www.skyebikeshack.com/hire-a-bike-on-skye **76 D4**

The Outer Islands

Bike Hebrides *6 Sand St, Stornoway* Stornoway is an ideal base for exploring the northern part of the island www.bikehebrides.com **97 D7**

BeSpoke Bicycles (Hebrides) *The Hub, Glen House, Willowglen Road, Stornoway, Isle of Lewis* Cycling is the best way to get around Lewis and appreciate the landscape. www.bespokebicycles.co.uk **97 D7**

Cycle Orkney *Tankerness Lane, Kirkwall, Mainland, Orkney.* Kirkwall is centrally placed on Mainland, giving easy access to a variety of rides through the rugged land. www.cycleorkney.com **99 B5**

Orkney Cycle Hire *54 Dundas St, Stromness, Mainland, Orkney* Located a few minutes walk from the ferry terminal at Stromness. A good starting point for rides to Skara Brae and Ring of Brodgar www.orkneycyclehire.co.uk **98 C3**

Grantfield Garage *Commercial Road, Lerwick, Mainland, Shetland.* Cycle hire giving access to Shetland's beautiful scenery. www.grantfield-garage.co.uk **101 B3**

Football

Glasgow and the Clyde

Celtic Football Club *Celtic Park, Parkhead, Glasgow, City of Glasgow.* Guided tours and visitor centre with museum. www.celticfc.net **28 A2**

Hampden Stadium *Hampden Park, Glasgow, City of Glasgow.* Scotland's national football stadium, which includes the Scottish Football Museum and guided tours. www.hampdenpark.co.uk **28 A2**

Rangers Football Club *Ibrox Stadium, 150 Edmiston Drive, Glasgow, City of Glasgow.* Tours of the stadium and trophy room. www.rangers.co.uk **28 A2**

Golf courses

Edinburgh and East Central

Muirfield *Duncur Road, Gullane, East Lothian.* Built by Tom Morris in 1891, overlooking the Firth of Forth and home to the Honourable Company of Edinburgh Golfers. It is a par 70 links course, has hosted the Open Championship more than 20 times and is consistently voted among the top five golf courses in the world. www.muirfield.org.uk **43 D5**

Royal Musselburgh *Prestongrange House, Musselburgh, East Lothian.* One of the oldest golf courses in the world, it is a demanding par-70. www.royalmusselburgh.co.uk **42 F2**

Perth, Angus, Dundee and Fife

Balcomie Golf Course *Craighead, Fife.* A beautiful 18-hole links set above the Fife coastline. It was designed by Tom Morris. www.crailgolfingsociety.co.uk **58 B4**

Carnoustie *Carnoustie, Angus.* The par-72 Championship Course at Carnoustie is among the best-known links courses in the world. The Burnside and Buddon courses form part of the complex. www.carnoustiegolflinks.co.uk **67 D5**

Gleneagles *Auchterarder, Perth and Kinross.* A complex of four courses, the Kings, Queens and Monarch courses and the 9-hole Wee Course. https://gleneagles.com/golf **56 A4**

St Andrews *St Andrews, Fife.* There are six public golf courses in and around the town: the par-72 Old Course, par-71 New Course, par-72 Jubilee Course, par-70 Eden Course, par-69 Strathtyrum Course and the par-30, 9-hole Balgove course. All except the Balgove course should be booked well in advance to make sure of playing. www.standrews.com **67 F4**

South of Scotland

Royal Troon *Craigend Road, Troon, South Ayrshire.* A complex of three courses, the testing par-71 Old Course, the par-71 Portland Course and the Par 3 Course, which is actually a 9-hole par-21 course. www.royaltroon.co.uk **17 D5**

Turnberry *Westin Turnberry Resort, South Ayrshire.* There are two courses, the famous par-69 Ailsa course and the new par-72 Kintyre course, against the backdrop of Ailsa Craig and the Turnberry lighthouse. www.turnberry.co.uk **6 C3**

Hang gliding and paragliding

Glasgow and the Clyde

Cloudbusters Paragliding School *2 Inchmurrin Drive, Cathkin, Glasgow, City of Glasgow.* Offers lessons in hang gliding and paragliding. www.cloudbusters.co.uk **28 A2**

The Highlands

Highland Hang Gliding and Paragliding Club *54 Culloden Road, Balloch, Highland.* Hang gliding and paragliding in spectacular surroundings. www.highlandhgpgclub.co.uk **80 D2**

Horseracing

Edinburgh and East Central

Musselburgh Racecourse *Musselburgh, East Lothian.* Flat racing in summer, National Hunt racing during winter. www.musselburgh-racecourse.co.uk **42 F2**

Glasgow and the Clyde

Hamilton Park Racecourse *Hamilton, South Lanarkshire.* Daytime and evening flat meetings take place from April to September. www.hamilton-park.co.uk **29 C5**

Perth, Angus, Dundee and Fife

Perth Racecourse *Scone Palace Park, Scone, Perth and Kinross.* Jump racing takes place during the summer season. www.perth-races.co.uk **66 E1**

South of Scotland

Ayr Racecourse *2 Whitletts Road, Ayr, South Ayrshire.* Flat racing takes place from May to October, with National Hunt usually in January, April and November. www.ayr-racecourse.co.uk **17 E6**

Kelso Racecourse *Kelso, Scottish Borders.* National Hunt racing takes place during the winter season – from October to May. www.kelso-races.co.uk **24 B3**

Motorsports

Glasgow and the Clyde

Scotkart Cambuslang *Westburn Road, Cambuslang, Glasgow, City of Glasgow.* Offers a variety of karting for all ages and abilities. www.scotkart.co.uk **28 A2**

Scotkart Clydebank *John Knox Street, Clydebank, Glasgow, City of Glasgow.* Karting for all ages and abilities on a 400-metre track featuring a flyover, tunnel and ramps www.scotkart.co.uk **28 A2**

Perth, Angus, Dundee and Fife

Scotkart Dundee *Myrekirk Road, Dundee,* Karting for all ages and abilities on a 400-metre track with a mixture of chicanes, hairpin bends and straights. www.scotkart.co.uk Knockhill Racing Circuit *Dunfermline, Fife.* Events at this circuit include British Touring Cars, British Superbikes plus driving experiences and track days. www.knockhill.com **40 B5**

Orienteering

The Highlands

National Orienteering Centre *Glenmore Lodge, Aviemore, Highland.* Provides training, maps, equipment and support for all levels. www.scottish-orienteering.org **72 A3**

Riding

Argyll, Bute, Stirling, Trossachs

Wilder Ways, Mull of Kintyre *Southend, Mull of Kintyre, Argyll* Riding lessons, trail riding holidays, day treks, and archery on horseback in the rugged landscape of the Mull of Kintyre www.wilderways.scot **50 F2**

The Highlands

Wilder Ways, Knoydart *Inverie, Highland.* Trail riding and day treks on the remote Knoydart Peninsua. Only accessible by ferry from Mallaig. www.wilderways.scot **69 C7**

South of Scotland

Blackstone Clydesdales Interact with rare-breed Clydesdale heavy horses. Short treks available on or off the farm. www.blackstoneclydesdales.co.uk/experience.html **18 E2**

Rugby

Edinburgh and East Central

Edinburgh Rugby *Edinburgh.* www.edinburghrugby.org **41 F8**

Murrayfield Stadium *Murrayfield, Edinburgh, City of Edinburgh.* The home of Scottish Rugby. Guided tours take visitors to the dressing rooms, royal box, hospitality suites and pitch. www.scottishrugby.org **41 F8**

Glasgow

Glasgow Warriors *Glasgow.* www.glasgowwarriors.org **28 A2**

Watersports

Argyll, Bute, Stirling, Trossachs

Loch Lomond Water Ski Club *Balloch, West Dunbartonshire.* Offers tuition in water skiing and wave boarding. www.lochlomondwaterskiclub.co.uk **37 D6**

Tighnabruaich Sailing School *Tighnabruaich, Argyll and Bute.* Lessons in dinghy sailing and windsurfing in the sheltered waters of the Kyles of Bute. www.tssargyll.co.uk **54 E2**

Edinburgh and East Central

Port Edgar Marina and Sailing School *Shore Road, South Queensferry, Edinburgh, City of Edinburgh.* Offers a wide variety of sailing courses to suit all abilities. www.portedgar.co.uk/activities **41 F8**

Perth, Angus, Dundee and Fife

Splash White-Water Rafting *Dunkeld Road, Aberfeldy, Perth and Kinross.* White-water rafting with experienced guides, as well as abseiling, bridge swinging and canyoning. www.rafting.co.uk **65 C6**

The Highlands

Loch Insh Watersports Centre *Kincraig, Highland.* Offers canoeing, sailing and windsurfing, as well as renting boats for fishing on the loch, mountain bikes. Ski instruction is offered on the 160ft dry ski slope. www.lochinsh.com **72 B3**

Loch Morlich Watersports Centre *Glenmore Forest Park, by Aviemore, Highland.* This centre offers sailing, windsurfing and canoeing in the spectacular surroundings of Loch Morlich. www.lochmorlich.com **72 B4**

Raasay House *Raasay House, Raasay, Highland.* Sailing and windsurfing courses for both children and adults as well as kayaking, rock climbing and abseiling. www.raasay-house.co.uk **77 E5**

▼ **Harness Racing at Musselburgh Racecourse** SJP / Alamy

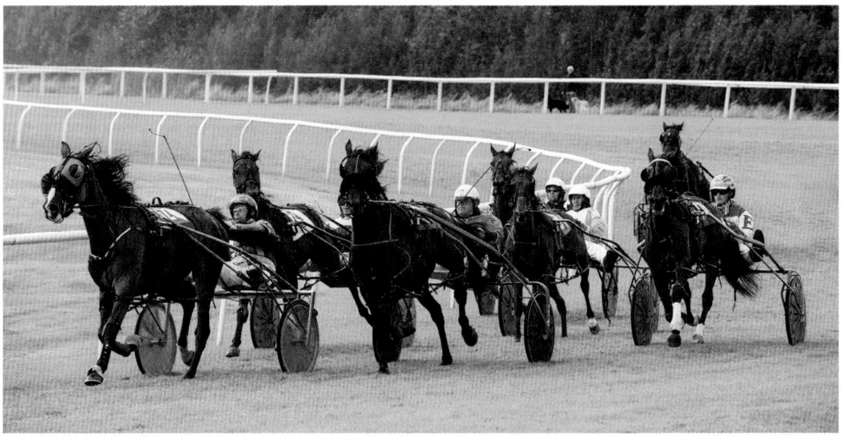

National route planning

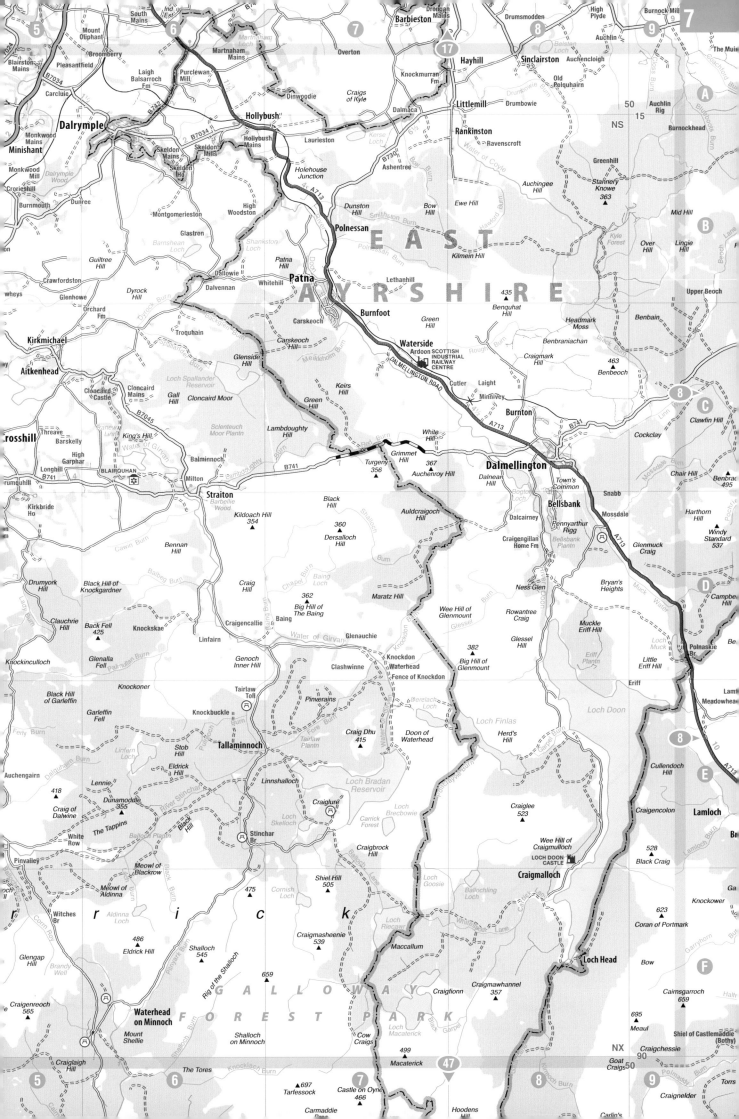

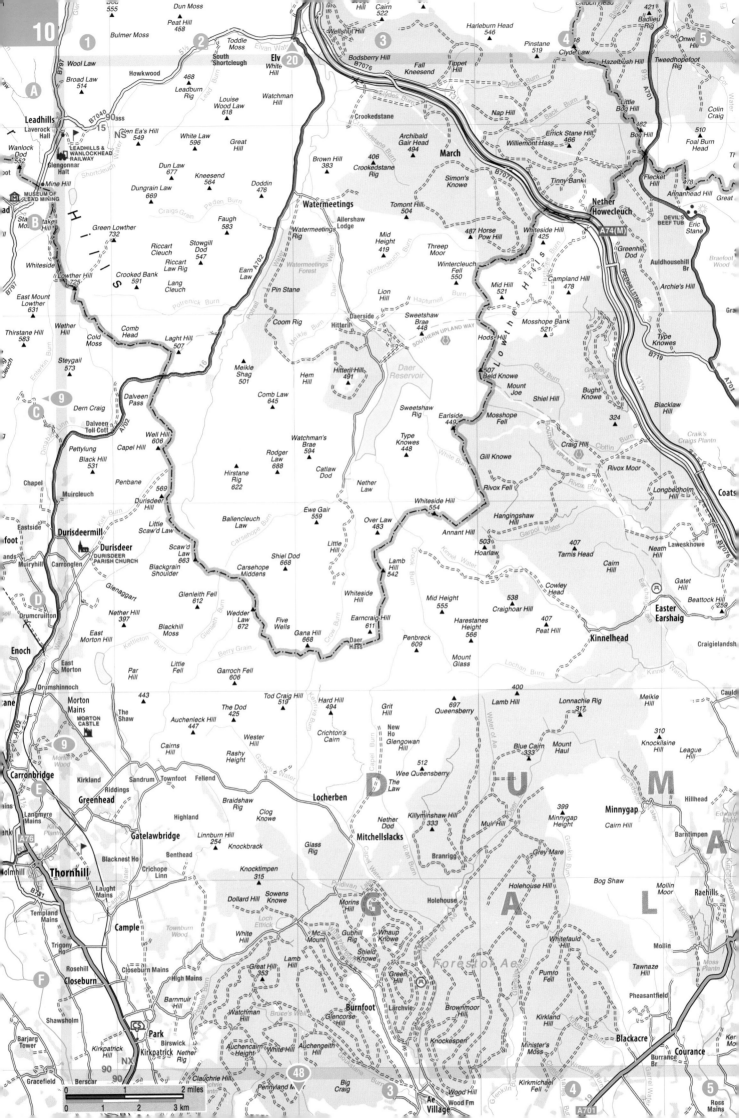

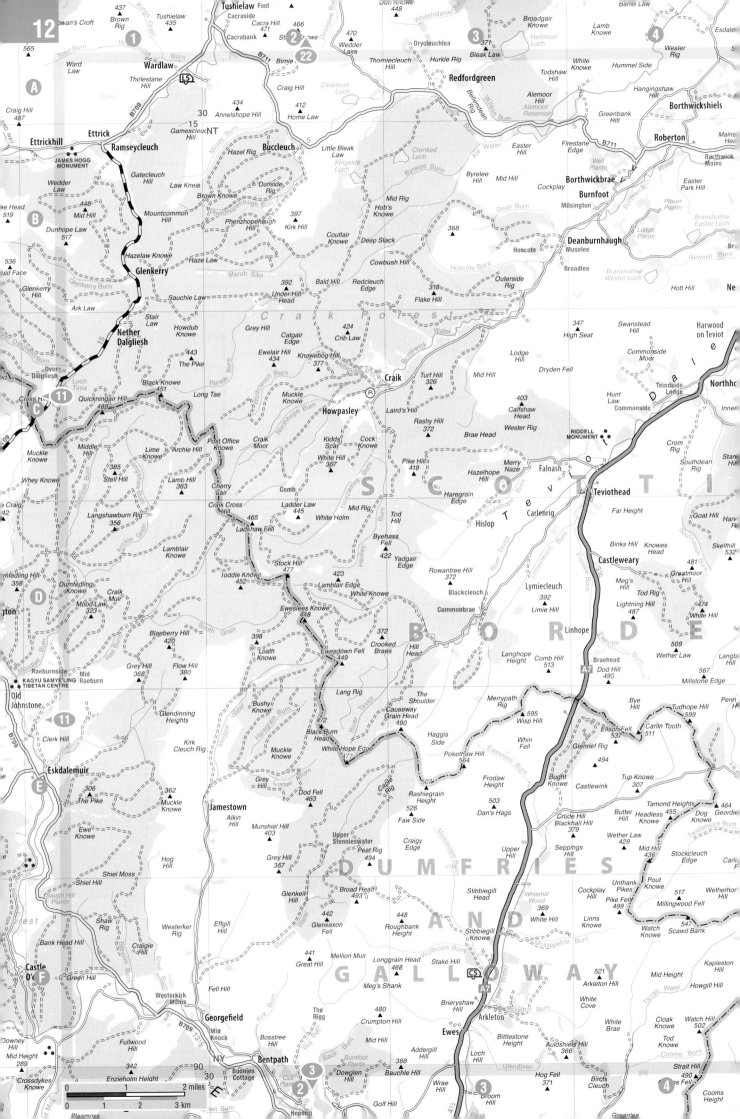

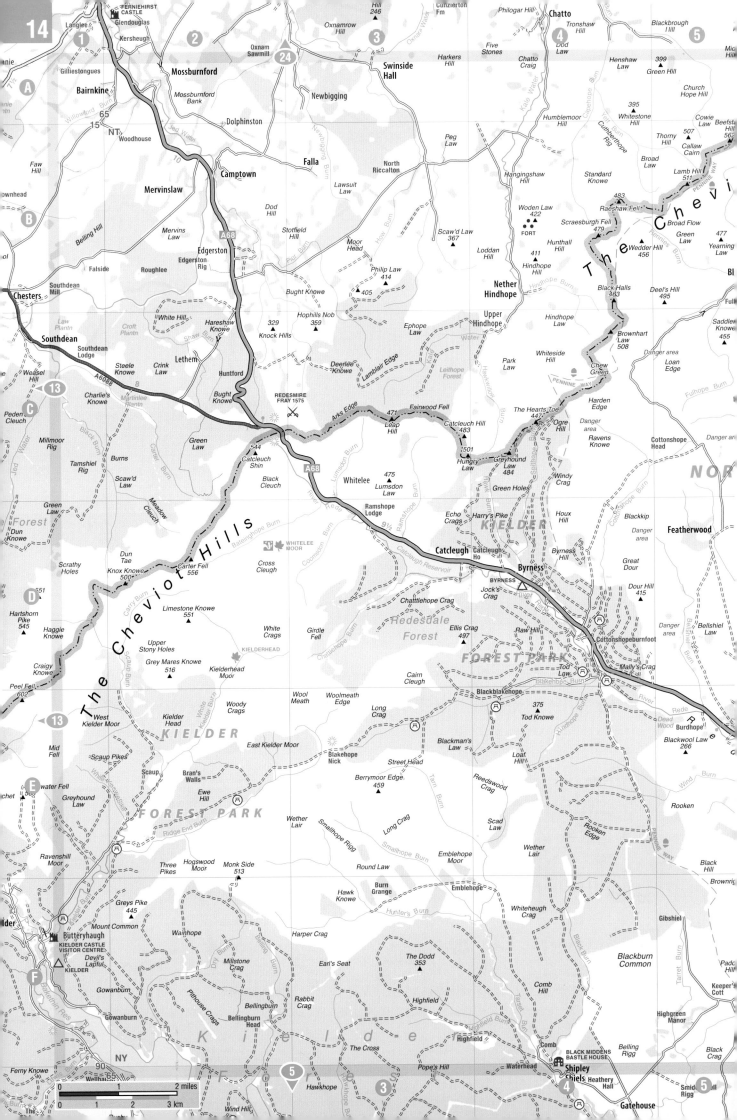

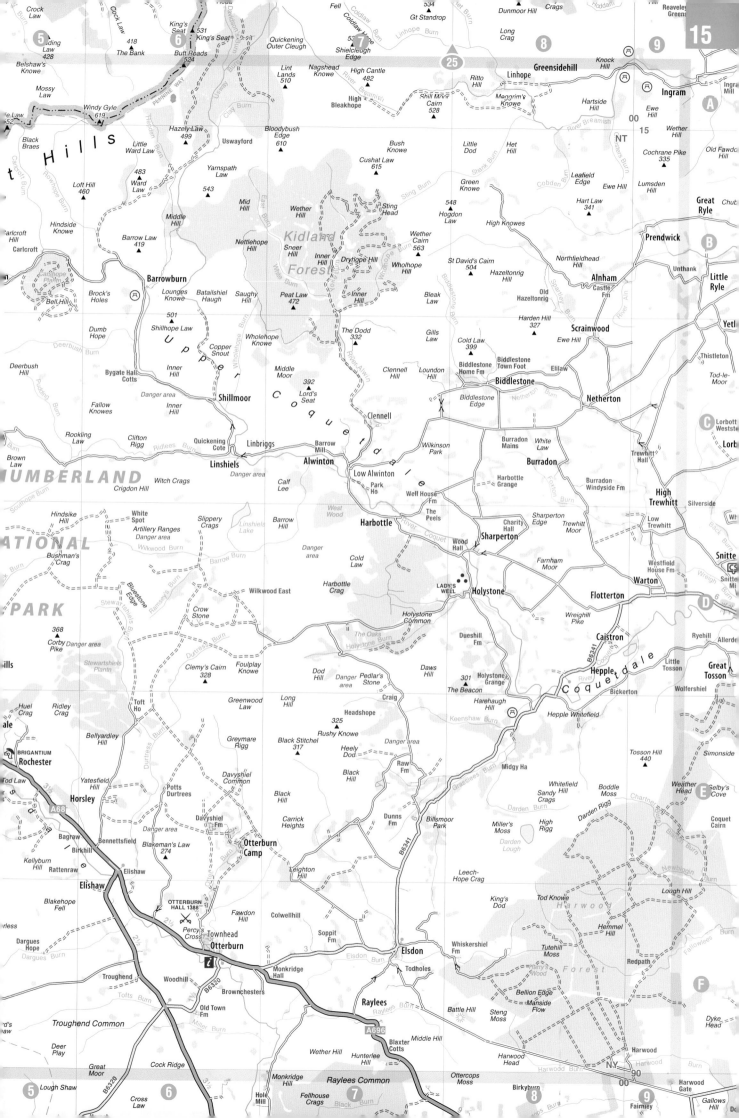

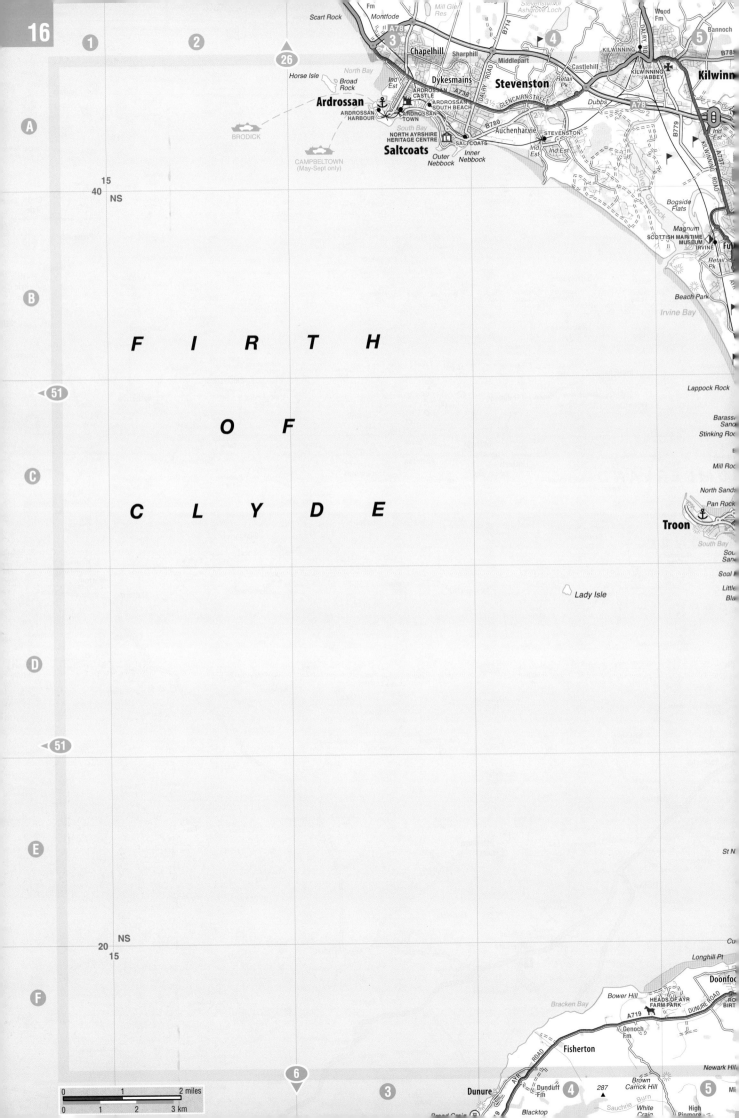

1   2   26   3   4   5

A

B

C

D

E

F

6

3

F I R T H

O F

C L Y D E

Scart Rock   Fm   Montfode   A78   Mill Glen Res

Stevenston Ashgrove Loch   Wood Fm   Bannoch

Chapelhill   Sharphill   Middlepart   B714   KILWINNING   DALRY ROAD

North Bay   Dykesmains   **Stevenston**   Castlehill   Retail Pk   KILWINNING ABBEY   **Kilwinn**

Horse Isle   Broad Rock   Ind Est   ARDROSSAN CASTLE   A738   Glencairn Street   Dubbs   A78   B780   B781

Ardrossan   ARDROSSAN SOUTH BEACH   3½   Ind Est

BRODICK   ARDROSSAN HARBOUR   ARDROSSAN TOWN   Auchenharvie   STEVENSTON   2½   B779

South Bay   NORTH AYRSHIRE HERITAGE CENTRE   Stevenston   Ind Est

CAMPBELTOWN (May-Sept only)   **Saltcoats**   SALTCOATS   Ind Est   Ind Est   Bogside Flats

Outer Nebbock   Inner Nebbock   Magnum   SCOTTISH MARITIME MUSEUM IRVINE   **Ful**

Retail Pk   Beach Park

Irvine Bay

◄ 51   Lappock Rock

Barass Sand

Stinking Roc

Mill Roc

North Sands

Pan Rock

Troon

South Bay   Sou Sand

Soal

Little Bla

15   40   NS

Lady Isle

◄ 51

St N

20   15   NS

Longhill Pt

Doonfo

Bower Hill   HEADS OF AYR FARM PARK   RO   BIRT

Bracken Bay   A719   DUNURE ROAD

Genoch Fm   **Fisherton**   Newark Hil

Dunure   AYR ROAD   Dunduff Fm   287   Brown Carrick Hill   High   **5**

Blacktop   Sauchrie Burn   White Craig   High Pinmore

0   1   2 miles
0   1   2   3 km

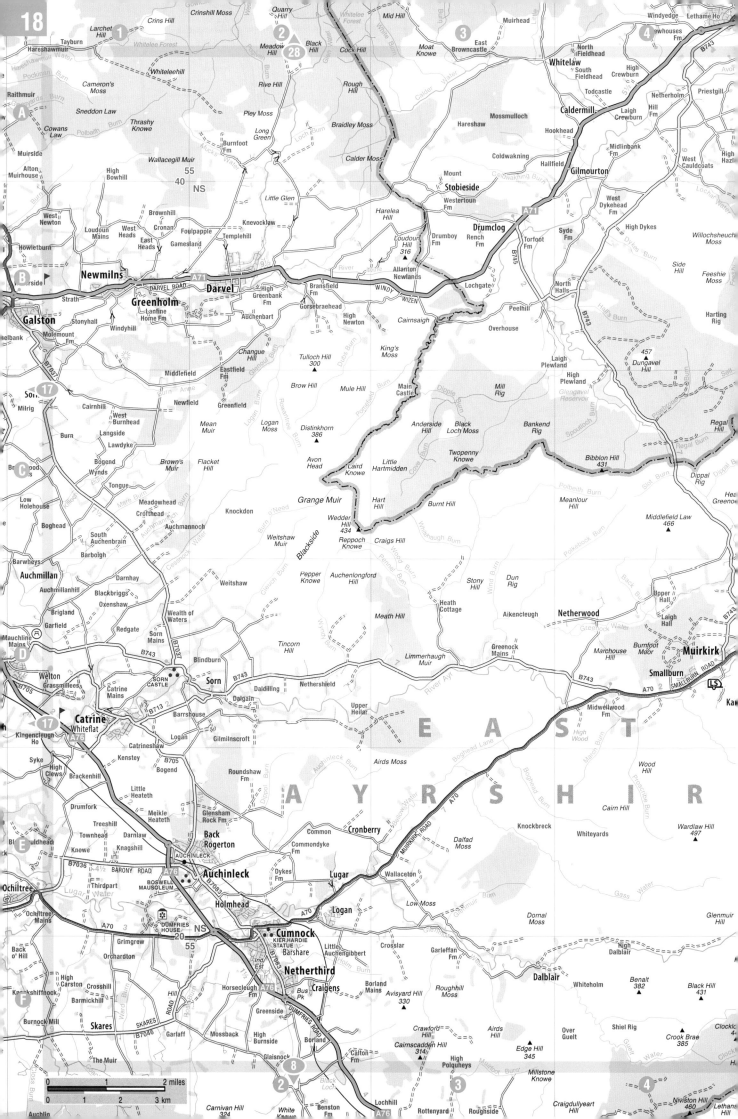

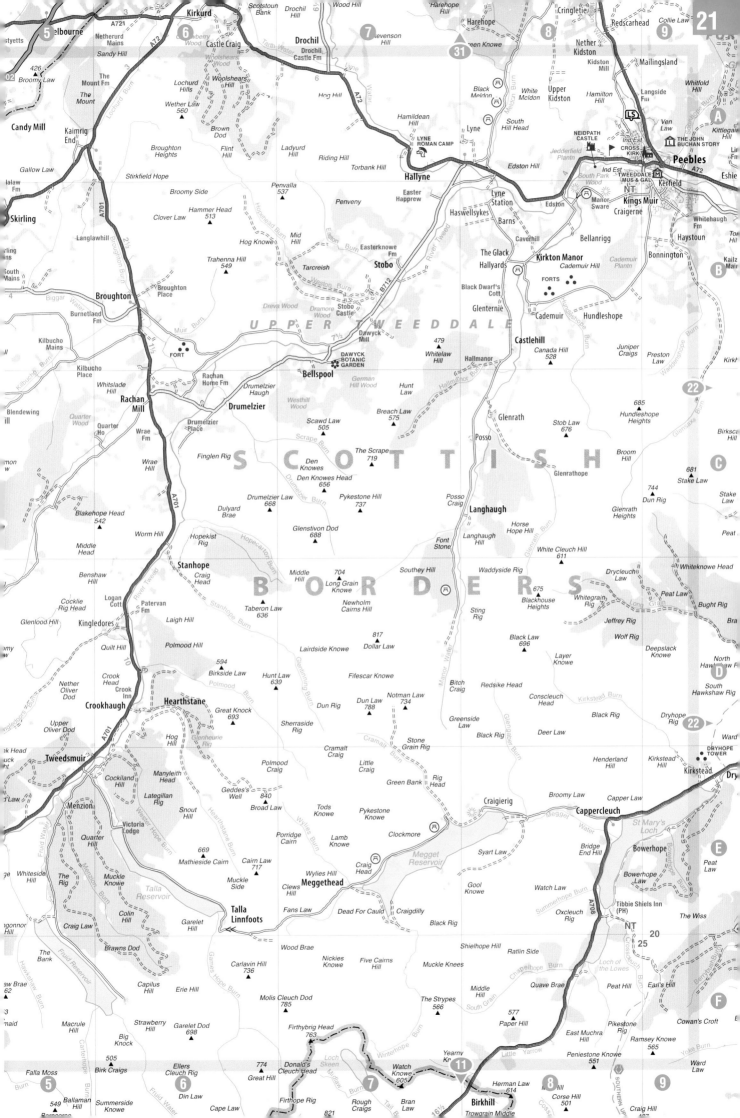

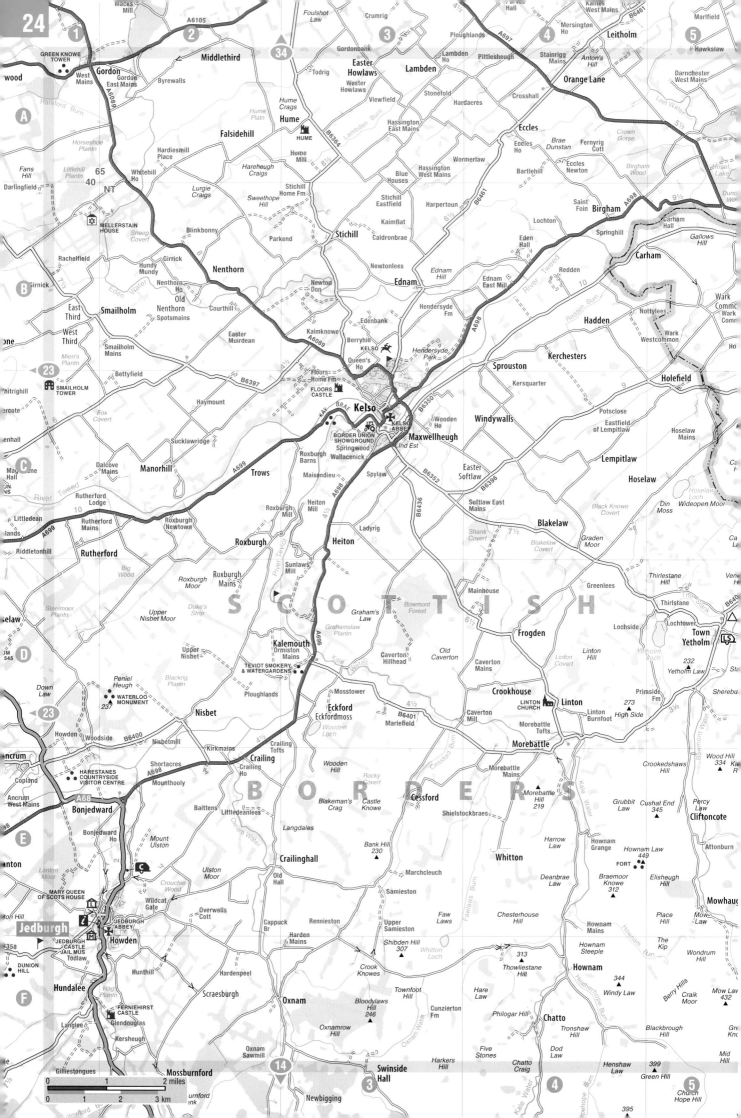

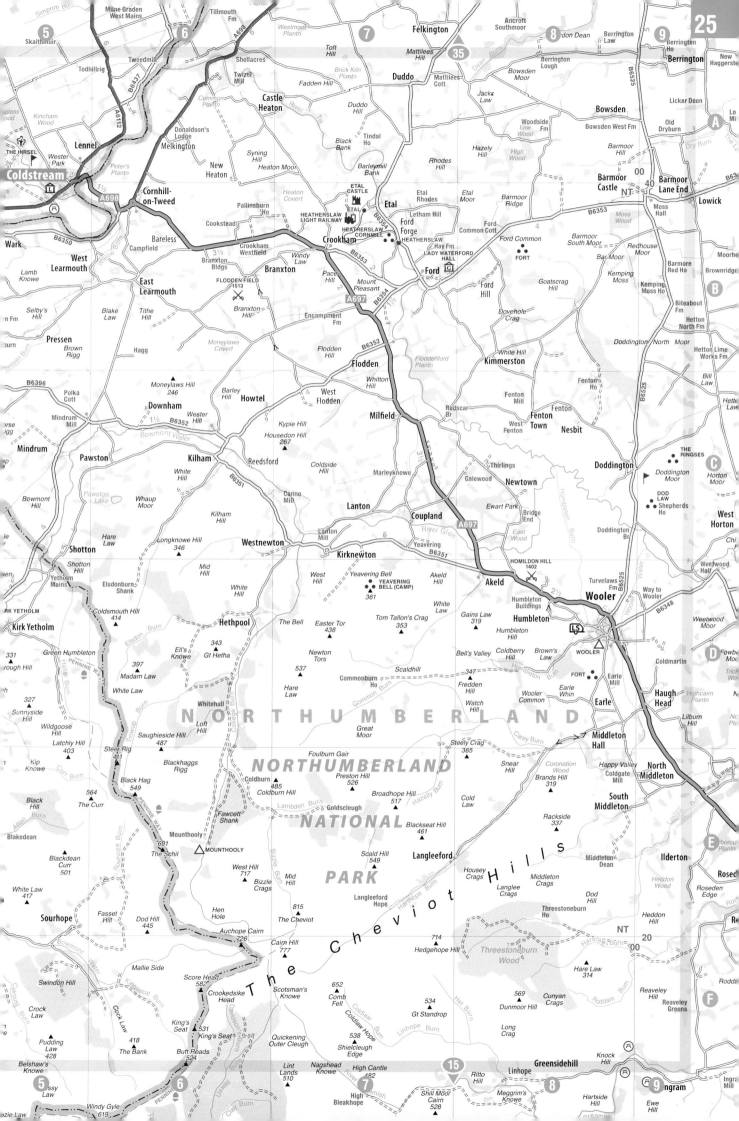

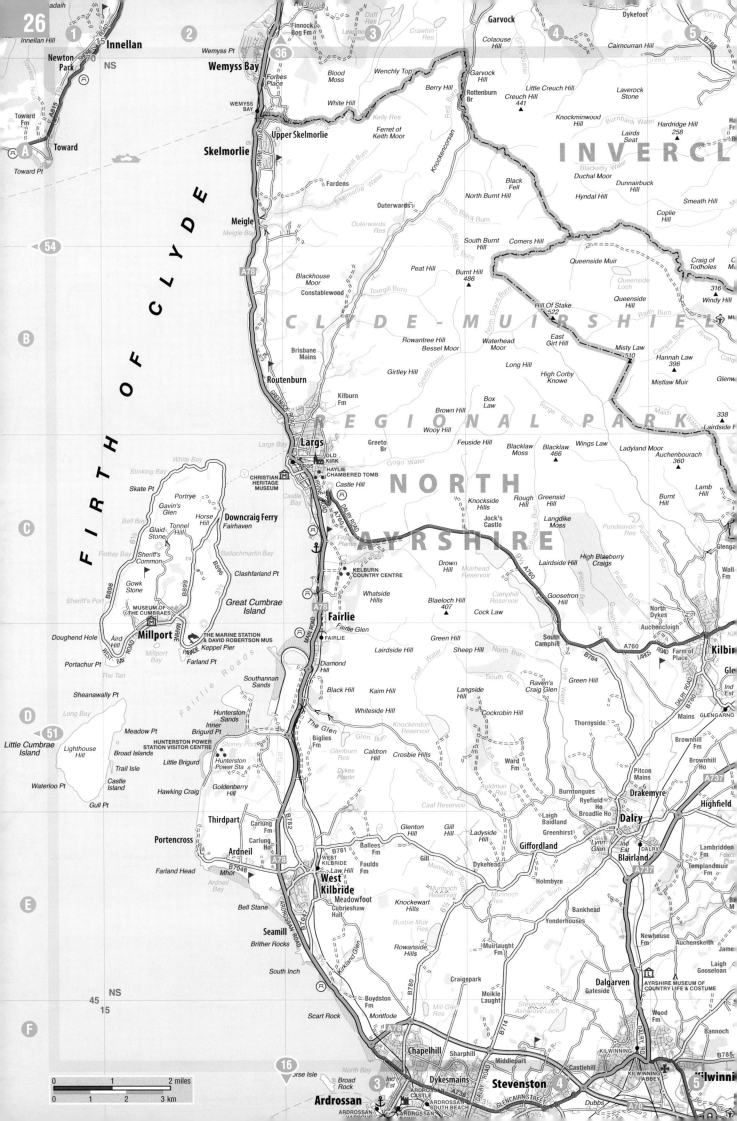

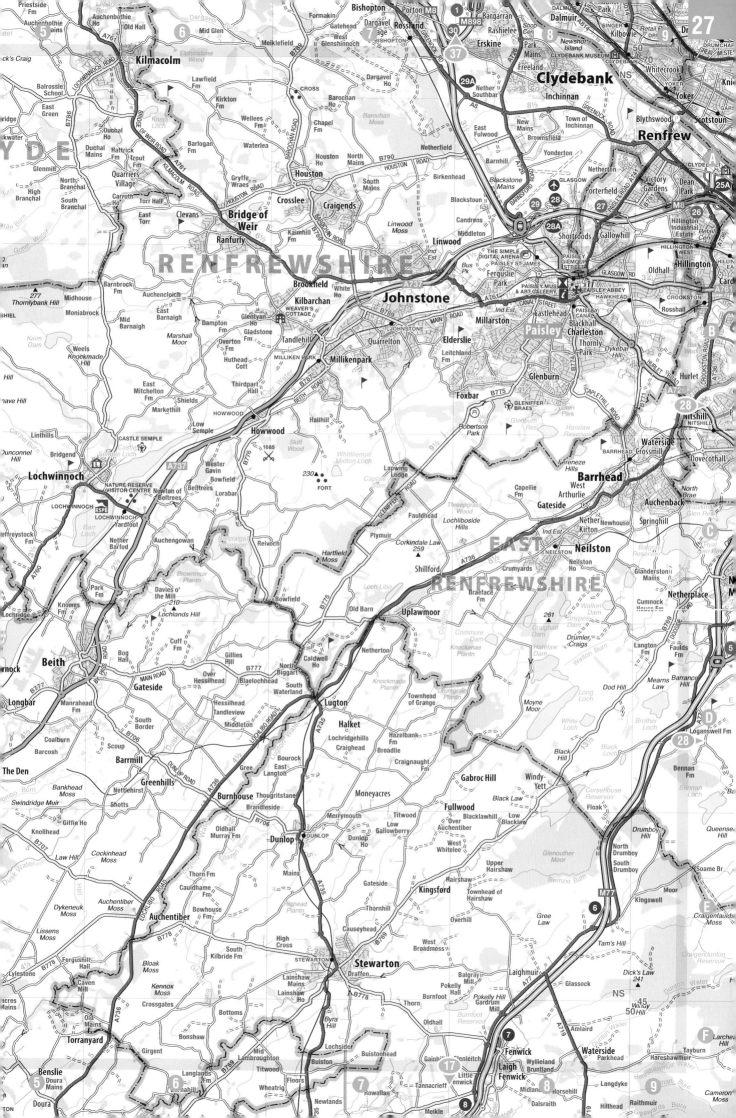

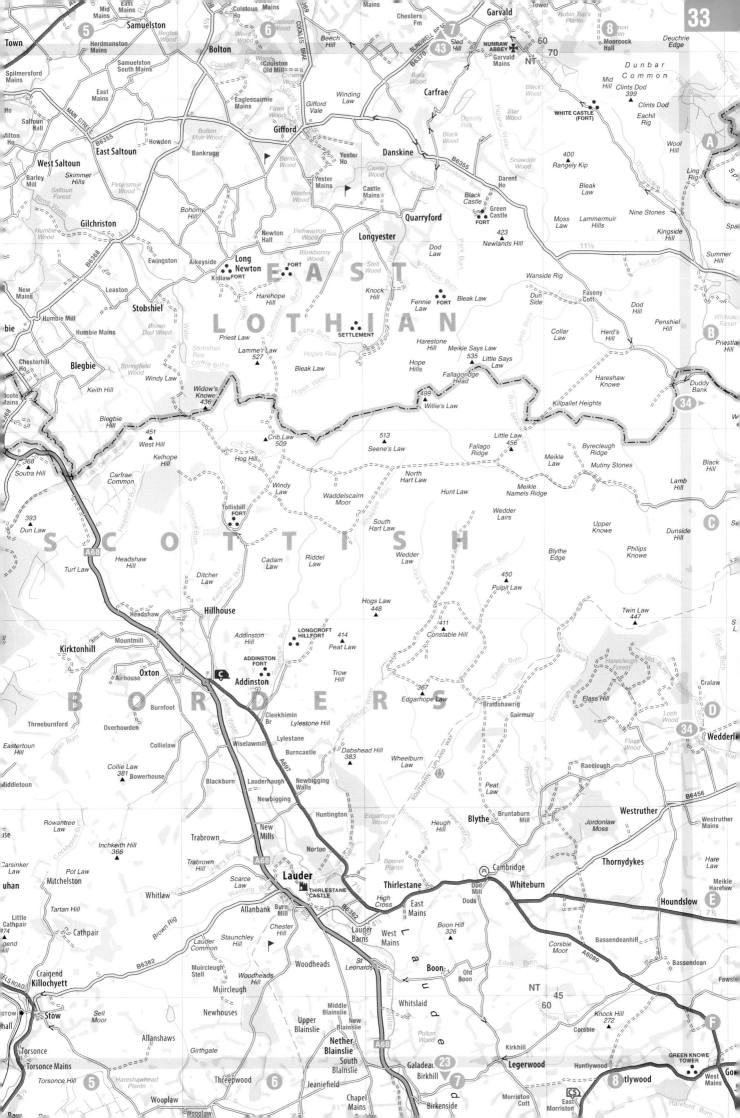

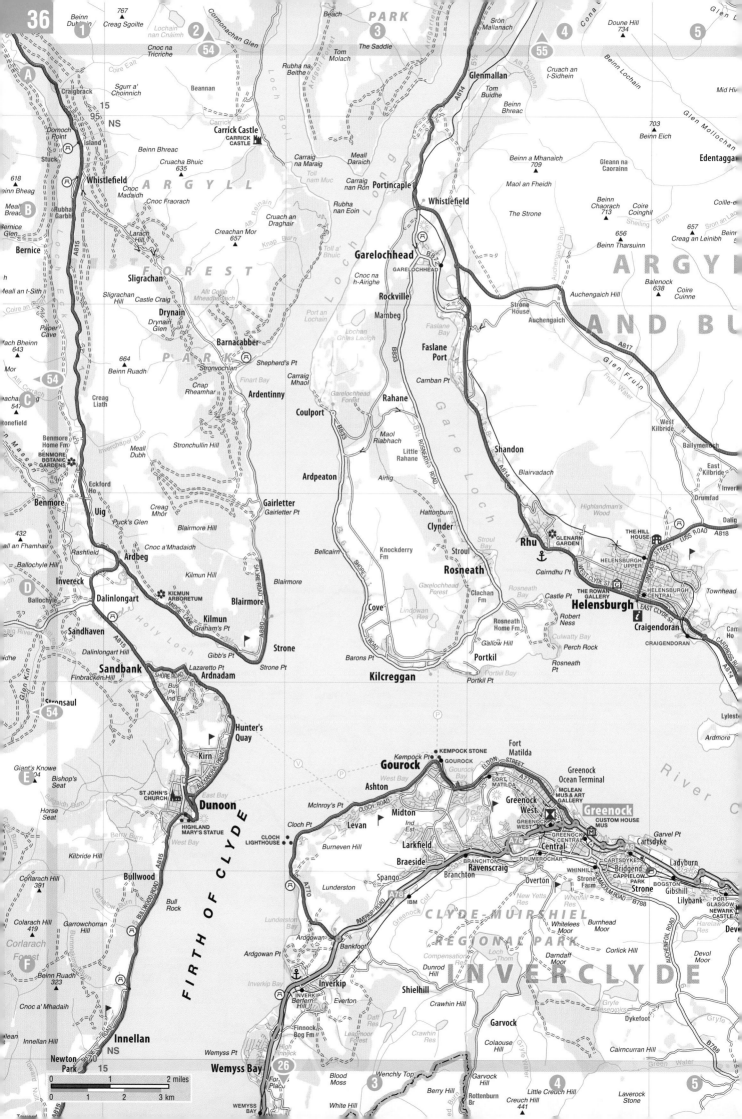

A

00
85
NT

B

S E A

C

D

Fast Castle
Head
Wheat Stack
Meikle Poo Craig
Hirst Rocks
Telegraph
Hill
**FAST
CASTLE**

Oatlee Hill

St Abb's Head

Lumsdaine

A1107

Coldingham
Loch

SETTLEMENT

ST ABB'S HEAD
Horsecastle Bay

Cambus
Wood

9½

Moor
Ho

Lumsdaine
Common

Lumsdaine
Moor

Cross
Law

Moorside
Plantn

Bell
Hill

Starney Bay

Long Latch

Coldingham
Moor

Buskinburn
Ho

Northfield

E

Bell
Hill

Drone
Hill

Huxton

SCHOOL   ROAD

B6438 1½

St Abbs
St Abb's Haven
Coldingham Bay
Yellow Craig

Mid Grange Burn

Atton
Cott

Dalks
Law

Three Burn
Grange

Press
Castle

Press
Mains

Temple
Hall

Abbey
Park

PRIORY

Coldingham

Callercove Pt

Hairy
Ness

**EYEMOUTH
MUSEUM**

Green
Wood

Grange
Plantn

Gallows
Law

B6438

Abbey   Burn

2½

3 Hallydown

A1107

Eyemouth

Houndwood

A1

Mount
Alban

Blackhill

Cairncross

North
Wood

Ale   Water

Ind
Est

B6355

Scout Pt
Horse Head

Fancove Head

F

Horseley
Hill

Howburn

Heugh
Head

MAIN   STREET

2

Eye Water

Fox
Covert

Littledean
Fm
Aytonwood
Ho

2½

Ayton
Mains

Breeches
Rock

B6437

B6438

A1

Reston
East
Reston Mill

3

Loanside

Auchencrow

Berrybank

Greenburn
Plantn

Peelwalls
Ho

Cocklaw

Ayton

**AYTON
CASTLE**

Peelwalls

Ayton Hill
19°
Chester
Hill

Burnmouth

Ross Pt
Ross

NT
60
00

Auchencrow
Mains

Bowie's
Plantn

Prenderguest

Millerton
Hill

35

Hill

Billiemains

Causeway Bank

Billiemire Burn

Horn Burn

Greenfield
Plantn

Lamberton
Moor

Lamberton

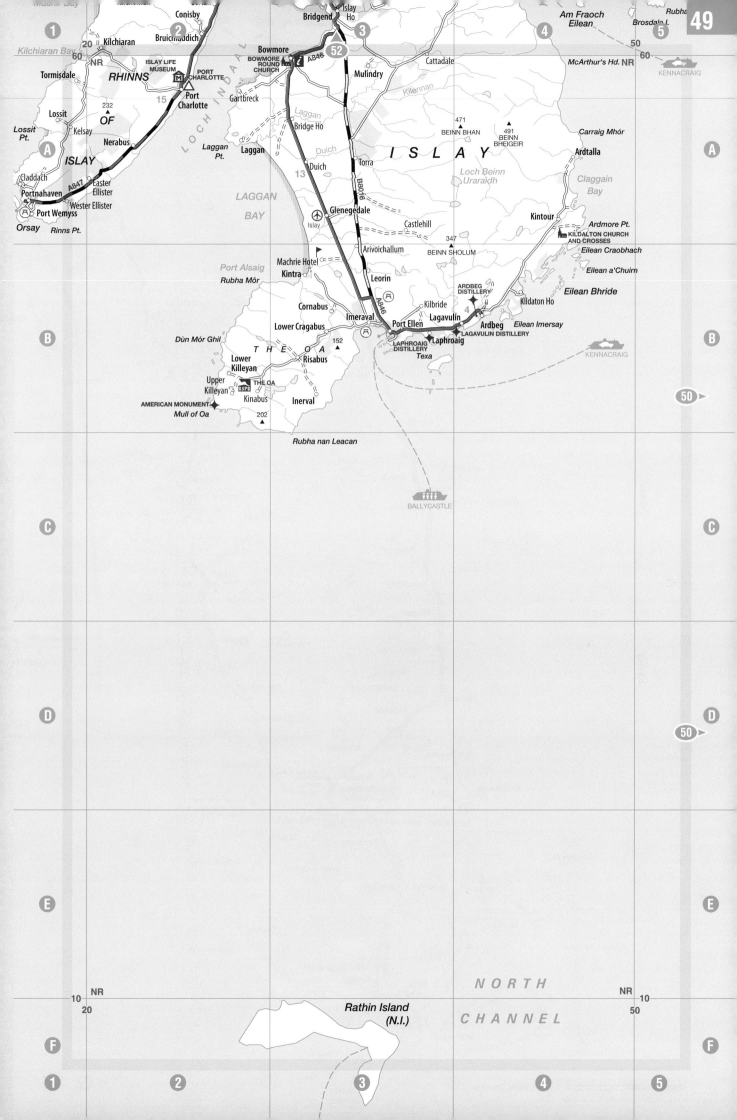

MULL OF KINTYRE

Gigha Island

Straad
Woodend Ho
Kerrycroy
Waterhead
HILL OF ST
Routenburn

Rubha Leatha 5
6
7
8
26

Northpark
60
Midpark
Scoulag
54
MOUNT STUART
HOUSE AND GARDEN
VIKINGAR!
Largs
OLD KIRK
Ladylane
Moo

Inchmarnock
Scalpsie
Piperhall
Tomont End
CHRISTIAN HERITAGE
MUSEUM
CLYDE-
IRISH LAW
484

SKIPNESS CASTLE
Skipness Pt.
Ardscalpsie
Pt.
Kingarth
Great
Cumbrae
Island
Downcraig
Ferry
KELBURN
COUNTRY CENTRE
MUIRSHIEL

Skipness Bay
Stravanan
Bay
Kilchattan
Bay
MUSEUM OF
THE CUMBRAES
Millport
Fairlie
387
KAIM HILL
Knockendon
Reservoir

SOUND OF BUTE
157
Kilchattan Bay
ST BLANE'S
CHAPEL
The Tan
Fairlie Roads
REGIONAL
8
26

(Oct-Mar)
Garroch Hd.
Little
Cumbrae
Island
HUNTERSTON
POWER STATION
VISITOR CENTRE
A78
PARK
Drakemyre

Cock of Arran
Thirdpart
Giffordland
Dalry

LOCHRANZA
CASTLE
Lochranza
Millstone Pt.
Portencross
Ardneil
West
Kilbride
B780
A737

L NAN DAMH
570
CLOCHRANZA
Catacol
ISLE OF ARRAN
DISTILLERY
444
Farland Hd.
Seamill
Dalgar
B

Fairhaven
A841
Seamill
Horse Isle
Chapelhill
Dykesmains

NORTH
AYRSHIRE
A738
2

NORTH
573
Sannox
Sannox Bay
Dalry

Loch Tanna
859
Glen Sannox
Scottish Maritime Museum

798
Corrie
Ardrossan
NORTH AYRSHIRE
HERITAGE CENTRE
Stevenston

ARRAIN
CIR MHOR
874
GOAT FELL
Saltcoats

ISLE
825
Merkland
Irvine Bay

ARRAN
BRODICK
BRODICK
CASTLE
SCOTTISH MARITIME MUSEUM

Glen Iorsa
Glenrosa
Brodick Bay
Irvine Bay
C

228
ISLE OF ARRAN
HERITAGE MUSEUM
Brodick
Strathwhillan
16

encar
Glenloig
A'CHRUACH
512
North
Corriegills

chrie
OF
South
Corriegills

MACHRIE MOOR
STANDING STONES
503
Clauchlands Pt.

Balmichael
Blairbeg
Margnaheglish
CAMPBELTOWN
(May-Sept
Sat only)

Shiskine
Birchburn
North Feorline
Lamlash
Lamlash
Bay
Holy Island
Lady Isle
D

Kilpatrick
KILPATRICK DUN
458
TIGHVEIN
Auchencairn
Kingscross Pt.
Kingscross
Whiting Bay

Corriecravie
Moor
Glenree
Clachaig
Knockenkelly
North Kiscadale
South Kiscadale
Whiting Bay

Corriecravie
Auchareoch
GLENASHDALE
FALLS
Largymore
Largymeanoch

Sliddery
Largybeg
Dippin

Lagg
Shannochie
Levencorroch
Dippin Head
Heads of Ayr
HEADS OF AYR FARM PARK
A719

TORRYLINN
CAIRN
Kilmory
Bennan
Kildonan
Fisherton
287
E

Bennan Hd.
Sound of Pladda
Dunure
ELECTRIC BRAE

Pladda
17

Culzean Bay
6

NS
CULZEAN CASTLE
270
B1023
Whitefaulds

20
CULZEAN
Maidenhead Bay
COLLEGE
CHUR
F

Maidens
A719
A77
CROSSRAGUEL
ABBEY

TURNBERRY
6
Kirkoswald
SOUTER JOHNNIE'S
COTTAGE

Turnberry Bay
Turnberry
Brest Rocks
252
Ruglen

5
6
7
8
Townhead

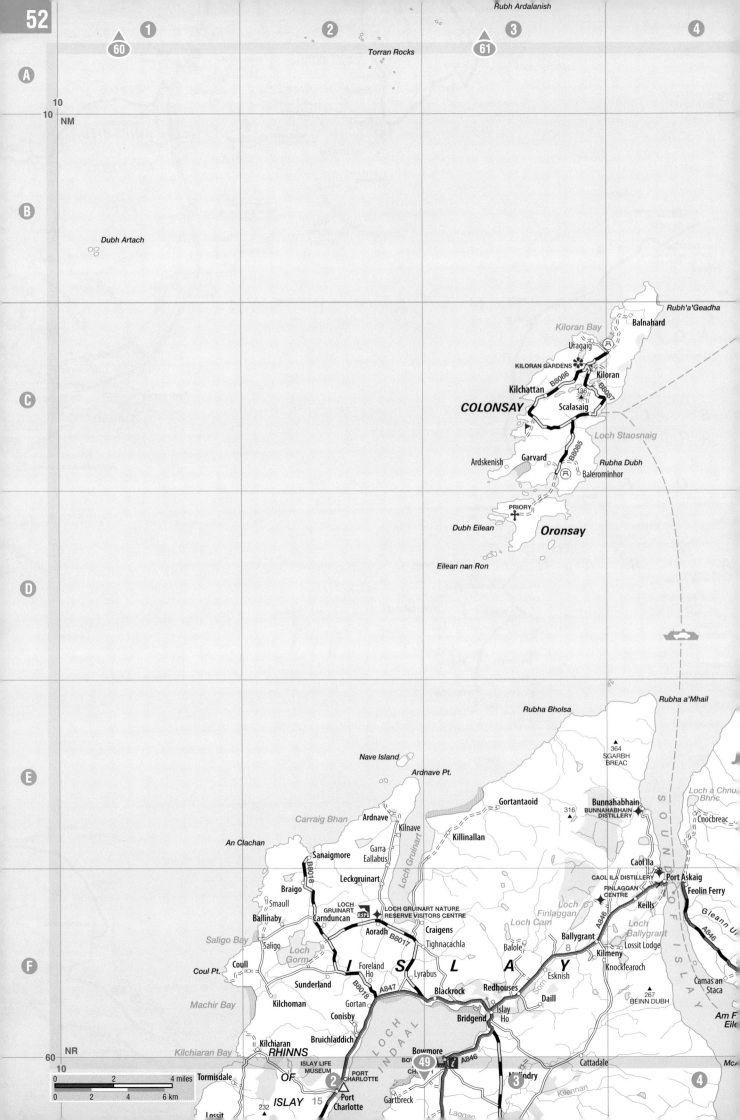

A   B   C   D   E   F

1   2   3   4

60   61

Rubh Ardalanish

Torran Rocks

10
NM

Dubh Artach

Rubh'a'Geadha

Kiloran Bay

Balnahard

Uragaig

KILORAN GARDENS

B8086   Kiloran

Kilchattan   L36   B8087

COLONSAY   Scalasaig   B8087

B8085

Ardskenish   Garvard

Rubha Dubh

Balerominor

Dubh Eilean   PRIORY

Oronsay

Eilean nan Ron

Rubha a'Mhail

Rubha Bholsa

Nave Island   364
SGARBH
BREAC

Ardnave Pt.

Gortantaoid   Bunnahabhain

316   BUNNAHABHAIN
DISTILLERY

Carraig Bhan   Ardnave   Kilnave

Killinallan   S
O
U
N
D

Loch a Chnu
Bhric

Cnocbreac

An Clachan

Sanaigmore   Garra
Eallabus

Caol Ila

CAOL ILA DISTILLERY   Port Askaig

B8018   Leckgruinart

Loch   FINLAGGAN
CENTRE   Feolin Ferry

Braigo   LOCH
GRUINART   LOCH GRUINART NATURE
RESERVE VISITORS CENTRE   Loch
Finlaggan   Keills   O
F

Smaull   RSPB   Loch Cam   Ballygrant   Loch
Ballygrant   I
S
L
A
Y

Ballinaby   Carnduncan   Aoradh   B8017   Craigens   8   Kilmeny   Lossit Lodge   Gleann U

Saligo Bay   Tighnacachla   Balole   Knockfearoch   A846

Coul Pt.   Coull   Saligo   Loch
Gorm   I S   L A   Y   Esknish   Camas an
Staca

Foreland
Ho   Lyrabus   267
BEINN DUBH   Am F
Eile

Sunderland   B8018   A847   Blackrock   Redhouses   Daill

Machir Bay   Gortan   Islay
Ho

Kilchoman   Bridgend

Conisby

Bruichladdich

60
NR   Kilchiaran   RHINNS   LOCH
INDAAL   Bowmore   Cattadale   Mc

10   Kilchiaran Bay   OF   ISLAY LIFE
MUSEUM   BO   49   A846

Tormisdale   ISLAY   PORT
CHARLOTTE   2   3   dry   Kilennan

0   2   4 miles   2   A846

0   2   4   6 km   Port
Charlotte   15   Gartbreck

Lossit   ISLAY   232   Laggan

1   2   3   4

A

B

C

D

44
45

arns Ness
rns
Skateraw
Thorntonloch

E

Reed Pt.
DUNGLASS
COLLEGIATE
CHURCH
Cove
Cockburnspath
Siccar Pt.
Wheat Stack
FAST CASTLE
ST ABB'S HEAD
stocks
St. Abb's Head
A1107
Lumsdaine
45
Ecclaw
245
Coldingham
Moor
Northfield
St Abbs
B6438
12
Coldingham Bay
SOUTHERN
UPLAND WAY
Grantshouse
Huxton
Coldingham
St. Abb's Haven
COLDINGHAM PRIORY
Nether
Monynut
SCOTTISH BORDERS
Ale Water
EYEMOUTH MUSEUM
Houndwood
Eye Water
12
Cairncross
Eyemouth
262
AYTON
CASTLE
Abbey
St. Bathans
A6112
R
Auchencrow
B6438
Reston
A1
Ayton
B6355
A1107
EDIN'S HALL
BROCH
12
Burnmouth
R
M
U
I
NU
60
10
B6438
Prenderguest
5
B6355
Lintlaw
Lamberton
Beach
21
7
8
Preston
B6355
Lamberton

F

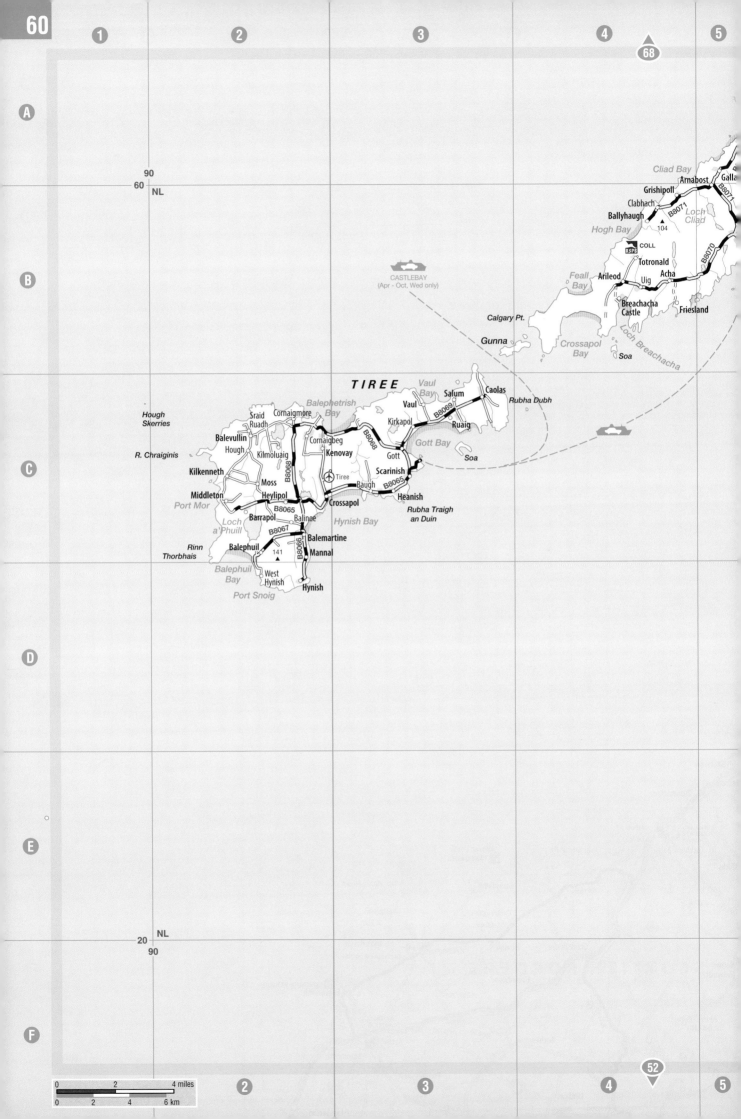

① ② ③ ④ ⑤

68

A

90
60
NL

Cliad Bay
Arnabost Galla
Grishipoll
Clabhach B8071
Ballyhaugh
Loch Cliad
Hogh Bay ▲104

B

CASTLEBAY
(Apr - Oct, Wed only)

COLL
RSPB

Totronald
Feall Bay
Arileod **Uig** **Acha**

Breachacha Castle **Friesland**

Calgary Pt.

Gunna

Crossapol Bay

Soa

Loch Breachacha

Vaul Bay

T I R E E

Salum **Caolas**
Vaul *Rubha Dubh*
Balephetrish Bay **Kirkapol** B8069
Cornaigmore **Ruaig**
Hough Skerries **Sraid Ruadh**
Balevullin **Cornaigbeg** *Gott Bay*
R. Chraiginis Hough **Kenovay** **Gott** *Soa*
Kilmoluaig B8068
Kilkenneth Tiree **Scarinish**

C

Moss **Baugh**
Middleton **Heylipol** B8065
Port Mor B8065 **Crossapol** **Heanish**
Barrapol Balinoe *Hynish Bay* *Rubha Traigh an Duin*
Loch a'Phuill B8067
Rinn Thorbhais **Balephuil** **Balemartine**
▲141 **Mannal**
Balephuil Bay West Hynish B8066
Port Snoig **Hynish**

D

E

20 NL
90

F

0   2   4 miles
0 2   4   6 km

52

② ③ ④ ⑤

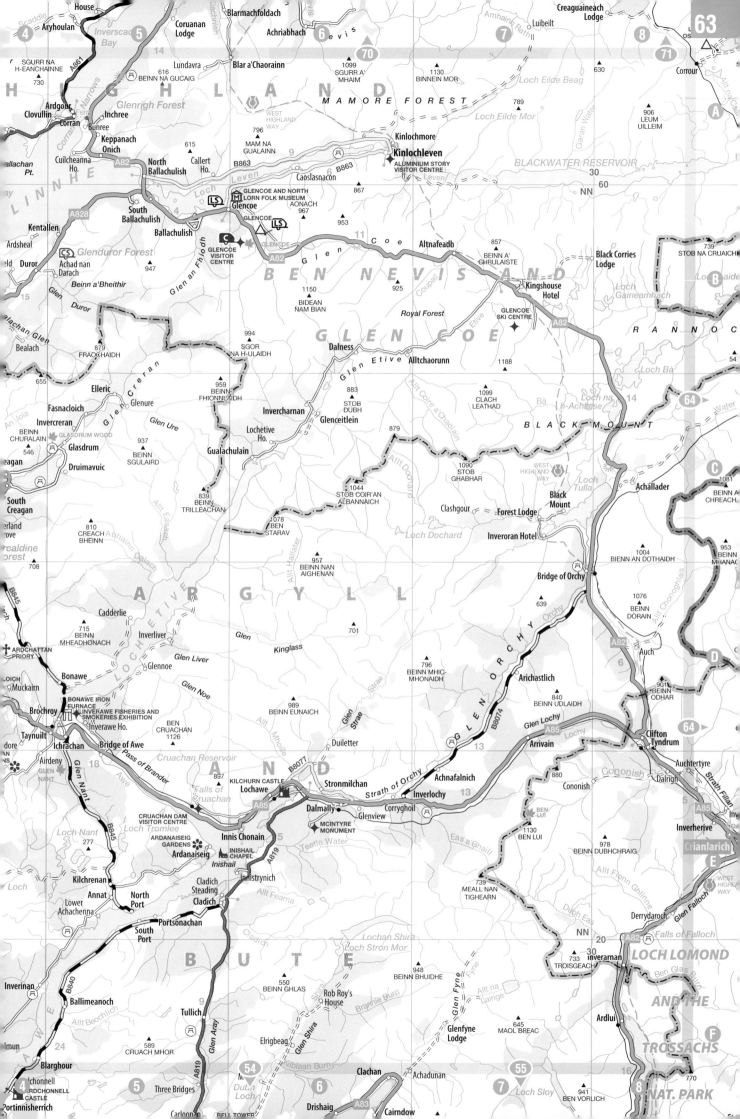

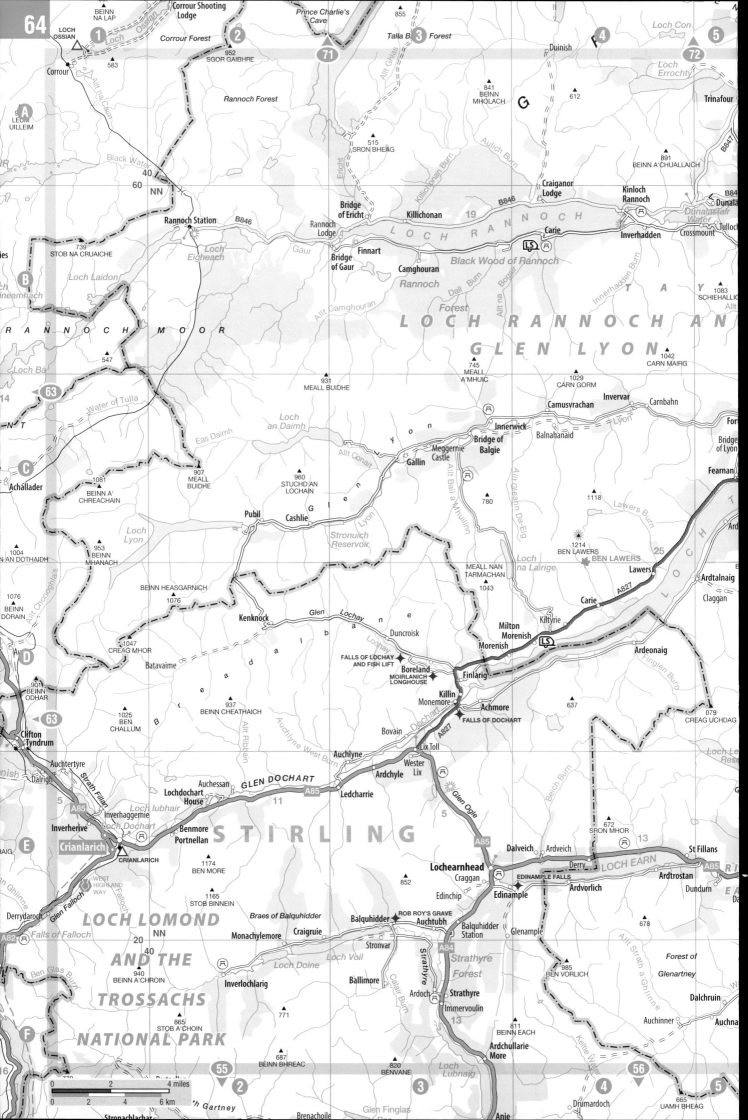

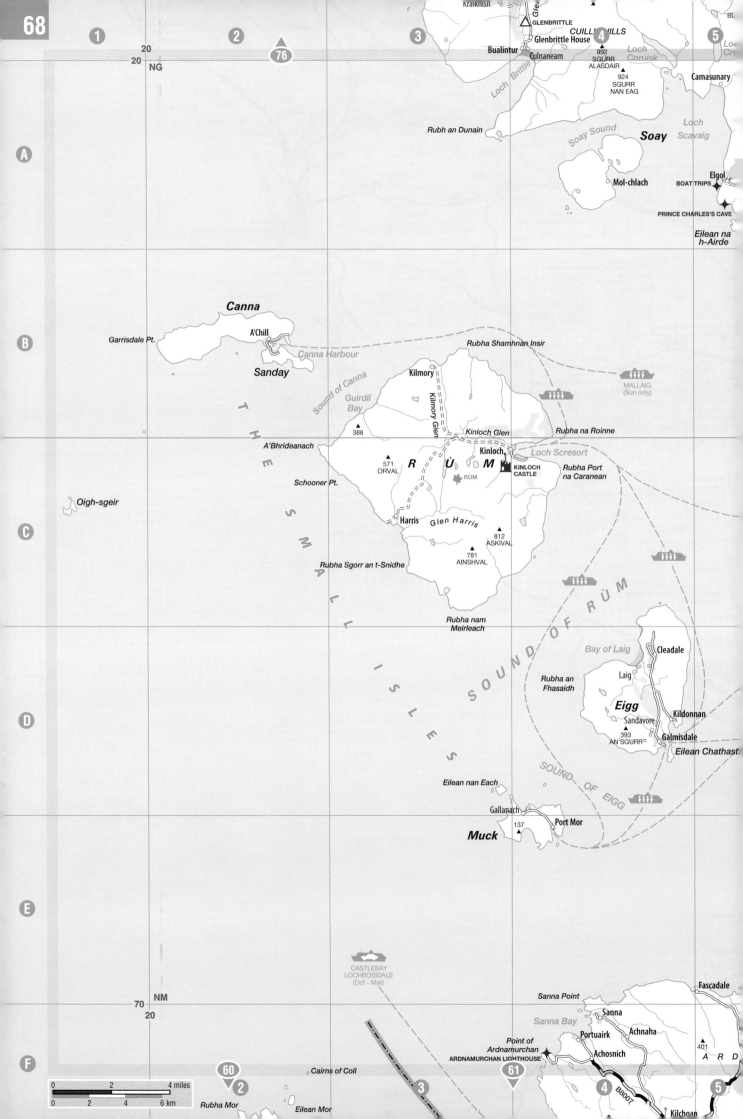

Kraiknish

GLENBRITTLE
Glenbrittle House
CUILL HILLS
Bualintur
Culnaneam
992
SGURR
ALASDAIR
924
SGURR
NAN EAG
Loch Coruisk
Camasunary
Loch
Cre
BL

Loch Brittle
Rubh an Dunain
Soay Sound
Soay
Loch
Scavaig

A

Mol-chlach
Elgol
BOAT TRIPS
PRINCE CHARLES'S CAVE
Eilean na
h-Airde

Canna
Garrisdale Pt.
A'Chill
Rubha Shamhnan Insir
Canna Harbour

B
Sanday
Sound of Canna
Kilmory
Guirdil
Bay
Kilmory Glen
Kinloch Glen
388
Rubha na Roinne
MALLAIG
(Sun only)

A'Bhrideanach
571
ORVAL
R   Ù   M
Kinloch
RÙM
KINLOCH
CASTLE
Loch Scresort
Rubha Port
na Caranean

Schooner Pt.

Oigh-sgeir

C
Harris
Glen Harris
812
ASKIVAL
Rubha Sgorr an t-Snidhe
781
AINSHVAL

Rubha nam
Meirleach

Bay of Laig
Cleadale
Rubha an
Fhasaidh
Laig
Eigg
Sandavore
Kildonnan

D
Eilean nan Each
393
AN SGURR
Galmisdale
Eilean Chathast
SOUND   OF   EIGG
Gallanach
137
Port Mor
Muck

THE   SMALL   ISLES

SOUND   OF   RÙM

E

NM
CASTLEBAY
LOCHBOISDALE
(Oct - Mar)

70
20

Sanna Point
Fascadale
Sanna
Sanna Bay
Portuairk
Achnaha
Point of
Ardnamurchan
ARDNAMURCHAN LIGHTHOUSE
Achosnich
401
A R D

F

0   2   4 miles
0   2   4   6 km

60
2
Rubha Mor
Cairns of Coll
Eilean Mor
3
61
Kilchoan
4
B8007
5

20
20
NG
76

1   2   3   4   5

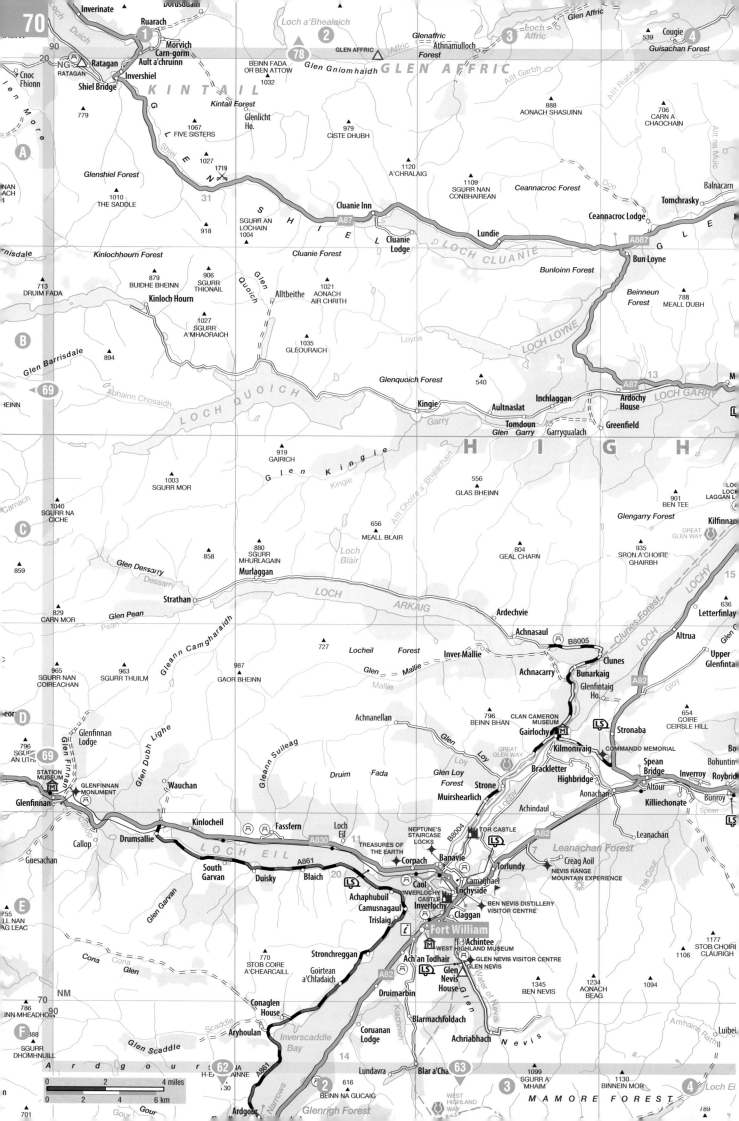

Loch ma Stac
Loch nan Eun
Loch na Beinne Baine
680
Dundreggan Forest
Dundreggan Lodge
Dundreggan
Torgyle
Dalchreichart
Munerigie
Faichem
Invergarry
Mandally
SADDLE MOUNTAIN
North Laggan
WELLS OF THE SEVEN HEADS
Laggan
LAND
815 CARN DEARG
Brae Roy Lodge
Annat
834 CARN DEARG
684
GLEN ROY
PARALLEL ROADS
915
Bohuntine
Bohenie
Achluachrach
Murlaggan
Roughburn
Tulloch
Braes o' Lochaber
MONESSIE FALLS
GLEN SPEAN
Fersit
724 BEINN CHLIANAIG
Bothy
1115 STOB COIRE EASAIN
630
Creaguaineach Lodge
937 BEINN NA LAP
1046 CHNO DEARG
LOCH TREIG
LOCH OSSIAN
Corrour
583
906

Loch a' Chrathaich
CHRATHAICH 679
Levishie Forest
Levishie
Bhlàraidh
Achnaconeran
FALLS OF MORISTON
Invermoriston
Portclair Forest
Portclair
607 BURACH
555
Inchnacardoch Hotel
FORT AUGUSTUS
Fort Augustus
CLANSMAN CENTRE
Auchteraw
CALEDONIAN CANAL VISITOR CENTRE
Bridge of Oich
Newtown
Aberchalder
Glendoe Lodge
Glendoebeg
CARN A'CHUILLINN 816
Glendoe Forest
779 CARN EASGANN BANA
Caledonian Canal
GREAT GLEN WAY
Loch Tarff
Glen Tarff
884 CARN LEAC
896 GAIRBEINN
Melgarve
Drummin
Corrieyairack Forest
Garvamore
Crathie
CARN LIATH 1006
Aberarder Forest
Aberarder Lodge
1128 CREAG MEAGAIDH
Aberarder
CREAG MEAGAIDH
LOCH LAGGAN
Kinloch Laggan
Moy Forest
1049 BEINN A' CHAORUINN
Moy
Moy Lodge
Ardverikie Forest
1049 GEAL CHARN
Loch Pattack
Ben Alder Lodge
Culra Lodge
1087 BEINN A'CHLACHAIR
Loch Ghuilbinn
1114 AONACH BEAG
1148 BEN ALDER
Corrour Shooting Lodge
Corrour Forest
952 SGOR GAIBHRE
Rannoch Forest

Boleskine
Foyers
Alltsigh
LOCH NESS
Loch Knockie
Knockie Lodge
Whitebridge
588
Knockcarrach
Glenbrein Lodge
Garrogie Lodge
Killin Lodge
Stronelairg Lodge
Glen Brein
Loch Killin
Glen Markie
MEALL NA H-AISRE 862
925 GEAL CHARN
Glenshero Lodge
622
Cromra
Gallovie
Feagour
Ardverikie
674 BEINN EILDE
Allt Cam
Allt na Glaise
Loch a' Bhealaich Bheithe
Prince Charlie's Cave
855
Talla Bheith Forest

FARIGAIG FOREST CENTRE
Errogie
79
e of Gorthleck
Farraline
Easter Aberchalder
Wester Aberchalder NH
Lochgarthside
Bailebeag
Corriegarth Lodge
Garthbeg
802 CARN ODHAR
MONADHLIATH MOUNTAINS
811 CARN NA SAOBHAIDHE
809 CARN NA LARAICHE MAOILE
828 BURRACH MOR
826 CARN COIRE NA CREICHE
942 CARN BAN
72
Gergask
Balgowan
Laggan
Drumgask
Catlodge
Strathmashie House
571
Crubenmore Lodge
BADENOCH
Cuaich
Dalwhinnie
DALWHINNIE DISTILLERY
72
Greagdhubh Lodge
Cluny Castle
Cruben
Creagan Mor
934
BEINN UDLAMAIN
774 Creagan Mor
Balsporran Cottages
North Drumachter Lodge
917
803 THE SOW OF ATHOLL
936 A'BHUIDHEANACH BHEAG
Dalnacaro
Dalnaspidal Lodge
775 MEALL NA LEITREACH
Dalnaspidal Forest
NN
841 BEINN MHOLACH
612
Duinish

Dunmaglass Lodge
A
Coignafearn Forest
Dalbeg
814 CALPA M
A'
B
Calder
Glen B
C
8
56
D
A9
E
Can
F
63
64
5
6
7
8

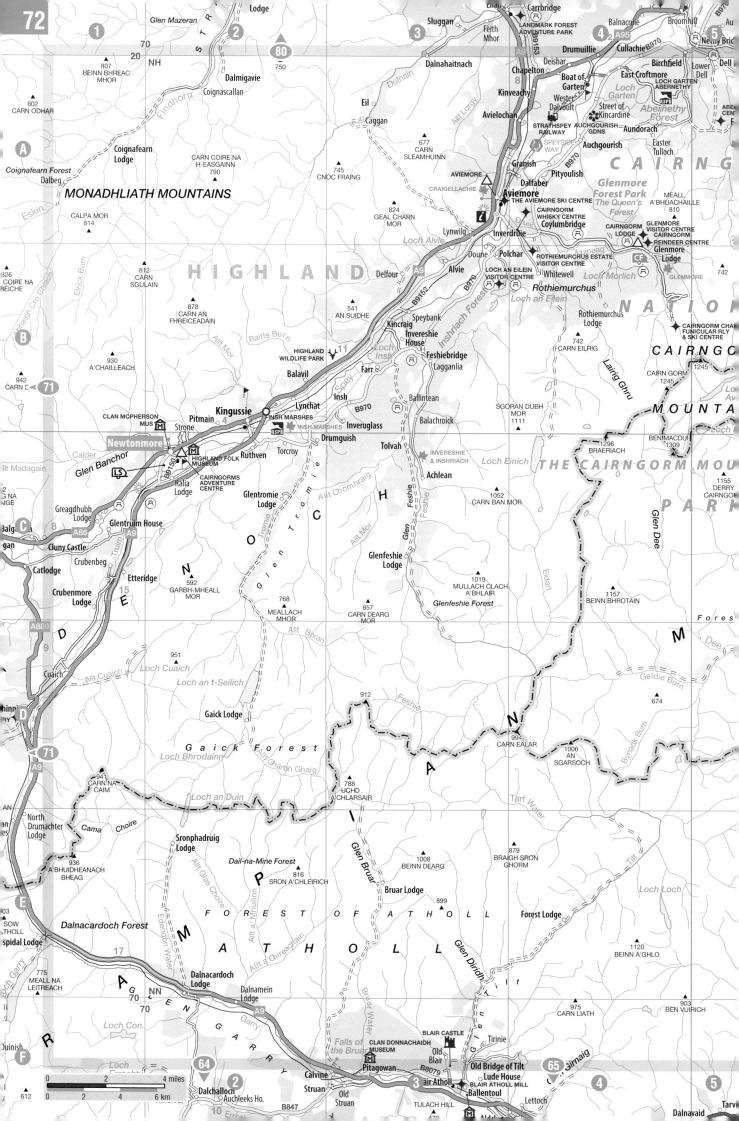

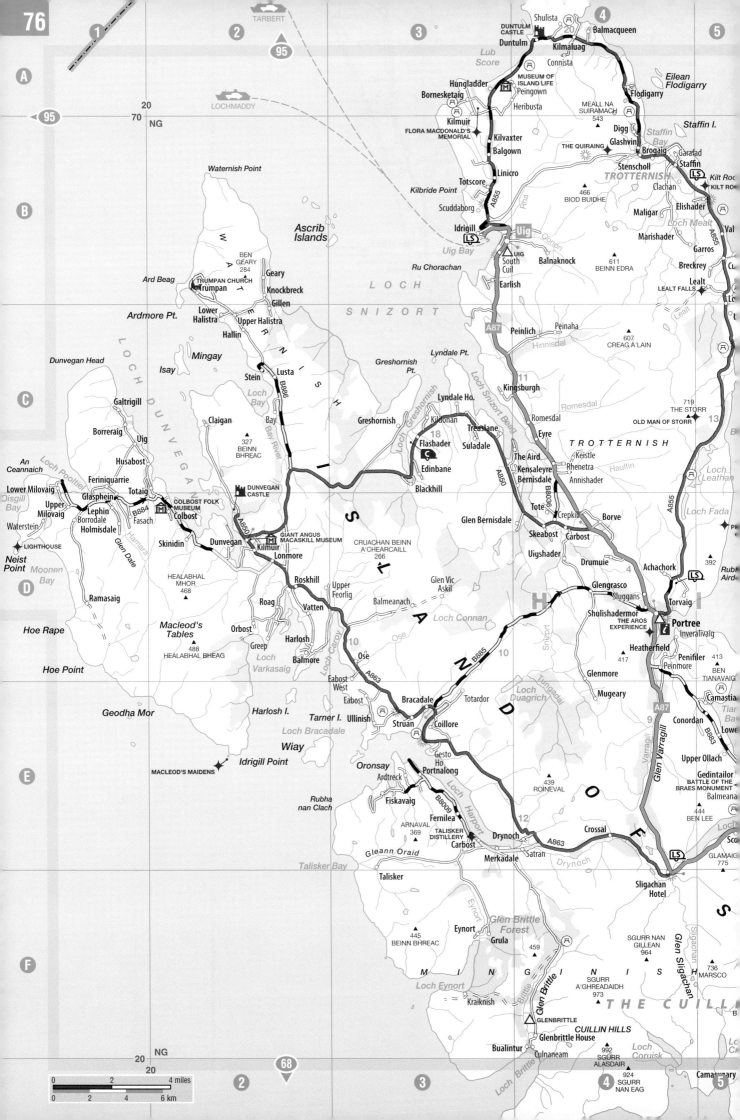

LOCH GAIRLOCH

420

Charlestown

A832

Bodantionail
Aird
Port
Henderson
7
Badachro
B8056
Leacnasaide
Ke
84

8

Opinan
Shieldaig
Kerry
Loch Bad
an Sgalaig

A

Eilear.
Subhainn

South
Erradale

Loch
Clàir

Erradale

Dubh
Loch

VICTORIA FALLS
90
Tall le
70

NG

Redpoint

Flowerdale
Forest

875
BAOSBHEINN
Forest

Loch na
h- Oidhch

B

Craig

624
BEINN BHREAC

Loch
a'Bhealaich

& MEALT FALLS

Rubha na
Fearn

Fearnmore

Loch

Torridon

Upper
Diabaig
Lower
Diabaig

Upper
Torridon
985
BEINN ALLIGIN

Torridon Forest

78

LIATH

r Tote
er Tote

Fearnbeg
Arinacrinachd

Reaulay
Rubha nam
Brathairean

Island of Rona

125

Cuaig
Kenmore

Ardheslaig

Loch a'
Chracaich

Alligin
Shuas
Rechullin

Inveralligin
Torridon Ho.

Fasag
TORRIDON

17

knock

Eilean Garbh

Callakille

Abhainn Chuaig

Upper
Loch
Torridon

Balgy
A896

TORRIDON
VISITOR
CENTRE

C

Annat

r Tote

Lonbain

Loch
Gaineamhach

Shieldaig

Ben-damph Forest

reraig
ay

Eilean Tigh
Garbh Eilean

An Caol

Loch a'
Sguirr

254

493
CROIC-BHEINN

Abhainn Dubh

BEN
SHIELDAIG
439

902
BEINN DAMH

993

MAOL
CHEAN-D

Holm I.

Eilean
Fladday

Torran

Manish Pt.

Loch
Arnish

Arnish

Glenshieldaig
Forest

Loch Lundie

513

Kinloch
Damph

Loch Coultrie

D

na h
laise

CE CHARLES'S
PE

BROCHEL CASTLE

Brochel

BEINN
A'CHLACHAIN
626

HARTFIELD
HOUSE
CHAPEL OF
ST.MAELRUBHA
Hartfield

Applecross Forest

896
BEINN BHAN

Couldoran

Rassal
Tornapress

Tullich

Loch nan
Eun

Applecross Ho.

G

Glame

ISLAND
OF
RAASAY

385

Applecross
Bay

Milton

Applecross

14

Kirkton

Balmeanach
Balachuirn

443
DUN CAAN

Camusteel
Camusterrach

BEALACH NA BA

Russel

Sanachan
Glen
Mor

A896

Lochcarron

78

Holman
aig
aig

RAASAY

Ard-dhubh
Culduie

710
MEALL GORM

Slumbay

Oskaig

Rubha na'Leac

Ardban

Toscaig

Ardarroch
Achintraid

A890

Raasay Ho.
Clachan

RAASAY
OUTDOOR
CENTRE

Eilean na Bà

Reraig
Cot

STROME
CASTLE
395

Ardnarff

The
Narrows
Braes of
Raasay

Inverarish

North Fearns

Stromemore
Ardaneaskan

Stromeferry

CARN NAN
IOMAIREAN

E

East
Suisnish

Eyre Point

Crowlin
Islands

Caolas Mór

Eilean Mór

Uags

An Dubh-aird

LOCH CARRON

Peinchorran
Eyre

Plockton

Achmore

Sligachan

Caol Mór

Longay

Port Cam

CRAIG HIGHLAND FARM

Braeintra

Duirinish

Gleann Udalain

Allt-nan-sùgh

Sallachy

Scalpay

Moll

Corran a Chan
Uachdaraich

Guillamon I.

Pabay

Black Is.

Drumbuie

Achnandarach

Loch
Long

Ca

Scalpay Ho.

Badicaul

Erbusaig

Balmacara Square

Auchertyre

Conchra

Bundalloch

Luib
Dunan

Caolas Scalpay

Kyle of Lochalsh

LS
Reraig

Avernish

Carndu
Ardelve

Loch
Duich

16

K

570
GLAS
BHEINN MHOR

RED HILLS

A87

Corry

Broadford
Bay

Waterloo

CS

Ashaig

CASTLE MOIL
Kyleakin

LOCHALSH
WOODLAND GARDEN
BRIGHT WATER
VISITOR CENTRE

Balmacara

Kirkton

Nostie

A87

Dornie

EILEAN DONAN
CASTLE

Glas
Eilean

F

Totaig

SG

BHEINN
928

15

Y

732

Old
Corry

Broadford

Lower Breakish

8

Upper Breakish

SGURR
NA COINNICH
739

Ardintoul Pt.

Ardintoul

603
BEINN A'CHUIRN

Letterfern

Keppoch

Inverina

na
each

Harrapool

INTERNATIONAL
OTTER SURVIVAL
FUND

Skulamus

A851

Glen Arroch

Allt Mór

KYLERHEA
OTTER HAVEN

Kyle Rhea

Bernera
Galltair

Scalasaig

NG

20
90
Rata

E
HILLS

Torrin

Suardal

B8083

Faoilean

Kilbride

trathaird

Kirkibost

Kilmarie

5

610
BEN ASLAK

6

Heast

301

Kinloch

69

7

8

Glenelg

BERNERA BARRACKS

Eilanreach

Còsag

Glenelg
Bay

Cnoc
Fhionn

CS

GLENELG BROCHS

Ratagan

RATAGAN

Shiel Bri

779

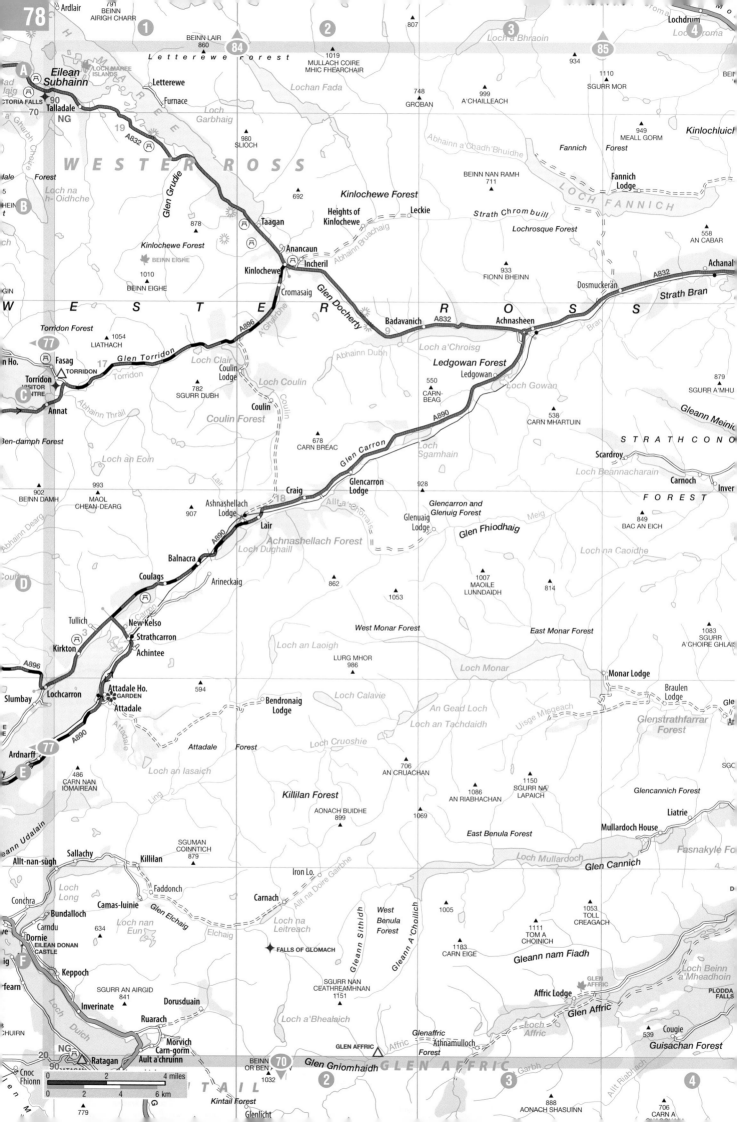

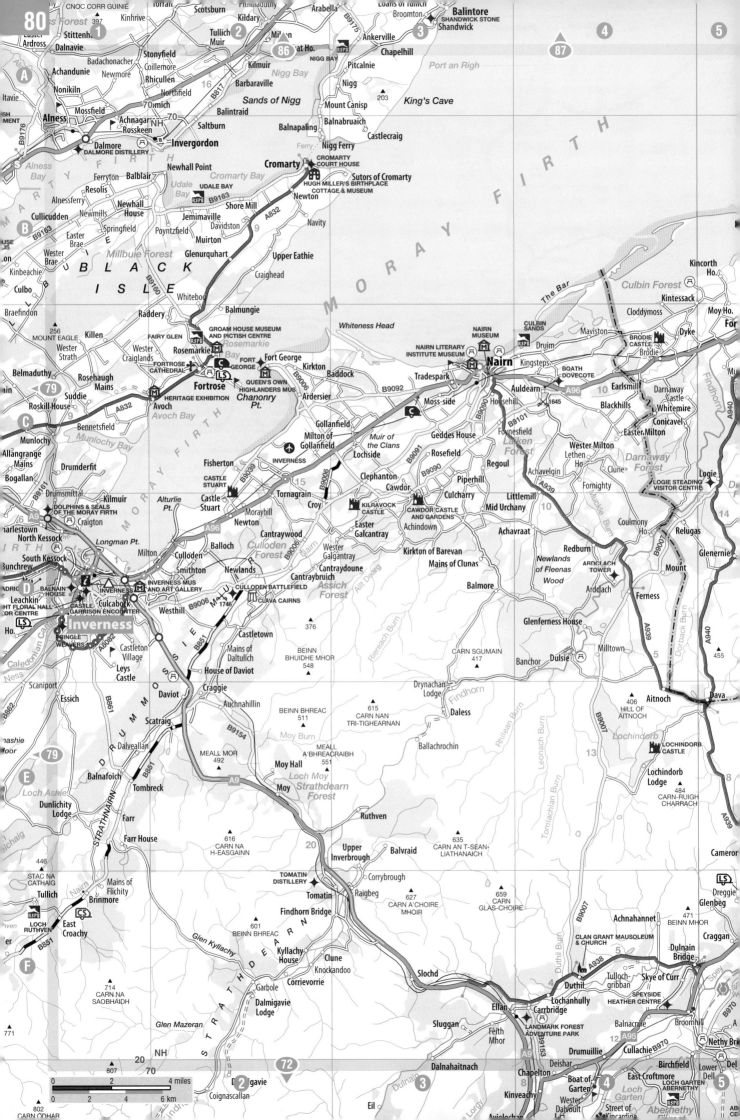

CAPE WRATH

Kearvaig

Geodha Ruadh na Fola

Bay of Keisgaig

Loch Keisgaig

Insho

Am Balg

Geodha Ruadh

423
BEINN DEARG

485
CREAG
RIABHACH

457
FASHVEN

SGRI
BHE

Rubh'an Fhir Léithe

Sandwood
Loch

Loch na Gàinimh

Strath Shinary

Sheigra
Balchrick
Blairmore
Droman Oldshore Beg
Oldshoremore

Eilean Roin Mor

521
FARRMHEALL

Loch Clash Kinlochbervie
Badcall B801
Rhivichie Inshegra
Achriesgill

Gualin Ho.

Bagh Loch an Roin

9

Achlyness

Loch Dughaill

Ceathramh Garbh

L. na Claise
Carnaich

Ardmore Pt.

Rubha Ruadh

Ardmore

Portlevorchy
Skerricha

Rhiconich

A838

GANU M
908
Foinav

Fanagmore
Tarbet

NORTH-WEST SUTHER

Loch Laxford *Loch a'Gàrbh-
bhaid Mòr*

Handa Island

Foindle

*Loch nam
Brac*

A894

Laxford Bridge

Badnabay

787
ARKLE

Scourie Bay

Scourie More
Rubh'Aird an t-Sionnaich

Scourie

A838

Lochstack Lodge

Loch Stack

Upper Badcall

Lower Badcall

Gorm Loch

719
BEN STACK

Strath Stack

Airdachuilin

Eil. a'Bhreitheimh

Badcall Bay

18

BEINN AUSKAIRD
386

332

Achfary

F O R

Duartbeg

Rubha a'Mhucard

Meall Mór

A894

*Loch
Crocach*

R E A Y

Lochmore Lodge

*Loch na Creige
Duibhe*

Calbha
Mòr

Calbha
Beag

Duartmore
Bridge

Duartmore
Forest

Loch a'Chàirn Bhàin

*Loch an Leathaid
Bhuain*

Eddrachillis Bay

Oldany
Island

Point of Stoer

R. nan Còsan

Eilean Chrona

Culkein
Drumbeg

Loch Nedd

Kylestrome

Kylesku

547
Forest

Glendhu

Cirean Geardail

161

Cluas Deas

Rubha
Stoer

Culkein

Clashnessie Bay

Oldany

Drumbeg

Ardvar

B869

Unapool

Loch Glendhu

Gleann Dubh

Achnacarnin

Clashmore

Clashnessie

Nedd
Glenleraig

Gleann

8

Newton

530

BEINN AIRD
DA LOCH

Loch Glencoul

Glen Coul

Balchladich

Rienachait

*Loch
Poll*

Leireag

NC

13

Stoer

Rubh'a'
Mhill Dheirg

Bay of Stoer

Clachtoll

*Loch
Crocach*

*Loch an
Leathaid*

5

808
QUINAG

Loch Beannach

Lochassynt Lodge

A894

EAS COUL AULIN
WATERFALL

776

7

BEINN
UIDHE
740

BEINN UIDHE

R. Leum

84

B869

2

Rhicarn

3

10

Little
Assynt

85

Skiag Bridge

4

Gorm Loch Mòr

Achmelvich

ACHMELVICH
BEACH

ASSYNT

A837

Inver

LOCHASSY

0   2   4 miles
0   2   4   6 km

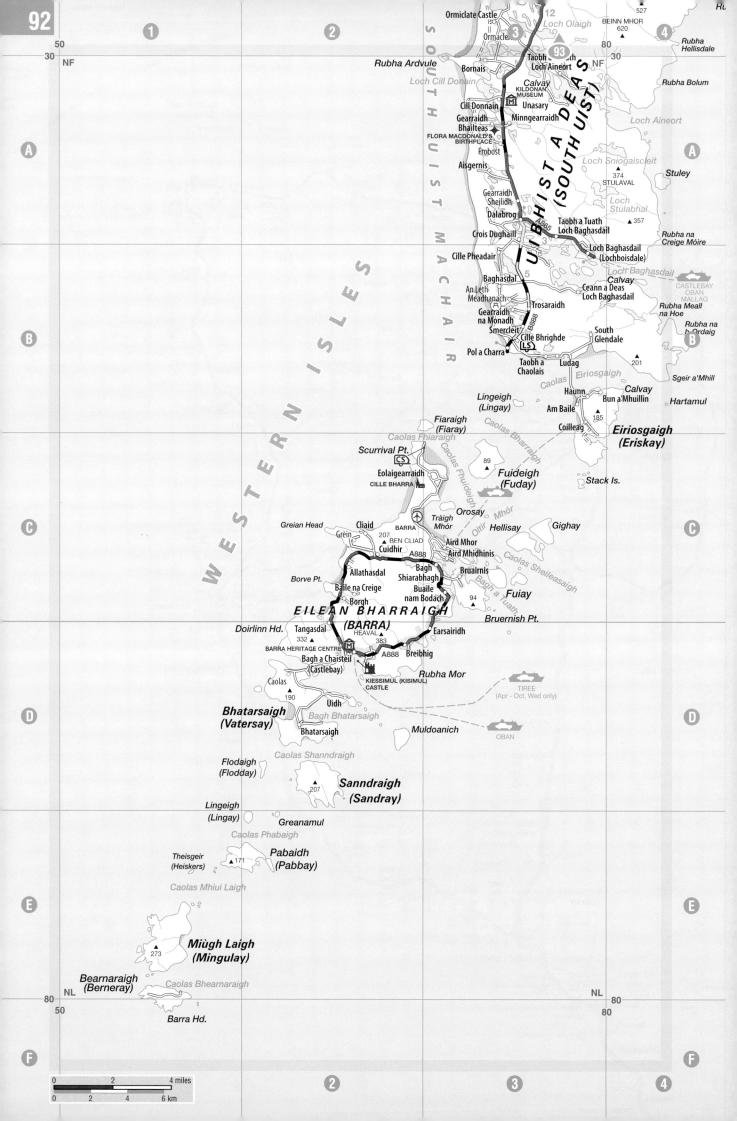

WESTERN ISLES

UIBHIST A DEAS (SOUTH UIST)

SOUTH UIST MACHAIR

Ormiclate Castle
Loch Olaigh
BEINN MHOR 620
527
Ru
Ormacle
12
93
Rubha Hellisdale
50
30
NF
Rubha Ardvule
Loch Cill Domain
Taobh a' Tuath
Loch Aineort
Bornais
Calvay
KILDONAN MUSEUM
NF
30
Rubha Bolum
Loch Aineort
Cill Donnain
Unasary
Gearraidh Bhailteas
Minngearraidh
Loch Sniogaiscleit
Stuley
FLORA MACDONALD'S BIRTHPLACE
Frobost
374 STULAVAL
Aisgernis
Gearraidh Shejlidh
Dalabrog
▲ 357
Crois Dughaill
Taobh a Tuath Loch Baghasdail
Rubha na Creige Móire
Cille Pheadair
Loch Baghasdail (Lochboisdale)
Baghasdal
5
Calvay
An Leth Meadhanach
Ceann a Deas Loch Baghasdail
CASTLEBAY OBAN MALLAG
Trosaraidh
3
Rubha Meall na Hoe
Gearraidh na Monadh
B888
Smercleit
Cille Brighde
South Glendale
Rubha na h'Ordaig
Pol a Charra
Ludag
201
Taobh a Chaolais
Caolas Eiriosgaigh
Haunn
Sgeir a'Mhill
Lingeigh (Lingay)
Am Baile
Calvay
Bun a'Mhuillin
Hartamul
Coilleag
185
Eiriosgaigh (Eriskay)
Fiaraigh (Fiaray)
Caolas Fhiaraigh
Caolas Bharralgh
Scurrival Pt.
89
Fuideigh (Fuday)
Stack Is.
Eolaigearraidh
CILLE BHARRA
Greian Head
Cliaid
BARRA
Orosay
Oitir Mhór
Grèin
Tràigh Mhór
Hellisay
Gighay
207 BEN CLIAD
Cuidhir
Aird Mhor
Caolas Sheileasaigh
Allathasdal
A888
Aird Mhidhinis
Borve Pt.
Bagh Shiarabhagh
Brualrnls
Baile na Creige
Buaile nam Bodach
Fuiay
Bagh a' Tuath
Borgh
94
EILEAN BHARRAIGH (BARRA)
Bruernish Pt.
Doirlinn Hd.
Tangasdal
HEAVAL
Earsairidh
332
383
BARRA HERITAGE CENTRE
Breibhig
A888
Bagh a Chaisteil (Castlebay)
Rubha Mor
KIESSIMUL (KISIMUL) CASTLE
TIREE (Apr - Oct, Wed only)
Caolas
190
Uidh
Bhatarsaigh (Vatersay)
Bagh Bhatarsaigh
Muldoanich
OBAN
Bhatarsaigh
Caolas Shanndraigh
Flodaigh (Flodday)
Sanndraigh (Sandray)
207
Lingeigh (Lingay)
Greanamul
Caolas Phabaigh
Theisgeir (Heiskers)
Pabaidh (Pabbay)
171
Caolas Mhiui Laigh
Miùgh Laigh (Mingulay)
273
Bearnaraigh (Berneray)
Caolas Bhearnaraigh
NL
80
50
Barra Hd.

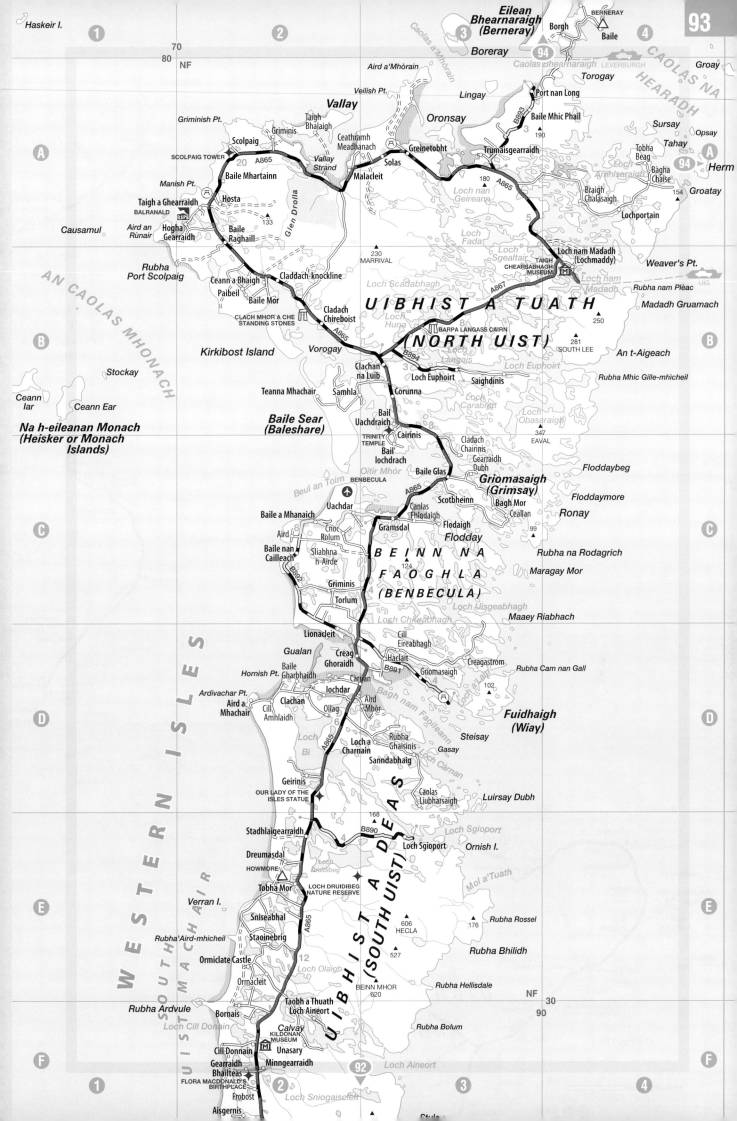

Scarp

Kearstay

308

Bràighe Mór

Huisinis

Hushinish Pt.

Beitearsaig

489

679
TIRGA MOR

Gobhaig

Horsanish

Arda Móra

Abhainn Suidh

Gaisgeir

Taransay Glorigs

Soay Beag

Cliasmol

Soay Mór

Camus an
t-suithean

Tarasaigh
(Taransay)

ST KILDA

Boreray

384

Soay

CNOC
GLAS
376

Loch a'
Ghlinne

CONACHAIR
376

MULLACH BI
358

ST KILDA

St Kilda or Hirta
(Hiort)

Bagh a
Bhaile

Dun

Paible

99

Rubha Sgeirigin

Seilebost

Horgabost

Borve Lodge
Buirgh

SCARISTA
STANDING STONE

23

Toe Head

Coppay

CHAIPAVAL
365

Sgarasta Mhor

398
BLEAVAL

Loch Lang

Shillay

Little Shillay

Sound of Shillay

Rubha'an Teampuill

Taobh Tuath

SEALLAM!

A859

An t-Ob (Leverburgh)

459

FIonnsbhagh

ROINEABHAL

Brenish Pt.

196

**Pabaidh
(Pabbay)**

Quinish

Ensay

Carminish Is.

Cairminis
Srannda

Borghasdal

ST CLEMENT'S
CHURCH

Roghadal

Valley
Renish Pt.

Sound of Spuir

Caolas Phabaidh

Spuir

**Eilean
Bhearnaraigh
(Berneray)**

Boreray

Ruisigearraidh

BERNERAY

Borgh

Baile

Killegray

Langay

CAOLAS NA HEARADH

Groay

Gilsay

Lingay

Scaravay

Aird a'Mhòrain

Caolas Bhearnaraigh

Torogay

Veilish Pt.

Lingay

Port nan Long

B893

Baile Mhic Phail

190

Sursay

Opsay

Tahay

Griminish Pt.

Taigh
Bhalaigh

Griminis

Oronsay

Trumaisgearraidh

Valley

Scolpaig

Ceathramh
Meadhanach

Greinetobht

Tobha
Beag

Bàgha
Chaise

Hermetray

SCOLPAIG TOWER

20

A865

Valley
Strand

Solas

Malacleit

3

Loch
Amhlasaraigh

Groatay

154

Baile Mhartainn

Manish Pt.

180

A865

Braigh
Chalasaigh

Lochportain

Hosta

Loch nan
Geireann

Taigh a Ghearraidh

BALRANALD

133

Glen Drolla

5

Baile
Raghaill

Aird an
Rùnair

Hogha
Gearraidh

70

230
MARRIVAL

Loch
Sgealtair

Loch
Sgeltair

TAIGH
CHEARSABHAGH
MUSEUM

Loch nam Madadh
(Lochmaddy)

Weaver's Pt.

Rubha
Port Scolpaig

Loch Scadabhagh

Loch nam
Madadh

Rubha nam Plèac

UIG

Ceann a'Bhaigh

Claddach-knockline

A867

Madadh Gruamach

Paibeil

Baile Mór

Claddach
Chireboist

UIBHIST A TUATH

250

CLACH MHOR A CHE
STANDING STONES

A865

Loch
Huna

BARPA LANGASS CAIRN

8

281
SOUTH LEE

An t-Aigeach

Kirkibost Island

(NORTH UIST)

Vorogay

Clachan
na Luib

93

ch Euphoirt

Saighdinis

Rubha Mhic Gille-mhicheil

Samhla

Corunna

2

Loch
Carabhat

Loch Euphoirt

Bail
Uachdraich

Baile Sear

Loch
Obasaraigh

0   2   4 miles

0   2   4   6 km

LEWIS, ISLAND

Beiniseabhal

Morsgail Forest

96

Strandabhat

Tabost

KERSHADER

13

Marbhig

Calbost

8

Ceann Tarabhaigh A859 6

Airidh a Bhruaich

Ceann Shiphoirt

97

7

Loch nan Eilean

Grabhair

Aird an Troim

Taobh a' Ghlinne

Tom an Fhuadain

B8060

Loch Odhairn

A

STULAVAL 579

Aline Lodge

Seaforth I.

PARK OR PAIRC

Orasaigh

Eisgean

Leumrabhagh

Kebock Head

Aird a' Mhulaidh

Scaladal

Loch Shell or Loch Sealg

40

10

ULLAVAL

UISGNAVAL MORE 729

572 BEINN MHOR

NB

Srianach

Eilean Iubhard

CLISHAM 799

17

CEANN A TUATH NA HEARADH

Loch Shiphoirt

470 CRIONAIG

449

Mol Truisg

B

13

Miabhag

Bun Abhainn Eadarra

A859

Maraig

Eilean Anabaich

559

RHENIGIDALE

Reinigeadal

Gob Rubh'Uisenis

Rubha Bhrollum

OLD WHALING STATION

Cul na h-Aird

Aird Asaig

3

Lochan Lacasdail

Urgha Beag

Oban

Loch Trollamarig

Rubha a'Bhaird

CAOLAS NAN EILEAN

Isay

Leacainn

Taobh Siar

Urgha

Carragraich

Garbh Eilean

Eilean Mhuire

436

LUSKENTYRE

467

Tairbeart (Tarbert)

Direcleit

Caolas Scalpaigh

Carnach

Sgeotasaigh

Rudha Crago

Na h-Eileanan Mòra (Shiant Islands)

Eilean an Tighe

South Harris Forest

A859

Loch Ceann Dibig

Miabhag

Loch an Tairbeart

Scalpay

Ceann a Bhàigh

Eilean Scalpaigh (Scalpay)

C

HEARADH (HARRIS)

Drinisiadar

Kennacley

LS

Plocropol Pt.

Plocrapol

Scadabhagh

Aird Mhighe

386

Liceasto

Geocrab

Greosabhagh

Leac a Li

Collam

Cliuthar

Loch Greosabhagh

Rubha Bhocaig

Beacrabhaic

Caolas Stocinis

Stockinish I.

eabhagh

Manais

Cuidhtinis

seam bhagh

rabay I.

WESTERN ISLES

Fladda-chùain

D

Eilean Troday

Rubha Hunish

Rubha na h-Aiseig

Eilean Troday

E

DUNTULM CASTLE

Shulista

20

Balmacqueen

Duntulm

Kilmaluag

Connista

LOCHMADDY

Hungladder

Bornesketaig

MUSEUM OF ISLAND LIFE

Peingown

Flodigarry

Kilmuir

Heribusta

TR

55

MEALL NA SUIRAMACH

543

Digg

FLORA MACDONALD'S MEMORIAL

Kilvaxter

45

Glashvin

Balgown

THE QUIRAING

Broga

Stenscholl

Linicro

TROTTERNISH

Waternish Point

Totscore

Kilbride Point

A855

466 BIOD BUIDHE

F

Ascrib Islands

76

Scuddaborg

Idrigill

LS

Uig

aligar

Marish

BEN ARY 284

Geary

Knockbreck

LOCH SNIZORT

Uig Bay

Ru Chorachan

South Cuil

Earlish

UIG

Baln ck

611 BEINN EDRA

Ard Beag

TRUMPAN CHURCH

Trumpan

4

5

6

7

8

WESTERN ISLES

An Caolas

Scarp

94

95

0 2 4 miles
0 2 4 6 km

RUBHA ROBHANAIS
(BUTT OF LEWIS)

CHURCH OF ST MOULAG
Cunndal
Eòropaidh
Coig Peighinnean
B8014
HARBOUR VIEW GALLERY

Cross Sands
Lional
Port Nis
Adabroc
Suainebost
Tàbost
Aird Dhail
Cros
Dail bho Dheas
Dail bho Thuath
Glen Cross
B8015
Sgiogarstaigh

Gabhsann bho Thuath
Gabhsann bho Dheas
A857
Cuiashader

Mealabost Bhuirgh
Loch
Langabhat
Cellar Head

Bail Àrd Bhuirgh
15
Coig Peighinnean Bhuirgh
Gabhsann bho Dheas
Siadar
Rubha Leathann
Siadar Iarach
Loch Mòr
Shanndabhat

Aird Barvas
Siadar Uarach
TRUSHAL STONE
Baile an Truiseil

Borgh
Abhainn Ghearadha

LOCH NA MUILNE
Barabhas Iarach
Barabhas Uarach
Bail' Ur Tholastaidh
BLACK HOUSE MUSEUM
Brù
Tolastadh bho Thuath
Labost
Barabhas
Arnol
RSPB
248
MUIRNEAG
Tolsta Head
Siabost bho Thuath
Bragar
A858
Gleann Mòr Barvas
A857
ST NORSE MILL
bho Dheas
SHAWBOST MUSEUM
Grìais
Pairc Shiaboist
Loch Urghag
Loch
Sgeireach
Mòr
Gleann Tholàstaidh
Port Bun
a'Ghlinne
B895
261
BEINN BRAGAR
Loch Breibhat
Gleann Bhruthadail
Griais
14
Creag Fhraoch
Loch
Scarabhat Mhòr

Col
Glen Bragar
Loch Mòr an Stàirr
12
Cnoc an
t-Solais
Bac
Col
Vatisker Pt.
292
BEINN MHOLACH
Col Uarach
Breibhig
Lacasdal
Coll Sands
BROAD BAY
OR
LOCH A TUATH
Port Nan Giùran
Rubha an t-Siumpain

Loch
nan Stearnag
Lacasdail
A857
Aird Thunga
Cnoc
Amhlaigh
Port Mholair
Loch Lacabhat
Ard
Tunga
Sròn Ruadh
Sulaisiadar
A866
Aird
cleit
Grianan
Newmarket
Seisiadar
CALANAIS VISITOR
CENTRE
An Gleann Ur
Cnoc Màiri
STORNOWAY
Garrabost
EYE
CALANAIS SMALL
STONE CIRCLES
LEWS CASTLE &
MUS NAN EILEAN
Lacasdal
Aiginis
PENINSULA
Gearraidh na
h-Aibhne
Loch Urabhal
LEWIS LOOM CENTRE
Mealabost
Pabail Uarach
223
Groba
Stornoway
Aird Thunga
10
A858
Loch a'
Ghainmhich
AN LANNTAIR
GALLERY
Sanndabhaig
A866
An Cnoc
Pabail Iarach
ST COLUMBA'S
ACHMORE
STONE CIRCLE
Tolm
Suardail
Bàgh Phabail
Acha Mor
14
A859
Arnish Moor
Airinis
Holm I.
A'Chearc
Loch
Orasaigh
Soval Lodge
10
Griomsidar
Raerinish Pt.
Liùrbost
Ben Casgro
B897
16
ULLAPOOL
Loch
Trealabhal
Ranais
Crosbost
Barkin Is.
Tabhaidh Mhor
Loch pam Falcag
Loch Tobhta
Bridein
Ceos
Eilean Chaluim
Chille
Lacasaidh
Eilean Orasaidh
Baile Ailein
Crobeag
Cromor
Sildinis
Cearsiadair
Gearraidh Bhaird
Eilean Thoraidh
Tabost
Cabharstadh
Loch
andabhat
B8060
KERSHADER
13
Marbhig
A859
Ceann
Shiphoirt
Loch
nan
Eilean
Calbost
Airidh a
Bhruaich
cleit
95
Kebock Head
ard an
roim
5
6
Taobh Ghlinne
Grabhair
B8060
7
8
Tom an
Loch Odhairn
Loch Shanndabhat

60
70
NB
A
B
C
D
E
F
NB
20
60

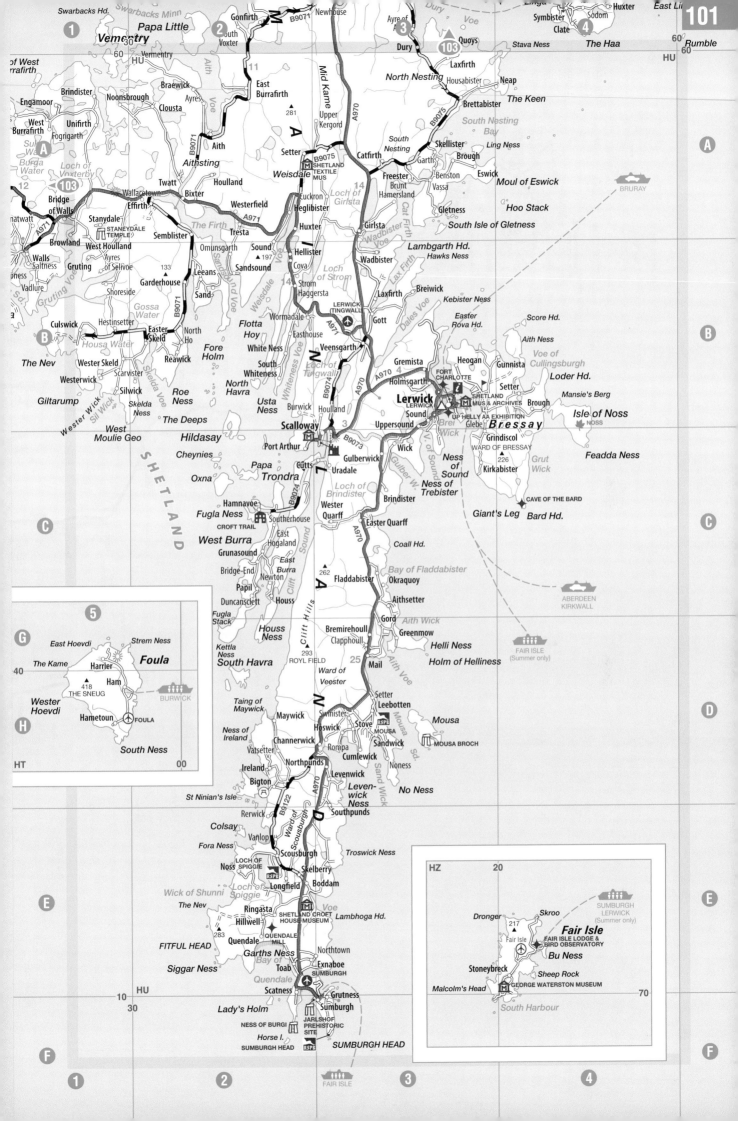

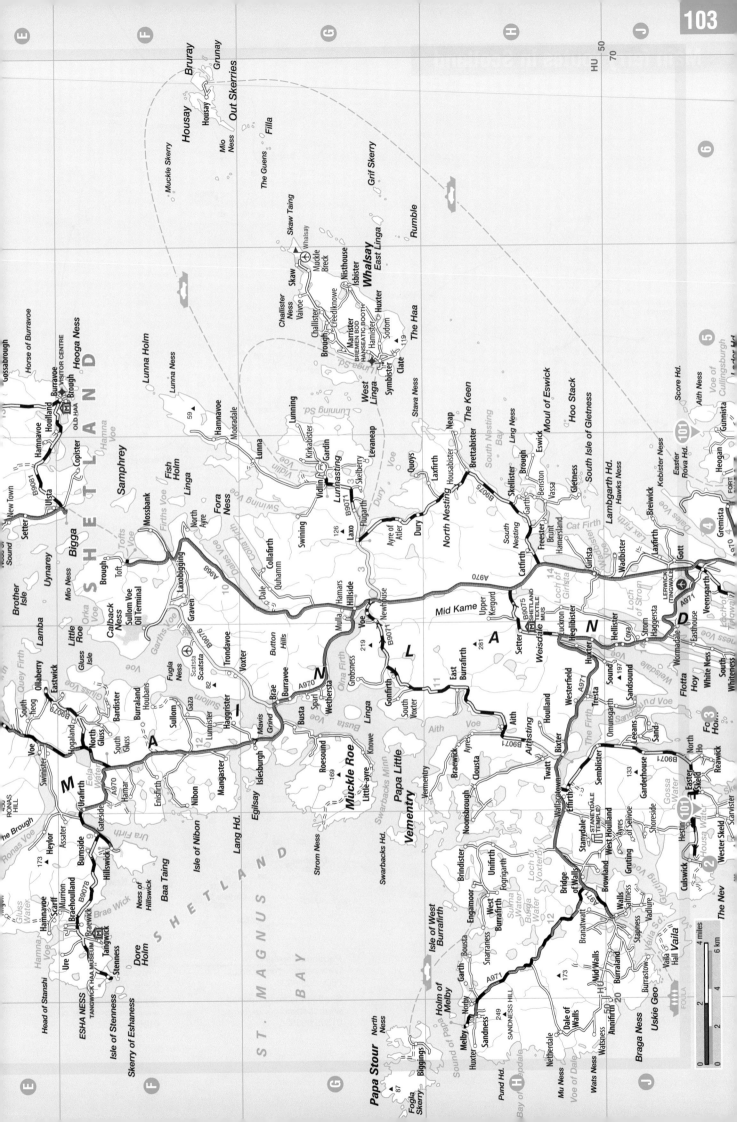

HU 50 70

Grid references (top)
E | F | G | H | J

Bruray
Grunay
Housay
Out Skerries
Housay
Mio Ness
Filla
Muckle Skerry
The Guens
Grif Skerry
Rumble

SHETLAND

Gossabrough
Horse of Burravoe
Heoga Ness
Burravoe
Brough
VISITOR CENTRE
Houlland
Hamnavoe
OLD HAA
Copister
Samphrey
Lunna Holm
Lunna Ness
Lunna Ness
Skaw Taing
Whalsay
Skaw Taing
Skaw
Whalsay
Muckle
Breck
Nisthouse
Isbister
East Linga
Challister
Ness
Vaivoe
Challister
Freediknowe
Brough
Marrister
BREMEN BÖD
HANSEATIC BOOTH
Huxter
Hamister
Sodom
The Haa
West
Linga
Symbister
Clate
119

New Town
B9081
Setter
Ulsta
Bigga
Mio Ness
Brough
Toft
Mossbank
North
Ayre
Fora
Ness
Collafirth
Ouhamm
Dale
Swining
Swining
Linga
Fish
Holm
Mooradale
Hamnavoe
Lunna
Lunning
Kirkabister
Gardin
Skelberry
Levaneap
Quoys
Stava Ness
Ling Ness
South Nesting
Bay
Neap
The Keen
Moul of Eswick
Eswick
Hoo Stack
South Isle of Gletness
Gletness
Brough
Vassa
Benston
Skellister
South
Nesting
North Nesting
Housabister
Brettabister
Laxfirth
Dury
Ayre of
Atler
Laxo
126
B9071
Flugarth
Vidlin
B9071
Lunnasting
Voe
Dury

Sound
Brother
Isle
Uynarey
Lamba
Little
Roe
Calback
Ness
Sullom Voe
Oil Terminal
Graven
Trondavoe
Voxter
Button
Hills
Hamars
Hillside
Mulla
Voe
B9071
Newhouse
Mid Kame
Upper
Kergord
219
Kergord
Luckron
Setter
Weisdale
281
A
L
M
East
Burrafirth
11
Gonfirth
South
Voxter
Freester
Brunt
Hamersland
Catfirth
14
A970
Loch of
Girlsta
Girlsta
Wadbister
Laxfirth
Gott
Strom
Haggersta
Hawks Ness
Kebister Ness
Breiwick
Lambgarth Hd.
Wadbister Ness
Easter
Rova Hd.
101
Aith Ness
Gunnista
Heogan
Gremista
Voe of
Cullingsburgh
Score Hd.
Leder Hd.

Head of Stanshi
Isle of Stenness
Skerry of Eshaness
ESHA NESS
TANGWICK HAA MUSEUM
Tangwick
Stenness
Dore
Holm
Baa Taing
Ness of
Hillswick
Isle of Nibon
Lang Hd.
Stram Ness
Swarbacks Hd.
Swarbacks Minn
Papa Little
Vementry
Vementry
Vementry
Noonsbrough
Clousta
Braewick
Ayres
Aith
Houlland
Westerfield
Tresta
Sand
Leans
Onunsgarth
Sandsound
Sound
Flotta
White Ness
South
Voe of
Tingwall
LERWICK
TINGWALL
A971
Normadale
Easthouse
Coya
Loch of
Strom
Stanydale
STANEYDALE
TEMPLE
West Houlland
Effirth
Wallacetown
Garderhouse
133
Sound
197
Hellister
Heglibister
Huxter
N
D
A971
B9071
Sandness
Walls
Bridge
of Walls
Browland
Saltness
Vadlure
Stapness
Burraland
Voe of
Dale
Vaila Sd.
Hall
Vaila
Gruting
Gruting Voe
Garderhouse
Shoreside
Loch of
Selivoe
Seli Voe
Easter
Skeld
North
Ho
B9071
Culswick
Wester Skeld
The Nev
2
Housa Voter
Fo 3
Ho
Gossa
Water
Scarvister
Skeld
101
Hestin
Easter
Skeld
Wallacetown

ST. MAGNUS BAY

Papa Stour
North Ness
Fogla Skerry
Biggings
Papa Stour
Holm of
Melby
Sound of Papa Stour
Melby
Notby
Sandness
SANDNESS HILL
249
Huxter
Mid Walls
Burrastow
173
Dale of Walls
Netherdale
Watsness
Wats Ness
Voe of Dale
Braga Ness
Mu Ness
Uskie Geo
FOULA
Pund Hd.
Bay of Deepdale
The Nev
Braewick

87

scale:
0 2 4 6 km
0   4 miles

E | F | G | H | J

Main ferry routes in Scotland

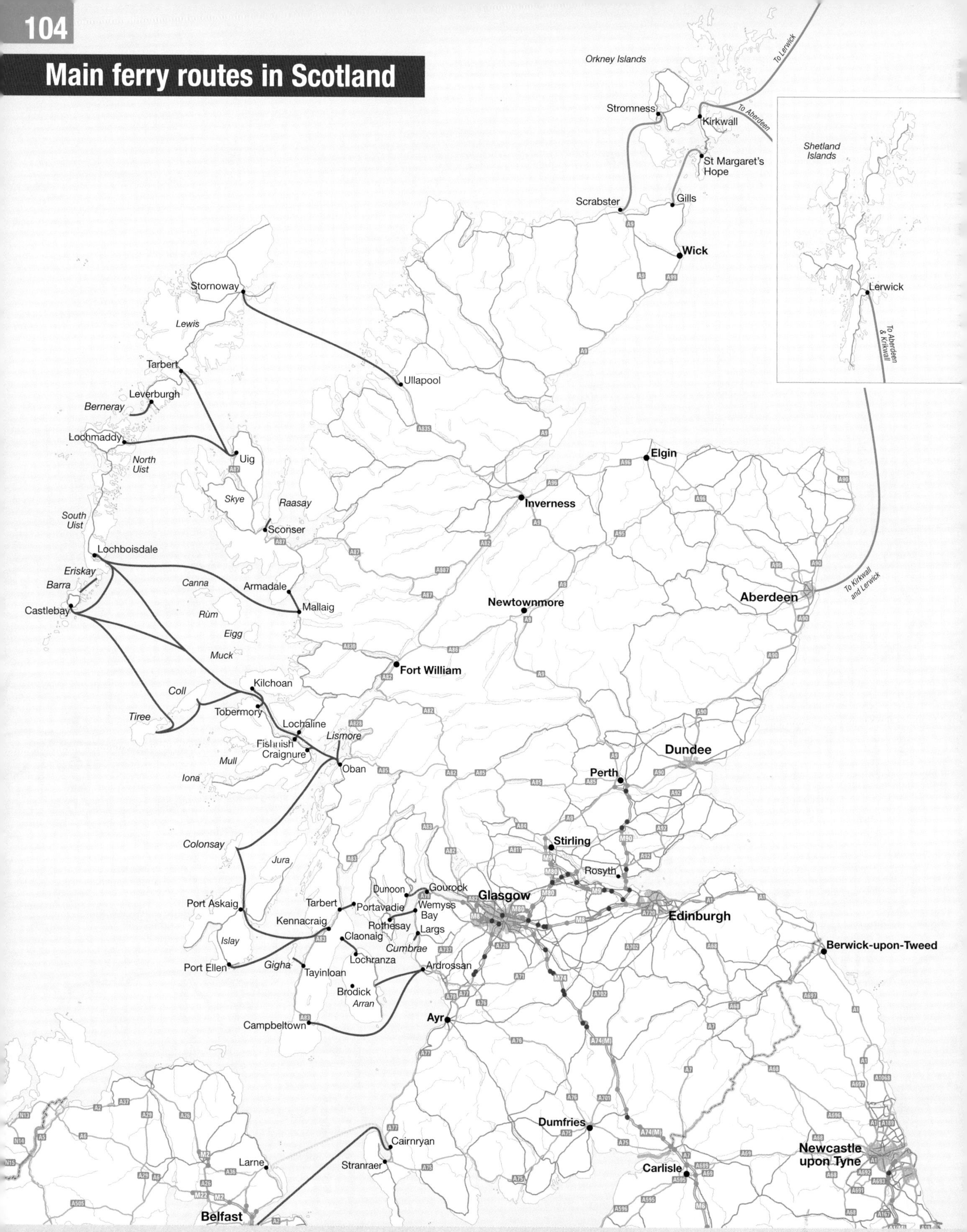

Orkney Islands

To Lerwick

Stromness
Kirkwall
St Margaret's Hope
Gills
Scrabster
Wick

To Aberdeen

Shetland Islands

Lerwick

To Aberdeen & Kirkwall

Stornoway

Lewis

Tarbert
Leverburgh
Berneray
Lochmaddy
Ullapool

North Uist

Uig
Skye
Raasay
Sconser

South Uist

Lochboisdale
Eriskay
Barra
Castlebay
Canna
Armadale
Mallaig
Rùm
Eigg
Muck
Kilchoan
Coll
Tobermory
Tiree
Lochaline
Fishnish
Craignure
Lismore
Mull
Iona
Oban

Elgin
Inverness

Newtownmore

Fort William

Aberdeen

To Kirkwall and Lerwick

Colonsay
Jura

Dundee
Perth
Stirling
Rosyth

Port Askaig
Tarbert
Kennacraig
Islay
Dunoon
Portavadie
Rothesay
Claonaig
Cumbrae
Lochranza
Port Ellen
Gigha
Tayinloan
Brodick
Arran
Campbeltown

Gourock
Wemyss Bay
Largs
Glasgow
Ardrossan

Edinburgh
Berwick-upon-Tweed

Ayr

Dumfries
Carlisle

Larne
Cairnryan
Stranraer

Newcastle upon Tyne

Belfast

Caledonian MacBrayne
www.calmac.co.uk
0800 066 5000

Northlink Ferries
www.northlinkferries.co.uk
0845 6000 449

Orkney Ferries
www.orkneyferries.co.uk
01856 872 044

P&O Irish Sea
www.poferries.com
0800 130 0030

Pentland Ferries
www.pentlandferries.co.uk
0800 688 8998

Shetland Islands Council
www.shetland.gov.uk/ferries
01595 693535

Stenaline
www.stenaline.co.uk
03447 70 70 70

Western Ferries
www.western-ferries.co.uk
01369 704452

Town plans

Town plan symbols

Motorway

Primary route – dual/single carriageway

A road –dual/single carriageway

B road – dual/single carriageway

Minor through road, one-way street

Pedestrian roads

Shopping streets

Railway

City Hall **Tramway with tram stop**

Railway or bus station

Shopping precinct or retail park

Park

Ⓗ **Hospital**

Ⓟ **Parking**

▽ **Police station**

PO **Post office**

♿ **Shopmobility**

Bank ●West **Underground or metro station**
St

▲ **Youth hostel**

Tourist information

✝ **Abbey or cathedral**

🏛 **Ancient monument**

🐠 **Aquarium**

🖼 **Art gallery**

🕊 **Bird garden**

🏛 **Building of public interest**

🏰 **Castle**

⛪ **Church of interest**

🎥 **Cinema**

✿ **Garden**

⚓ **Historic ship**

🏠 **House**

🏡 **House and garden**

🏛 **Museum**

✦ **Other place of interest**

🚂 **Preserved railway**

🚉 **Railway station**

🏛 **Roman antiquity**

🎭 **Theatre**

ℹ **Tourist information centre**

🐘 **Zoo**

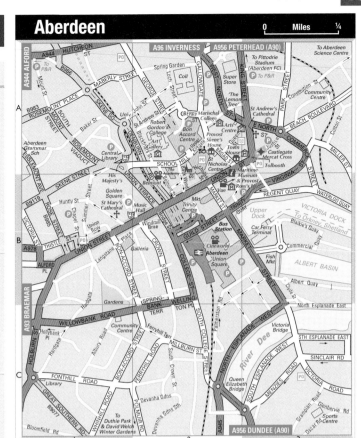

Aberdeen

Aberdeen ⇌ B2	Constitution St A3	Maritime Museum	School Hill A2
Aberdeen Grammar	Cotton St A3	& Provost Ross's	Sinclair Rd C3
School A1	Crown St B2	House 🏛 B2	Skene Sq A1
Academy, The B2	Denburn Rd A2	Market B2	Skene St B1
Albert Basin B3	Devanha Gdns C2	Market St B2/B3	South College St. . . . C2
Albert Quay B3	Devanha Gdns	Menzies Rd C3	South Crown St C2
Albury Rd C1	South C2	Mercat Cross ✦ . . A3	South Esp East C3
Alford Pl B1	East North St A3	Millburn St C2	South Esp West C3
Art Gallery 🖼 A2	Esslemont Ave A1	Miller St A3	South Mount St A1
Arts Centre 🏛 A2	Ferryhill Rd C2	Mount St A1	Sports Centre C3
Back Wynd. A2	Ferryhill Terr. C2	Music Hall 🎭 B1	Spring Garden A2
Baker St A1	Fish Market B3	North Esp East C3	Springbank Terr C2
Beach Blvd. A3	Fonthill Rd. C1	North Esp West C2	Summer St. B1
Belmont 🎥 B2	Galleria B1	Oscar Rd C3	Superstore A2
Belmont St. B2	Gallowgate A2	Palmerston Rd C2	Thistle St B1
Berry St A2	George St. A2	Park St A3	Tolbooth 🏛 A3
Blackfriars St A2	Glenbervie Rd C3	Police Station ▽ . . A2	Town House 🏛 A2
Blaikie's Quay B3	Golden Sq B1	Polmuir Rd. C2	Trinity Centre B2
Bloomfield Rd. C1	Grampian Rd C3	Post Office	Union Row B1
Bon Accord	Great Southern Rd . C1	PO . . A1/A2/A3/B1/C3	Union Square B2
Centre A2	Guild St. B2	Provost Skene's	Union St. B1/B2
Bon-Accord St .B1/C1	Hardgate B1/C1	House 🏛 A2	University A2
Bridge St B2	His Majesty's	Queen Elizabeth Br C2	Upper Dock B3
Broad St A2	Theatre 🎭 A1	Queen St A2	Upper Kirkgate. . . . A2
Bus Station B2	Holburn St. C1	Regent Quay B3	Victoria Bridge. . . . C3
Car Ferry Terminal. B3	Hollybank Pl C1	Regent Road B3	Victoria Dock B3
Castlegate. A3	Huntly St B1	Robert Gordon's	Victoria Rd. C3
Central Library A1	Hutcheon St A1	College. A2	Victoria St B2
Chapel St B1	Information Ctr ℹ . B2	Rose St B1	Virginia St A3
Cineworld 🎥 B2	John St. A2	Rosemount Pl A1	Vue 🎥 B2
Clyde St B3	Justice St. A3	Rosemount	Waterloo Quay B3
College. A2	King St A2	Viaduct. A1	Wellington Pl C2
College St B2	Langstane Pl B1	St Andrew St A2	West North St A2
Commerce St A3	Lemon Tree, The. . . A2	St Andrew's	Whinhill Rd C1
Commercial Quay . . B3	Library C1	Cathedral ✝ A3	Willowbank Rd C1
Community	Loch St A2	St Mary's	Windmill Brae. B2
Centre A3/C1	Maberly St A1	Cathedral ✝ B1	
	Marischal	St Nicholas Centre . A2	
	College 🏛 A2	St Nicholas St A2	

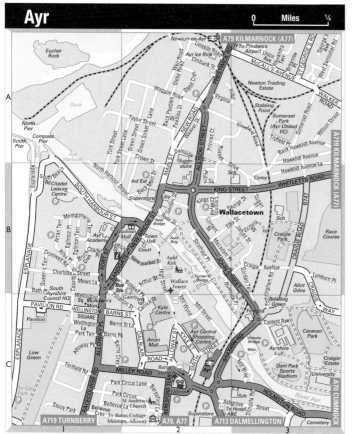

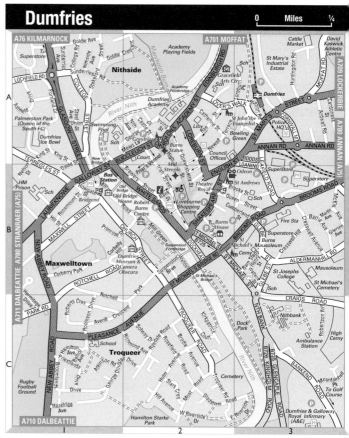

Ayr

Ailsa Pl B1	Charlotte St B1	James St B3	Queen's Terr B1
Alexandra Terr A3	Citadel Leisure	John St B2	Racecourse Rd C1
Allison St B2	Centre B1	King St B2	River St B2
Alloway Pk C1	Citadel Pl B1	Kings Ct C2	Riverside Pl B2
Alloway Pl C1	Compass Pier A1	Kyle Centre C2	Russell Dr A2
Alloway St C2	Content Ave C3	Kyle St C2	St Andrews
Arran Mall C2	Content St B2	Library B2	Church C2
Arran Terr B1	Craigie Ave B3	Limekiln Rd A2	St George's Rd B1
Arthur St B2	Craigie Rd B3	Limonds Wynd B2	Sandgate B1
Ashgrove St C2	Craigie Way B3	Loudoun Hall . . . B2	Savoy Park C1
Auld Brig B2	Cromwell Rd B1	Lymburn Pl B3	Smith St C2
Auld Kirk B2	Crown St A2	Macadam Pl B2	Somerset Park
Ayr C2	Dalblair Rd C2	Main St B2	(Ayr United FC) . . . A3
Ayr Academy B1	Dam Park Sports	Mcadam's	Somerset Rd A2
Ayr Central	Stadium C3	Monument C1	South Beach Rd . . . B1
Shopping Centre . C2	Damside A2	Mccall's Ave A3	South Harbour St . . B1
Ayr Harbour A1	Dongola Rd C3	Mews La A3	South Pier A1
Ayr Ice Rink A2	Eglinton Pl B1	Mill Brae C3	Station Rd C2
Ayrshire Coll C3	Eglinton Terr B1	Mill St C2	Strathayr Pl B2
Back Hawkhill Ave . . A3	Elba St B2	Mill Wynd C2	Superstore A2/B2
Back Main St B2	Elmbank St A2	Miller Rd C1	Taylor St B2
Back Peebles St . . . A2	Esplanade B1	Montgomerie Terr . . B1	Town Hall B2
Barns Cres C1	Euchar Rock A1	New Bridge B2	Tryfield Pl A3
Barns Pk C1	Farifield Rd C1	New Bridge St B2	Turner's Bridge B2
Barns St C1	Fort St B2	New Rd A3	Union Ave A3
Barns Street La C1	Fothringham Rd . . . C3	Newmarket St B2	Victoria Bridge C2
Bath Pl B1	Fullarton St C1	Newton-on-Ayr	Victoria St B3
Bellevue Cres C1	Gaiety C2	Station B1	Viewfield Rd A3
Bellevue La C1	Garden St B2	North Harbour St . . . B1	Virginia Gdns A2
Beresford La C2	George St B2	North Pier A1	Waggon Rd A2
Beresford Terr C2	George's Ave A3	Odeon C1	Walker Rd C1
Boswell Pk B2	Glebe Cres A2	Park Circus C1	Wallace Tower . . B2
Britannia Pl A3	Glebe Rd A2	Park Circus La C1	Weaver St A2
Bruce Cres B1	Gorden Terr B3	Park Terr C1	Weir Rd A2
Burns Statue . . . B2	Green St A2	Pavilion Rd C1	Wellington La C1
Bus Sta B1	Green Street La A2	Peebles St A2	Wellington Sq C1
Carrick St C2	Hawkhill Ave B3	Philip Sq B2	West Sanouhar Rd . . A3
Cassillis St B1	Hawkhill Ave Lane . . B3	Police Station . . . B2	Whitletts Rd A3
Cathcart St B1	High St B2	Prestwick Rd B1	Wilson St A3
	Holmston Rd C3	Princes Ct A2	York St A1
	Information Ctr . . B1	Queen St B3	York Street La B1

Dumfries

Academy St A2	David Keswick	Irving St A2	Queen St B3
Aldermanhill Rd . . . B3	Athletic Centre . . . A3	King St A1	Queensberry St A2
Ambulance	David St B1	Kingholm Rd A3	Rae St A2
Station C3	Dock Park C3	Kirkpatrick Ct C2	Richmond Ave C2
Annan Rd A3	Dockhead B2	Laurieknowe B1	Robert Burns
Ardwall Rd A3	Dumfries A3	Leafield Rd B3	Centre B2
Ashfield Dr A1	Dumfries Academy A2	Library A2	Roberts Cres C1
Atkinson Rd C1	Dumfries Ice Bowl . . A1	Lochfield Rd A1	Robertson Ave C3
Averill Cres C1	Dumfries Museum &	Loreburn Pk A2	Robinson Dr C1
Balliol Ave C1	Camera Obscura	Loreburn St A2	Rosefield Rd C2
Bank St B2	. . . . B2	Loreburne	Rosemount St B1
Bankend Rd C1	Dumfries & Galloway	Shopping Centre . B2	Rotchell Park C1
Barn Slaps B3	Royal Infirmary	Lover's Walk A2	Rotchell Rd B1
Barrie Ave B3	(A&E) C3	Martin Ave B3	Rugby Football
Beech Ave A1	East Riverside Dr . . C3	Mausoleum B3	Ground C2
Bowling Green A3	Edinburgh Rd A2	Maxwell St B2	Ryedale Rd C2
Brewery St B2	English St B2	McKie Ave B3	St Andrews A2
Bridgend	Fire Station B3	Mews La B2	St John the
Theatre B1	Friar's Vennel A2	Mid Steeple B2	Evangelist A2
Brodie Ave C2	Galloway St B1	Mill Green B2	St Josephs College . . A3
Brooke St B2	George Douglas Dr C1	Mill Rd B1	St Mary's
Broomlands Dr C1	George St A2	Moat Rd C2	Industrial Estate . . A3
Brooms Rd B3	Gladstone Rd C2	Moffat St A2	St Mary's St A3
Buccleuch St A2	Glasgow St A1	Mountainhall Pk . . . C2	St Michael St B2
Burns House B2	Glebe St B3	Nelson St B1	St Michael's B2
Burns Mausoleum . . B3	Glencaple Rd C2	New Abbey Rd . . B1/C1	St Michael's Bridge . C1
Burns St B2	Goldie Ave A1	New Bridge B1	St Michael's Bridge
Burns Statue A2	Goldie Cres A1	Newall Terr A2	Rd B2
Bus Station B1	Golf Course C3	Nith Ave A3	St Michael's
Cardoness St A3	Gracefield Arts	Nith Bank C3	Cemetery B3
Castle St A2	Centre A2	Nithbank	Shakespeare St B2
Catherine St C1	Greyfriars A2	Hospital C3	Solway Dr C2
Cattle Market A3	Grierson Ave B3	Nithside Ave A1	Stakeford St A1
Cemetery B3	Hamilton Ave C1	Odeon B2	Stark Cres C2
Cemetery C2	Hamilton Starke	Old Bridge A3	Station Rd A3
Church Cres A2	Park C2	Old Bridge	Steel Ave A1
Church St B2	Hazelrigg Ave C1	House B1	Sunderries Ave A1
College Rd A1	Henry St B3	Palmerston Park	Sunderries Rd A1
College St A1	Hermitage Dr C1	(Queen of the	Superstore B3
Corbelly Hill B1	High Cemetery C3	South FC) A1	Suspension Brae . . . B2
Corberry Park B1	High St A2	Park Rd C2	Swimming Pool A1
Cornwall Mt A3	Hill Ave C2	Pleasance Ave C1	Terregles St B1
Council Offices A2	Hill St B2	Police HQ A3	Theatre Royal . . . B2
Court A2	HM Prison B1	Police Station	Troqueer Rd C1
Craigs Rd C3	Holm Ave C2	. . . . A2/A3	Union St A1
Cresswell Ave B3	Hoods Loaning A3	Portland Dr A1	Wallace St B3
Cresswell Hill B3	Howgate St A3	Post Office	Welldale B2
Cumberland St B3	Huntingdon Rd A3	. . . . B1/B2/B3	West Riverside Dr . . C2
	Information Ctr . . B2	Priestlands Dr C1	White Sands B2
	Irish St B2	Primrose St B1	

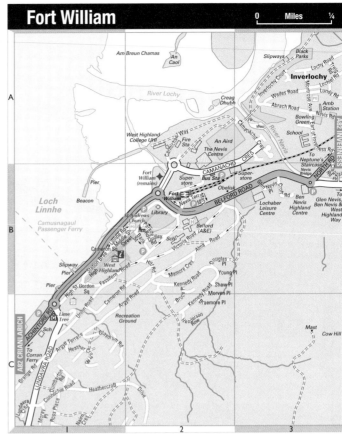

Dundee

Abertay University	B2	Drummond St	A1
Adelaide Pl	A1	Dudhope Castle	A1
Airlie Pl	C1	Dudhope St	A2
Albany Terr	A1	Dudhope Terr	A1
Albert St	A3	Dundee ≥	C2
Alexander St	A2	Dundee	
Ann St	A2	Contemporary	
Arthurstone Terr	A3	Arts ✦	C2
Bank St	B2	Dundee High	
Barrack Rd	A1	School	B2
Barrack St	B2	Dundee Law ✦	A1
Bell St	B2	Dundee	
Blinshall St	B1	Repertory	C2
Broughty Ferry Rd	A3	Dunhope Park	A1
Brown St	B1	Dura St	A3
Bus Station	B3	East Dock St	B3
Caird Hall	B2	East Marketgait	B3
Camperdown St	B3	East Whale La	B3
Candle La	B3	Erskine St	A3
Carmichael St	A1	Euclid Cr	A2
City Churches	B2	Forebank Rd	A2
City Quay	B3	Foundry La	A3
City Sq	B2	Gallagher Retail	
Commercial St	B2	Park	B3
Constable St	A3	Gellatly St	B3
Constitution Cres	A1	Government	
Constitution Ct	A1	Offices	C2
Constitution St	A1/B2	Guthrie St	B1
Cotton Rd	A3	Hawkhill	B1
Courthouse Sq	B1	Hilltown	A2
Cowgate	A3	HMS Unicorn ✦	B3
Crescent St	A3	Howff Cemetery,	
Crichton St	B2	The	B2
Dens Brae	A3	Information Ctr	B2
Dens Rd	A3	Keiller Shopping	
Discovery Point ✦	C2	Centre	B2
Douglas St	B1	Keiller Ctr, The	B2
		King St	A3
		Kinghorne Rd	A1

Ladywell Ave	A3	Rosebank St	A2
Laurel Bank	A2	RRS Discovery	C2
Law Rd	A1	St Andrew's †	C2
Law St	A1	St Pauls	
Library	A2/A3	Episcopal †	B3
Library and Steps		Science Centre ✦	C2
Theatre	A2	Seagate	B2
Little Theatre,		Sheriffs Court	B1
The	A2	Shopmobility	B2
Lochee Rd	B1	South George St	A2
Lower Princes St	A3	South Marketgait	B2
Lyon St	A3	South Tay St	B2
McManus Art Gallery		South Victoria Dock	
& Museum, The	B2	Road	B3
Meadow Side	B2	South Ward Rd	B2
Meadowside		Tay Road Bridge ✦	C3
St Pauls	B2	Thomson Ave	B2
Mercat Cross ✦	B2	Trades La	B3
Murraygate	B2	Union St	B2
Nelson St	A2	Union Terr	A1
Nethergate	B2/C1	University Library	B2
North Lindsay St	B2	University of	
North Marketgait	B2	Dundee	B1
Old Hawkhill	B1	Upper	
Olympia Leisure		Constitution St	A1
Centre	B3	Verdant Works ✦	B1
Overgate Shopping		V&A Museum of	
Centre	B2	Design	C2
Park Pl	B1	Victoria Dock	B3
Perth Rd	C1	Victoria Rd	A2
Police Station	B1	Victoria St	A3
Post Office	B2	Ward Rd	B1
Princes St	A3	Wellgate	B2
Prospect Pl	A2	West Bell St	B1
Reform St	B2	West	
Riverside Dr	C2	Marketgait	B1/B2
Riverside		Westfield Pl	C1
Esplanade	C2	William St	A3
Roseangle	C1	Wishart Arch ✦	A3

Fort William

Abrach Rd	A3	Connochie Rd	C1
Achintore Rd	C1	Cow Hill	C3
Alma Rd	B2	Creag Dhubh	A2
Am Breun Chamas	A2	Croft Rd	B3
Ambulance Station	A3	Douglas Pl	B2
An Aird	A2	Dudley Rd	B2
Argyll Rd	C1	Dumbarton Rd	C1
Argyll Terr	C1	Earl of Inverness	
Belford Hospital	B2	Rd	A3
Ben Nevis Highland		Fassifern Rd	B1
Centre	B3	Fire Station	A2
Black Parks	A3	Fort William ≥	B2
Braemore Pl	C2	Fort William	
Bruce Pl	C2	(Remains) ✦	B2
Bus Station	B2	Glasdrum Rd	C1
Camanachd Cr	A3/B2	Glen Nevis Pl	B3
Cameron Rd	C1	Gordon Sq	B1
Cameron Sq	B1	Grange Rd	C1
Carmichael Way	A2	Heathercroft Dr	C1
Claggan Rd	B3	Heather Croft Rd	C1
		Henderson Row	C1
		High St	B1
		Hill Rd	B2

Information Ctr	A3	Nevis Rd	A3
Inverlochy Ct	A3	Nevis Terr	B2
Kennedy Rd	B2/C2	North Rd	B3
Library	B2	Obelisk	B2
Lime Tree		Parade Rd	B2
Gallery ✦	C1	Police Station	C1
Linnhe Rd	B1	Post Office	A3/B2
Lochaber Leisure		Ross Pl	C1
Centre	B3	St Andrews	B2
Lochiel Rd	A3	Shaw Pl	B2
Lochy Rd	A3	Station Brae	B1
Lundavra Cres	C1	Superstore	B3
Lundavra Rd	C1	Treig Rd	A3
Lundy Rd	A3	Union Rd	C1
Mamore Cr	C2	Victoria Rd	B2
Mary St	B2	Wades Rd	A3
Middle St	C2	West Highland	B1
Montrose Ave	A3	West Highland	
Moray Pl	C1	College UHI	A2
Morven Pl	C2	Young Pl	B2
Nairn Cres	C1		
Nevis Bridge	B3		
Nevis Centre, The	A2		

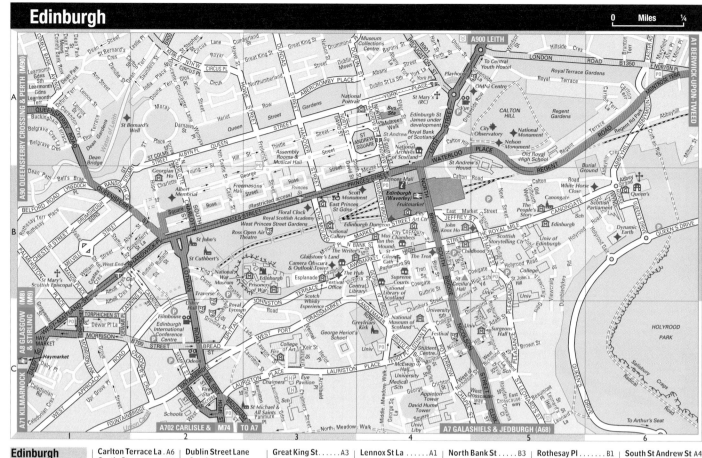

Glasgow

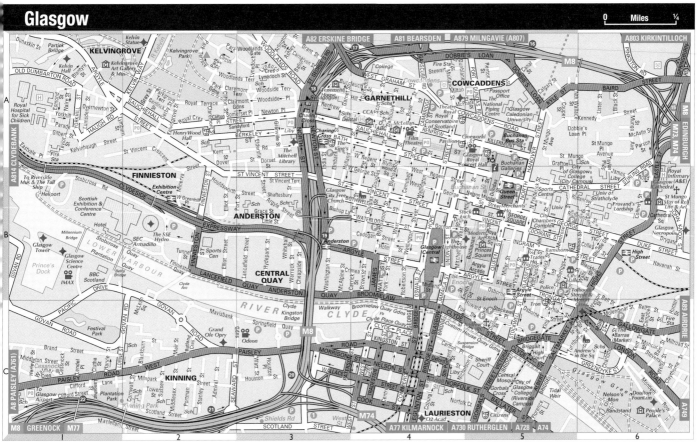

Glasgow

Admiral St C2
Albert Bridge C5
Albion St B5
Anderston ⩘ B3
Anderston Quay B3
Argyle Arcade B5
Argyle
St . . A1/A2/B3/B4/B5
Argyle Street ⩘ A3
Arlington St A3
Arts Centre 🏛 B3
Ashley St A3
Bain St C6
Baird St A6
Baliol St A3
Ballater St C5
Barras (Market),
The C6
Bath St A3
BBC Scotland B1
Bell St B5
Bell's Bridge B1
Bentinck St A2
Berkeley St A3
Bishop La B3
Black St A6
Blackburn St C2
Blackfriars St B6
Blantyre St A1
Blythswood Sq A4
Blythswood St B4
Bothwell St B4
Brand St C2
Breadalbane St A2
Bridge St C4
Bridge St M C4
Bridgegate C5
Briggait C5
Broomielaw B4
Broomielaw Quay
Gdns B3
Brown St B4
Brunswick St B5
Buccleuch St A3
Buchanan
Bus Station A5
Buchanan
Galleries B5
Buchanan St B5
Buchanan St M B5
Cadogan St B4
Caledonian
University A5
Calgary St A5
Cambridge St A4
Canal St A5

Candleriggs B5
Carlton Pl C4
Carnarvon St A3
Carrick St B4
Castle St B6
Cathedral Sq B6
Cathedral St B5
Central Mosque C5
Centre for
Contemporary
Arts 🏛 A4
Centre St C4
Cessnock M C1
Cessnock St C1
Charing Cross ⩘ . . . A3
Charlotte St C6
Cheapside St B3
Cineworld 🎬 A4
Citizens' Theatre 🎭 C5
City Chambers B5
City Halls 🏛 B5
City of Glasgow
College
(City Campus) B5
City of Glasgow
College (Riverside
Campus) C5
Clairmont Gdns A2
Claremont St A2
Claremont Terr A2
Claythorne St C6
Cleveland St A3
Clifford La C1
Clifford St C1
Clifton Pl A2
Clifton St A2
Clutha St C1
Clyde Arc B2
Clyde Pl C4
Clyde Place Quay . . . C4
Clyde St C5
Clyde Walkway C3
Clydeside
Expressway B2
Coburg St C4
Cochrane St B5
College St B6
Collins St B6
Commerce St C4
Cook St C4
Cornwall St C2
Couper St A5
Cowcaddens M A4
Cowcaddens Rd A4
Crimea St B3
Custom House
Quay Gdns C4

Dalhousie St A4
Dental Hospital Ⓗ . . A4
Derby St A2
Dobbie's Loan . . A4/A5
Dobbie's Loan
Place A5
Dorset St A3
Douglas St B4
Doulton
Fountain ✦ C6
Dover St A2
Drury St B4
Drygate B6
Duke St B6
Dunaskin St A1
Dunblane St A4
Dundas St B5
Dunlop St C5
East Campbell St . . . C6
Eastvale Pl A1
Eglinton St C4
Elderslie St A3
Elliot St B2
Elmbank St A3
Esmond St A1
Exhibition
Centre ⩘ B2
Festival Park C1
Film Theatre 🎭 A4
Finnieston Quay . . . B2
Finnieston St B2
Fire Station C6
Florence St C5
Fox St C5
Gallowgate C6
Garnet St A3
Garnethill St A4
Garscube Rd A4
George Sq B5
George St B5
George V Bridge . . . C4
Gilbert St A1
Glasgow
Bridge C4
Glasgow
Cathedral † B6
Glasgow Central ⩘ . B4
Glasgow City
Free Church B4
Glasgow Green C6
Glasgow
Necropolis ✦ B6
Glasgow Royal
Concert Hall A5
Glasgow Science
Centre ✦ B1
Glasgow Tower ✦ . . B1
Glassford St B5
Glebe St A6

Gorbals Cross C5
Gorbals St C5
Gordon St B4
Govan Rd . . . B1/C1/C2
Grace St B3
Grafton Pl A5
Grand Ole Opry ✦ . . C2
Grant St A3
Granville St A3
Gray St A2
Greendyke St C6
Grey Eagle St B7
Harley St C1
Harvie St C1
Haugh Rd A1
Havanah St B6
Heliport B2
Henry Wood Hall 🎵 . A2
High Court C5
High St B6
High Street ⩘ B6
Hill St A3
Holland St A3
Holm St B4
Hope St A5
Houldsworth St A2
Houston Pl C3
Houston St C3
Howard St C5
Hunter St C6
Hutcheson St B5
Hydepark St B3
Imax Cinema 🎬 B1
India St A3
Information Ctr 🅲 . . B5
Ingram St B5
Jamaica St B4
James Watt St B4
John Knox St B6
John St B5
Kelvin Hall ✦ A1
Kelvin Statue ✦ . . . A2
Kelvin Way A2
Kelvingrove Art
Gallery & Museum
🏛 A1
Kelvingrove Park . . . A2
Kelvingrove St A1
Kelvinhaugh St A1
Kennedy St A6
Killermont St A5
King's, The 🎭 A3
Kingston Bridge . . . C3
Kingston St C4
Kinning Park M C2
Kyle St A5

Lancefield Quay B2
Lancefield St B3
Langshot St C1
Lendel Pl C1
Lighthouse, The ✦ . . B4
Lister St A6
Little St B3
London Rd C6
Lorne St C1
Lower Harbour B1
Lumsden St A1
Lymburn St A1
Lyndoch Cr A3
Lynedoch Pl A3
Lynedoch St A3
Maclellan St C1
Mair St C2
Maitland St A4
Mansell St C7
Mavisbank Gdns . . . C2
Mcalpine St B3
Mcaslin St A6
McLean Sq C2
McLellan
Gallery 🏛 A4
McPhater St A4
Merchants'
House 🏛 B5
Middlesex St C1
Middleton St C1
Midland St B4
Miller St B5
Millennium Bridge . . B1
Millroad St C6
Milnpark St C2
Milton St A4
Minerva St B2
Mitchell St West . . . B4
Mitchell Library,
The ✦ A3
Modern
Art Gallery 🏛 . . . B5
Moir St C6
Molendinar St C6
Moncur St C6
Montieth Row C6
Montrose St B5
Morrison St C3
Nairn St A1
Nelson Mandela
Square B5
Nelson St C4
Nelson's
Monument C6
Newton Pl A3
Newton St A3

Nicholson St C4
Nile St B5
Norfolk Court C4
Norfolk St C4
North Frederick St . . B5
North Hanover St . . . B5
North Portland St . . B6
North St A3
North Wallace St . . . A5
O2 ABC A4
O2 Academy ✦ . . . C4
Odeon C3
Old Dumbarton Rd . . A1
Osborne St B5/C5
Oswald St B4
Overnewton St A1
Oxford St C4
Pacific Dr B1
Paisley Rd C3
Paisley Rd West C1
Park Circus A2
Park Gdns A2
Park St South A3
Park Terr A2
Parkgrove Terr A1
Parnie St C5
Parson St A6
Partick Bridge A1
Passport Office A5
Pavilion Theatre 🎭 . A4
Pembroke St A3
People's Palace 🏛 . . C6
Pinkston Rd A6
Pitt St A4/B4
Plantation Park C1
Plantation Quay . . . B1
Police Mus 🏛 B5
Police Station . . A4/A5
Port Dundas Rd . . . A5
Port St B2
Portman St C2
Prince's Dock B1
Princes Sq B5
Provand's
Lordship 🏛 B6
Queen St B5
Queen Street ⩘ . . . B5
Ramshorn St B5
Renfrew St A3/A4
Renton St A5
Richmond St B5
Robertson St B4
Rose St A4
Rottenrow B5
Royal Concert
Hall ✦ A5
Royal Conservatoire
of Scotland A4

Royal Crescent A2
Royal Exchange
Square B5
Royal Highland
Fusiliers
Museum 🏛 A3
West Glasgow
Ambulatory
Care A1
Royal Infirmary Ⓗ . . B6
Royal Terr A2
Rutland Crescent . . . C2
St Andrew's in the
Square C6
St Andrew's (RC) † . C5
St Andrew's St C5
St Enoch M B5
St Enoch Shopping
Centre B5
St Enoch Sq B5
St George's Rd A3
St James Rd B6
St Kent St C5
St Mungo Ave . . A5/A6
St Mungo Museum
of Religious Life
& Art B6
St Mungo Pl A6
St Vincent Cr A2
St Vincent Pl B5
St Vincent St . . B3/B4
St Vincent Terr B3
Saltmarket C5
Sandyford Pl A3
Sauchiehall St . . A2/A4
SEC Armadillo B1
School of Art A4
Sclater St B7
Scotland St C2
Scott St A4
Scottish Exhibition &
Conference
Centre B1
Seaward St C2
Shaftesbury St B3
Sheriff Court C5
Shields Rd M C2
Shopmobility A5
Shuttle St B6
Somerset Pl A3
South Portland St . . C4
Springburn Rd A6
Springfield Quay . . . C3
SSE Hydro The 🏛 . . B2
Stanley St C2
Stevenson St C6
Stewart St A4
Stirling Rd B6

Stobcross Quay B1
Stobcross Rd B1
Stock Exchange 🏛 . . B5
Stockwell Pl C5
Stockwell St C5
Stow College A4
Sussex St C2
Synagogue A3
Taylor Pl A6
Tenement
House 🏛 A4
Teviot St A1
Theatre Royal 🎭 . . . A4
Tolbooth Steeple &
Mercat Cross ✦ . . C6
Tower St C2
Trades House 🏛 . . . B5
Tradeston St C4
Transport
Museum ✦ A1
Tron 🎭 C5
Trongate B5
Turnbull St C5
Union St B4
University of
Strathclyde B6
Victoria Bridge C5
Virginia St B5
Wallace St C3
Walls St B6
Walmer Cr C1
Warrock St B3
Washington St B3
Waterloo St B4
Watson St B6
Watt St C3
Wellington St B4
West Campbell St . . B4
West George St . . . B4
West Graham St . . . A4
West Greenhill Pl . . . B2
West Regent St . . . A4
West Regent St . . . B4
West St C4
West St M C4
Whitehall St B3
Wilkes St C7
Wilson St B5
Woodlands Gate . . . A2
Woodlands Rd A3
Woodlands Terr . . . A2
Woodside Pl A3
Woodside Terr A3
York St B4
Yorkhill Parade . . . A1
Yorkhill St A1

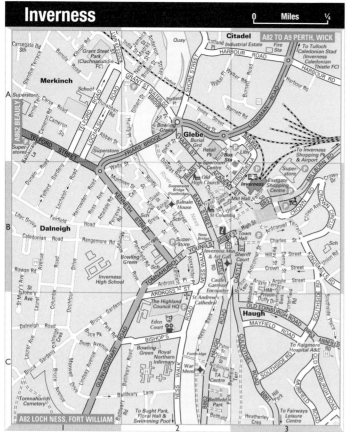

Inverness

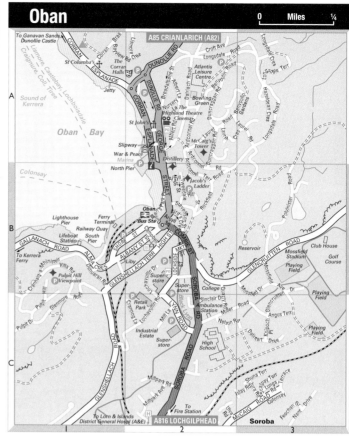

Oban

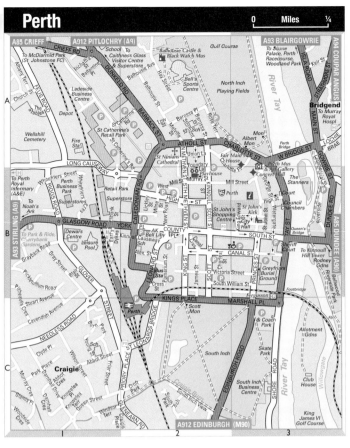

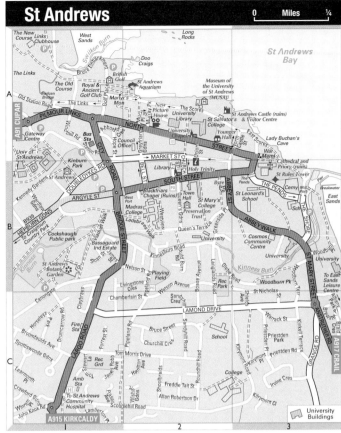

Perth

AK Bell Library B2
Abbot Cres. C1
Abbot St C1
Albany Terr A1
Albert Monument . . A3
Alexandra St B2
Atholl St A2
Balhousie Ave A2
Balhousie Castle
 & Black Watch
 Museum A2
Balhousie St A2
Ballantine Pl A1
Barossa Pl A2
Barossa St A2
Barrack St A2
Bell's Sports
 Centre A2
Bellwood B3
Blair St B1
Burn Park C1
Bus Station B2
Caledonian Rd B2
Canal Cres B2
Canal St B3
Cavendish Ave. C1
Charles St B2
Charlotte Pl. A2
Charlotte St. A3
Church St. A1
City Hall B3
Club House C3
Clyde Pl C1
Coach Park C3
Commercial St A3
Concert Hall ✦ B3
Council
 Chambers B3
County Pl A2
Court B3
Craigie Pl C2
Crieff Rd. A1
Croft Park C2

Cross St B2
Darnhall Cres C1
Darnhall Dr C1
Dewars Centre B1
Dundee Rd. C1
Dunkeld Rd A1
Earl's Dykes. B1
Edinburgh Rd C2
Elibank St. B1
Fair Maid's
 House ✦ A3
Fergusson ⌂ B3
Feus Rd A1
Fire Station A1
Foundary La A2
Friar St B2
George St. B3
Glamis Pl C1
Glasgow Rd B1
Glenearn Rd C2
Glover St B1/C1
Golf Course A2
Gowrie St A3
Gray St B1
Graybank Rd B1
Greyfriars Burial
 Gd B3
Hay St A2
High St B2/B3
Inchaffray St A1
Industrial/Retail
 Park B1
Information Ctr ⓘ . . B2
Isla Rd A3
James St B3
King Edward St B3
King James VI
 Golf Course C3
King St B2
Kings Pl C2
Kinnoull
 Causeway B2
Kinnoull St B2
Knowelea Pl C1

Knowelea Terr C1
Ladeside Business
 Centre A1
Leisure Pool B1
Leonard St. B2
Lickley St B2
Lochie Brae A3
Long Causeway A1
Low St. A3
Main St A3
Marshall Pl C3
Melville St B2
Mill St. B3
Milne St B3
Murray Cres. C1
Murray St B2
Needless Rd C1
New Rd B2
North Inch A3
North Methven St. . A2
Park Pl C1
Perth ✦ B2
Perth Bridge A3
Perth Business
 Park A1
Perth Museum &
 Art Gallery ⌂ B3
Perth Station ≥ . . . B2
Pickletulllum Rd. . . B1
Pitheavlis Cres C1
Playhouse ⚏ B2
Police Station ⌂. . . A2
Pomarium St B2
Post Office ⓟ . . . B2/C2
Princes St B3
Priory Pl C2
Queen St C1
Queen's Bridge B3
Riggs Rd B1
Riverside B3
Riverside Park A3
Rodney Gdns B3
Rose Terr A2
St Catherine's
 Rd A1/A2

St Catherine's
 Retail Park. A1
St John St. B3
St John's Kirk ⛪ . . . B3
St John's Shopping
 Centre B2
St Leonards Bridge C2
St Ninians
 Cathedral † A2
Scott Monument . . C2
Scott St C2
Sheriff Court. B3
Shore Rd C3
Skate Park C3
South Inch C2
South Inch
 Business Centre . . C3
South Inch Park . . . C2
South Inch View . . . C2
South Methven St. . B2
South St B3
South William St. . . B2
Stables, The A1
Stanners, The B3
Stormont St B2
Strathmore St A3
Stuart Ave C1
Superstore B1/B2
Tay St B3
Union La. A2
Victoria St B2
Watergate B3
Wellshill Cemetery A1
West Bridge St A3
West Mill St A2
Whitefriars Cres. . . B1
Whitefriars St B1
Wilson St C1
Windsor Terr. C1
Woodside Cres C1
York Pl B2
Young St. C1

St Andrews

Abbey St. B2
Abbey Walk B3
Abbotsford Cres. . . A1
Albany Pk. C3
Allan Robertson Dr C2
Ambulance Station . C3
Anstruther Rd. C3
Argyle St B1
Auld Burn Rd B2
Bassaguard
 Industrial Estate. . B2
Bell St. B2
Blackfriars Chapel
 (Ruins) B2
Boase Ave B2
Braid Cres C3
Brewster Pl C3
Bridge St B1
British Golf
 Museum ⌂ A1
Broomfaulds Ave . . C1
Bruce
 Embankment B1
Bruce St C2
Bus Station A1
Byre Theatre ⚏ B2
Canongate C1
Cathedral and
 Priory (Ruins) † . . B3
Cemetery. A3
Chamberlain St. . . . C1
Church St. B2
Churchill Cres. C2
City Rd A1
Claybraes. C2
Cockshaugh Public
 Park B1
Cosmos Community
 Centre B1
Council Office. A2
Crawford Gdns C1
Doubledykes Rd . . . B1

Drumcarrow Rd . . . C1
East Sands. B3
East Scores A3
Fire Station C1
Forrest St. C1
Fraser Ave C1
Freddie Tait St. C2
Gateway Centre . . . A1
Glebe Rd. B2
Golf Pl A1
Grange Rd C2
Greenside Pl B2
Greyfriars Gdns . . . A2
Hamilton Ave. B1
Hepburn Gdns B1
Holy Trinity ⛪ B2
Horseleys Park A1
Information Ctr ⓘ . . B2
Irvine Cres. C3
James Robb Ave . . . C1
James St B1
John Knox Rd C3
Kennedy Gdns B1
Kilrymont Cl C3
Kilrymont Pl C3
Kilrymont Rd C3
Kinburn Park B1
Kinkell Terr C3
Kinnesburn Rd B2
Ladebraes Walk . . . B2
Lady Buchan's
 Cave A3
Lamberton Pl C1
Lamond Dr. C2
Langlands Rd C2
Largo Rd. C1
Learmonth Pl C1
Library B2
Links Clubhouse. . . A1
Links, The A1
Livingstone Cres . . C2
Long Rocks A2
Madras College B2
Market St. A2

Martyr's
 Monument. A1
Murray Pk A2
Murray Pl A2
Museum of the
 University of
 St Andrews
 (MUSA) ✦ A2
Nelson St C1
New Course, The . . A1
New Picture
 House ⚏ A2
North Castle St A3
North St A2
Old Course, The . . . A1
Old Station Rd. A1
Pends, The. B3
Pilmour Links A1
Pipeland Rd B2/C2
Police Station
 ⌂ A2/C1
Post Office ⓟ B2
Preservation
 Trust ⌂ B2
Priestden Pk C3
Priestden Pl C3
Priestden Rd C3
Queen's Gdns B2
Queen's Terr B2
Roundhill Rd C2
Royal & Ancient
 Golf Club A1
St Andrews ⌂ B1
St Andrews
 Aquarium ⬯ A2
St Andrews Botanic
 Garden ❀ B1
St Andrews Castle
 (Ruins) & Visitor
 Centre ✦ A3
St Leonard's
 School B3
St Mary St. B3
St Mary's College . . B2

St Nicholas St C3
St Rules Tower ✦ . . B3
St Salvator's
 College. A2
Sandyhill Cres. C2
Sandyhill Rd C2
Scooniehill Rd C2
Scores, The A2
Shields Ave C3
Shoolbraids. C2
Shore, The B3
Sloan St B1
South St B2
Spottiswoode Gdns C1
Station Rd A1
Swilcen Bridge A1
Tom Morris Dr C2
Tom Stewart La. . . . C1
Town Hall A2
Union St A2
University
 Chapel ⛪ A2
University Library . A2
University of
 St Andrews A1
Viaduct Walk. B1
War Memorial. A3
Wardlaw Gdns B1
Warrack St C3
Watson Ave B2
West Port. B2
West Sands A1
Westview. B2
Windmill Rd. A1
Winram Pl C1
Wishart Gdns C2
Woodburn Pk B3
Woodburn Pl. B3
Woodburn Terr. . . . B3
Younger Hall ⌂ A2

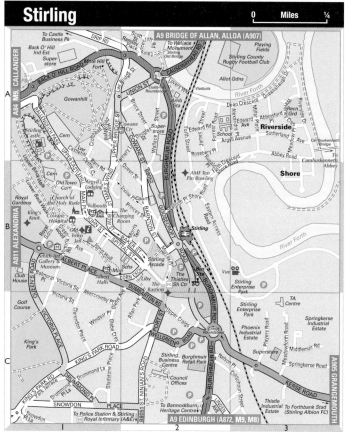

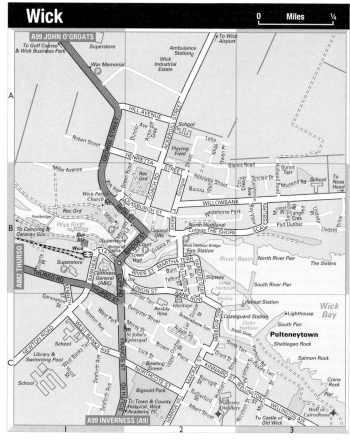

Stirling

Abbey Rd	A3
Abbotsford Pl	A3
Abercromby Pl	C1
Albert Halls	B1
Albert Pl	B1
Alexandra Pl	A3
Allan Park	C2
Ambulance Station	A2
AMF Ten Pin Bowling	B2
Argyll Ave	C2
Argyll's Lodging	B1
Back O' Hill Industrial Estate	A1
Back O' Hill Rd	A1
Baker St	B2
Ballengeich Pass	A1
Balmoral Pl	B1
Barn Rd	B1
Barnton St	B2
Bastion, The	C2
Bow St	B1
Bruce St	B1
Burghmuir Retail Park	C2
Burghmuir Rd	A2/B2/C2
Bus Station	B2
Cambuskenneth Bridge	A3
Castle Ct	B1
Causewayhead Rd	A2
Cemetery	A1
Changing Room, The	B1
Church of the Holy Rude	B1
Clarendon Pl	C1
Club House	B1
Colquhoun St	C3
Corn Exchange	B2
Council Offices	C2
Court	B2
Cowane Ctr	A2
Cowane St	A2
Cowane's Hospital	B1
Crofthead Rd	A1
Dean Cres	A3
Douglas St	A2
Drip Rd	A1
Drummond La	C1
Drummond Pl	C1
Drummond Pl La	C1
Dumbarton Rd	C1
Eastern Access Rd	B2
Edward Ave	A3
Edward Rd	A2
Forrest Rd	A2
Fort	A1
Forth Cres	B2
Forth St	A2
Gladstone Pl	C1
Glebe Ave	C1
Glebe Cres	C1
Golf Course	C1
Goosecroft Rd	B2
Gowanhill	A1
Greenwood Ave	B1
Harvey Wynd	A1
Information Ctr	B1
Irvine Pl	B2
James St	A2
John St	B1
Kerse Rd	C3
King's Knot	B1
King's Park	C1
King's Park Rd	C1
Laurencecroft Rd	A2
Leisure Pool	B2
Library	B2
Linden Ave	C2
Lovers Walk	A2
Lower Back Walk	B1
Lower Bridge St	A2
Lower Castlehill	A1
Mar Pl	B1
Meadow Pl	A3
Meadowforth Rd	C3
Middlemuir Rd	C3
Millar Pl	A3
Morris Terr	B2
Mote Hill	A1
Murray Pl	B2
Nelson Pl	C2
Old Town Cemetery	B1
Old Town Jail	B1
Park Terr	C1
Phoenix Industrial Estate	C3
Players Rd	C3
Port St	C2
Post Office	B2
Princes St	B2
Queen St	B2
Queen's Rd	B1
Queenshaugh Dr	A3
Ramsay Pl	A2
Riverside Dr	A3
Ronald Pl	A1
Rosebery Pl	A2
Royal Gardens	B1
Royal Gdns	B1
St Ninian's Rd	C2
Scott St	A2
Seaforth Pl	B2
Shore Rd	B2
Smith Art Gallery & Museum	B1
Snowdon Pl	C1
Snowdon Pl La	C1
Spittal St	B2
Springkerse Industrial Estate	C3
Springkerse Rd	C3
Stirling Arcade	B2
Stirling Business Centre	C2
Stirling Castle	A1
Stirling County Rugby Football Club	A1
Stirling Enterprise Park	C2
Stirling Old Bridge	A2
Stirling Station	B2
Superstore	A1/A2
Sutherland Ave	A3
TA Centre	C3
Tannery La	A2
Thistle Industrial Estate	C3
Thistles Shopping Centre, The	B2
Tolbooth	B1
Town Wall	B1
Union St	A2
Upper Back Walk	B1
Upper Bridge St	A1
Upper Castlehill	B1
Upper Craigs	C2
Victoria Pl	C1
Victoria Rd	C1
Victoria Sq	B1/C1
Vue	B2
Wallace St	A2
Waverley Cres	A3
Wellgreen Rd	C2
Windsor Pl	C1
YHA	B1

Wick

Ackergill Cres	A2
Ackergill St	A2
Albert St	A2
Ambulance Station	A2
Argyle Sq	C2
Assembly Rooms	C2
Bank Row	C2
Bankhead	B1
Barons Well	C2
Barrogill St	C2
Bay View	B3
Bexley Terr	C3
Bignold Park	C2
Bowling Green	C2
Breadalbane Terr	C2
Bridge of Wick	B1
Bridge St	B2
Brown Pl	C2
Burn St	C2
Bus Station	B2
Caithness General Hospital (A&E)	B1
Cliff Rd	B1
Coach Rd	C2
Coastguard Station	C3
Corner Cres	B3
Coronation St	C1
Council Offices	B2
Court	B2
Crane Rock	C3
Dempster St	C2
Dunnet Ave	A2
Fire Station	B2
Francis St	C1
George St	A1
Girnigoe St	B2
Glamis Rd	B2
Gowrie Pl	B1
Grant St	C2
Green Rd	B2
Gunns Terr	B3
Harbour Quay	B2
Harbour Rd	C2
Harbour Terr	C2
Harrow Hill	C2
Henrietta St	A2/B2
Heritage Museum	C2
High St	B2
Hill Ave	A2
Hillhead Rd	B3
Hood St	C2
Huddart St	C2
Kenneth St	C1
Kinnaird St	C2
Kirk Hill	B1
Langwell Cres	B3
Leishman Ave	B3
Leith Walk	A2
Library	B2
Library & Swimming Pool	C1
Lifeboat Station	C3
Lighthouse	C3
Lindsay Dr	B3
Lindsay Pl	B3
Loch St	B2
Louisburgh St	B2
Lower Dunbar St	C2
Macleay La	B1
Macleod Rd	B3
MacRae St	C2
Martha Terr	B2
Miller Ave	B1
Miller La	B2
Moray St	C2
Mowat Pl	B3
Murchison St	C3
Newton Ave	C1
Newton Rd	C1
Nicolson St	C3
North Highland College	B2
North River Pier	B3
Northcote St	C2
Owen Pl	A2
Police Station	B2
Port Dunbar	B3
Post Office	B2/C2
Pulteney Distillery	C2
River St	B2
Robert St	A1
Rutherford St	C2
St John's Episcopal	B2
Sandigoe Rd	B3
Scalesburn	B3
Seaforth Ave	C1
Shore La	C2
Shore, The	B2
Sinclair Dr	B3
Sinclair Terr	C2
Smith Terr	C3
South Pier	C3
South Quay	C3
South Rd	C1
South River Pier	B3
Station Rd	B1
Superstore	A1/B2
Telford St	B2
Thurso Rd	B1
Thurso St	B1
Town Hall	B2
Union St	A2
Upper Dunbar St	C2
Vansittart St	C3
Victoria Pl	C3
War Memorial	A1
Well of Cairndhuna	C3
Wellington Ave	C3
Wellington St	C3
West Banks Ave	C1
West Banks Terr	C1
West Park	C1
Whitehorse Park	B2
Wick Harbour Bridge	B2
Wick Industrial Estate	A2
Wick Parish Church	B1
Wick Station	B1
Williamson St	B2
Willowbank	B2

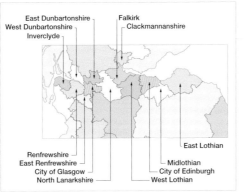

Index to road maps

How to use the index

Example

Benmore Lodge Highland **85** B7

- grid square
- page number
- county or unitary authority